CONSCIOUSNESS

This book presents a novel and comprehensive theory of consciousness. The initial chapter distinguishes six main forms of consciousness and sketches an account of each one. Later chapters focus on phenomenal consciousness, consciousness *of*, and introspective consciousness. In discussing phenomenal consciousness, Hill develops the representational theory of mind in new directions, arguing that all awareness involves representations, even awareness of qualitative states like pain. He then uses this view to undercut dualistic accounts of qualitative states. Other topics include visual awareness, visual appearances, emotional qualia, and meta-cognitive processing. This important work will interest a wide readership of students and scholars in philosophy of mind and cognitive science.

CHRISTOPHER S. HILL is Professor of Philosophy at Brown University. His past publications include *Sensations* (Cambridge, 1991) and *Thought and World* (Cambridge, 2002).

D0041447

CONSCIOUSNESS

CHRISTOPHER S. HILL

Brown University

CAMBRIDGE UNIVERSITY PRESS

Cambridge, New York, Melbourne, Madrid, Cape Town, Singapore, São Paulo, Delhi

Cambridge University Press
The Edinburgh Building, Cambridge CB2 8RU, UK

Published in the United States of America by Cambridge University Press, New York

www.cambridge.org
Information on this title: www.cambridge.org/9780521110228

First published 2009

Printed in the United Kingdom at the University Press, Cambridge

A catalog record for this publication is available from the British Library

Library of Congress Cataloguing in Publication data
Hill, Christopher S.
Consciousness / Christopher S. Hill.
p.   cm.
ISBN 978-0-521-11022-8
1. Consciousness.   I. Title.
BF311.H46917 2009
153–dc22   2009025733

ISBN 978-0-521-11022-8 hardback
ISBN 978-0-521-12521-5 paperback

For Lee Warren
Wise, generous, antic

Contents

Figures

Acknowledgments

I have been helped tremendously, at several stages, by conversations with Anil Gupta. He has played two roles – that of critic and that of midwife. I am deeply grateful for his advice and support. I have also been helped considerably by conversations and e-mail exchanges with David Bennett, Ned Block, Justin Broackes, Anthony Brueckner, Alex Byrne, David Chalmers, Paul Coppock, Ivan Fox, Christopher Frey, Jeremy Goodman, Anjana Jacob, Sean Kelly, Jaegwon Kim, Uriah Kriegel, Joseph Levine, Heather Logue, William Lycan, Jack Lyons, Brian McLaughlin, Kevin Morris, Maxwell Pines, Jeffrey Poland, Eoin Ryan, Joshua Schechter, Eric Schwitzgebel, Thomas Senor, Sydney Shoemaker, Susanna Siegel, Ernest Sosa, Michael Tarr, James Van Cleve, Barbara Von Eckardt, and William Warren. I am especially indebted to Bennett and Warren.

Several chapters and parts of chapters provided the basis for talks at the Australian National University, Cornell University, Monash University, the University of Arizona, the University of Arkansas, the University of Connecticut, the University of California, Davis, the University of Manitoba, the University of Melbourne, the University of Pittsburgh, and the University of Sydney. Questions and comments from audiences at these institutions improved my understanding of the issues considerably, as did the questions and comments following talks at the Pacific Division of the American Philosophical Association, the Southern Society for Philosophy and Psychology, and a conference at the University of Magdeburg. I remember with particular appreciation an observation by John Bigelow following my talk at Monash.

Anil Gupta, Joseph Levine, and two anonymous referees for Cambridge University Press read the penultimate version of the manuscript and provided extremely insightful criticisms and suggestions. Their comments have resulted in many improvements, both great and small.

I gratefully acknowledge financial support from Brown University, which granted me two leaves of absence while I was working on this project, the Centre for Consciousness at the Australian National University, and the Center for Philosophy of Science at the University of Pittsburgh.

Early versions of the ideas in this work appeared in books or journals edited by Murat Aydede, Alex Byrne, Rocco Gennaro, Uriah Kriegel, David Sosa, and Ernest Sosa. I very much appreciate their encouragement, insight, and patience.

I am grateful to Blackwell Publishing and to the MIT Press for permitting me to reprint portions of the following papers: "Remarks on David Papineau's *Thinking about Consciousness*," *Philosophy and Phenomenological Research* LXXI (2005), 147–158; "The Perception of Size and Shape," *Philosophical Issues* 18 (2008), 294–315 (written with David Bennett); and "OW! The Paradox of Pain," in Murat Aydede (ed.), *Pain: New Essays on Its Nature and the Methodology of Its Study* (Cambridge, MA: MIT Press, 2005), pp. 75–98.

The photographs reproduced in Chapter 5 and Chapter 7 were taken by Barbara Von Eckardt.

CHAPTER I

Forms of consciousness

It is customary to distinguish five forms of consciousness: *agent consciousness* (which is what we have in mind when we say of an agent that he is "losing consciousness" or "regaining consciousness"), *propositional consciousness* (which is expressed by the "conscious *that*" construction), *introspective consciousness* (which is what we have in mind when we say things like "His affection for me is fully conscious, but his hostility is not"), *relational consciousness* (which is expressed by the "conscious *of*" construction), and *phenomenal consciousness* (which is a property that mental states possess when they have a phenomenological dimension – that is, when they present us with such qualitative characteristics as pain and the taste of oranges).

I will have something to say about all of these forms of consciousness in the present work, though some of them will receive much more attention than others. To be more specific, I will have very little to say about agent consciousness and propositional consciousness, for insofar as the philosophical problems associated with these two forms of consciousness are problems of mind (as opposed to problems associated with agency and problems associated with knowledge), they are reducible to problems that arise in connection with other forms of consciousness. They are not in need of separate treatment. I will have more to say about all of the three remaining forms, but one of them, phenomenal consciousness, will be considered at much greater length than the others. The reason for this inequity is that phenomenal consciousness has a disproportionately large ability to produce philosophical puzzlement. Historically the task of explaining phenomenal consciousness has been thought to be the most challenging responsibility in philosophy of mind, and perhaps even the most challenging responsibility in all of philosophy. This view is also widely held by contemporary philosophers.

In addition to the five forms of consciousness that have just been identified, I will also discuss what I take to be a sixth form – a form that can reasonably be called *experiential consciousness*.

I

It seems that we have at least two notions of experience. One of these applies to mental states that have proprietary phenomenology, and therefore comes to much the same thing as phenomenal consciousness. The other notion of experience has a more general significance. It applies to states with a proprietary phenomenology, just as the first notion does, but it also applies to thoughts, judgments, suppositions, volitions, and all other mental states that count as *occurrent propositional attitudes*. (As is customary, I use the term "propositional attitude" to refer to mental states that can be described by verbs that take a sentential complement. Believing is a mental state of this sort, because beliefs can be described by combining "believes that" with a declarative sentence. I say that a propositional attitude is occurrent if it is an event. A thought is an event, and so is a volition, but most beliefs and desires are enduring states that remain with one even when one is asleep.)

Now when we reflect on the broader notion of experience, we find, I suggest, that it entails that the items to which it applies are conscious. To be an experience is to be conscious. This intuition is ratified by dictionaries. Thus, the third entry for "experience" in my *Webster's* says that experiences are "the conscious events that make up an individual's life,"[1] and the fourth entry in the *OED* says that to have an experience is to be "consciously the subject of a state or condition."[2] I will take this testimony at face value – experiential consciousness really is a form of consciousness. And I will assume that experiential consciousness cannot be reduced to any of the other forms. It poses problems of its own and requires separate treatment.

Finally, it is sometimes maintained that there is a seventh form of consciousness, *access consciousness*, which is possessed by all and only those higher mental states that are poised for control of speech, reasoning, and intentional action.[3] There will be some consideration of this proposal in the present chapter, but it will not figure prominently in later discussions. For reasons that will emerge, the standard characterizations of access consciousness are best seen as approximations to a correct account of experiential consciousness. They are suggestive, but problems emerge if we try to think of them as picking out a form of consciousness that is independent of the others.

[1] *Webster's Ninth New Collegiate Dictionary* (Springfield, MA: Merriam-Webster Inc., 1989), p. 437.
[2] *The Oxford English Dictionary*, 2nd edition (Oxford: Oxford University Press, 1989), Volume 5, p. 563.
[3] Ned Block, "On a Confusion about a Function of Consciousness," *Behavioral and Brain Sciences*, 18 (1995), 227–247. Reprinted with some changes in Ned Block, Owen Flanagan, and Güven Güzeldere (eds.), *The Nature of Consciousness* (Cambridge, MA: MIT Press, 1997), 375–415.

I have been speaking thus far of different *forms* of consciousness, but it is in some ways preferable to speak of different *concepts* or *notions* of consciousness. I will often adopt the latter mode of expression. This will be done partly for stylistic reasons, but also with a view to highlighting the fact that our concepts of consciousness may partially misrepresent the phenomena to which they refer.

The ensuing sections of this chapter will expand on the present descriptions of the various forms of consciousness, characterize some of the problems to which they give rise, and sketch the main themes of later chapters.

1.1   AGENT CONSCIOUSNESS

Agent consciousness is a property that adult human beings possess throughout their waking lives, and also when they are dreaming. It can be possessed by agents other than adult humans, but it presupposes the ability to have experiences and to engage in various forms of reasonably high level cognitive activity. We are sure that a slug does not enjoy agent consciousness, and we are reluctant to attribute it to insects.

Consider an agent who is waking up, or who is coming out of a coma. We describe the agent as regaining consciousness. In what exactly does this transition consist? Surely what we have in mind, when we say that the agent is regaining consciousness, is that he is starting to think and feel again, to perceive the world, and to experience bodily sensations. If conscious states of these sorts were not occurring, then, I suggest, the concept of agent consciousness could not get a foothold. In short, it seems that enjoying conscious mental states is a *necessary* condition of agent consciousness. But it is also a *sufficient* condition. It would be absurd to deny consciousness of someone who is consciously thinking about a topic, or consciously perceiving an object or an event. When there is a stream of conscious events, or even a tiny rivulet, agent consciousness is necessarily present as well.

In view of these facts, we can appreciate that the notion of agent consciousness is not a basic or foundational concept. It can be explained in terms of the concepts we use to attribute consciousness to individual mental states. It appears that there are just three concepts that have this role – the concept of introspective consciousness, the concept of phenomenal consciousness, and the concept of experiential consciousness. Accordingly, it is possible to explain agent consciousness by saying that an agent is conscious just in case he is in one or more mental states that are introspectively conscious or phenomenally conscious or experientially conscious.

It is sometimes maintained that agent consciousness comes in degrees, and that this fact should be explicitly recognized in any explanation of its nature. Insofar as this is the case, however, it can be accommodated by appealing to the number, variety, and internal complexity of conscious states that an agent is enjoying. When someone says, for example, that Bill is gradually losing consciousness, what the speaker seems to mean is that there is a decrease in the number and/or variety of Bill's conscious states, and/or that his experiences are less complex. Equally, an increase in the level of one's consciousness is a swelling of one's stream of consciousness – that is, an increase in the number of events in the stream, or in the number of kinds of events in the stream, or in the complexity of the individual events.

I.2   PROPOSITIONAL CONSCIOUSNESS

Attributions of propositional consciousness are tantamount to attributions of propositional *knowledge*. Thus, generally speaking, when it is appropriate to say that someone is conscious that *p*, it also appropriate to say that he knows that *p*; and when it is appropriate to say that someone knows that *p*, it is also appropriate to say that he is conscious that *p*.

This equivalence thesis is occasionally challenged on the grounds that propositional consciousness is a *special kind* of propositional knowledge. More specifically, it is sometimes said that propositional consciousness is propositional knowledge that is *active* or *operative* – propositional knowledge that is currently on line and immediately available for use by a range of high level cognitive faculties. But this is not true. Thus, it can make perfectly good sense to say that a soldier is conscious that there will be a battle tomorrow even though the soldier is asleep. Further, consider the following exchange:

JACK: Is Bill conscious of the fact that Mary dislikes him?
JILL: As far as I can tell, Bill doesn't think about Mary much these days, if indeed he thinks about her at all; but yes, I'm sure he's still conscious that she dislikes him. It's hardly the kind of thing that he would forget.

Jill's reply to Jack strikes us as a bit awkward – we would find the exchange a bit more natural if Jill had said that Bill *knows* that Mary dislikes him. Even so, however, we have no trouble finding an interpretation of the exchange on which Jill's reply is literally true. And of course, if the reply is literally true, then it cannot be the case that "conscious that" is used only to attribute *operative* knowledge.

It appears, then, that this objection to the equivalence thesis is mistaken. But it is understandable, for there is a secondary sense of "conscious that" on which it does carry the suggestion that knowledge is currently operative. Thus, it would be quite natural to say the following: "Bill knows that he's supposed to be home by midnight, but he isn't presently *conscious* that this is so – at present he has no mind for anything but the music and his dancing." Statements of this sort are often regarded as true. But this could not be the case unless "conscious that" *can* be used to attribute active knowledge. Accordingly, it must be the case that there are two senses of "conscious that," a primary one on which it is equivalent to "knows that," and a secondary one on which it has a more narrowly circumscribed use. (I say that the latter sense is secondary because it is generally necessary to stress "conscious" in order to bring it to the fore.)

With these observations in mind, we can easily see that the primary sense of "conscious that" presents no special challenges to someone who is trying to understand consciousness. Of course, it presents plenty of interesting problems to someone who is trying to understand *knowledge*; but a philosopher of consciousness is interested principally in the nature of the mind, not in the ability to acquire knowledge of the world. Hence, unless he is also an epistemologist, a philosopher of consciousness should set the primary sense of "conscious that" aside as irrelevant to his main concerns.

The same applies, with a qualification, to the secondary sense of "conscious that." To understand the nature of *active* propositional knowledge, one should focus principally on propositional knowledge. But one should also consider what it is for a mental state to be active or operative. Because of this, the task of explaining the secondary sense is not the sole responsibility of epistemologists. Part of it belongs to philosophers of mind. Even so, however, I think that the philosopher of consciousness can set the secondary sense of "conscious that" aside. Insofar as it involves the notion of an active mental state, it presents some problems that are relevant to his main concerns. But as we will see, those problems arise independently in connection with experiential consciousness and access consciousness. These are no additional problems that are proprietary to the secondary sense of "conscious that."

1.3 INTROSPECTIVE CONSCIOUSNESS

A mental state counts as introspectively conscious if it is *actually* an object of introspective awareness, but it seems that we are also willing to ascribe introspective consciousness to mental states if the relevant agents could easily *become* aware of them, whether by simply redirecting their attention, or by asking a question like "What exactly is it that I am perceiving now?" Thus, we are quite prepared to say something like, "All of John's feelings about his sister are conscious, though some of his feelings about his brother are repressed." When we say something of this sort, we don't mean to imply that all of the mental states to which we are attributing consciousness are objects of explicit introspective awareness. Rather, we mean that the states would easily become objects of awareness if the agent would turn his attention to them. In general, we distinguish between *actual introspective consciousness* and *potential introspective consciousness*, and we apply this distinction both to mental events and to continuing states like one's attitudes toward one's siblings.

It seems that the states that are characterized by actual introspective consciousness are highly circumscribed, at least in comparison to the states that have potential introspective consciousness. Thus, there is very little introspective evidence for the idea that we are always actively monitoring our mental processes, taking explicit note of their nature, and it seems very unlikely that the brain would find it advantageous to expend energy on constant monitoring of this sort. On the other hand, it seems likely that potential introspective consciousness is distributed quite widely. Indeed, in adult human beings, at any rate, it may well be true that all experiences, including both occurrent propositional attitudes and events with a qualitative dimension, could easily become objects of introspective awareness. Still, actual introspective consciousness is more fundamental than potential introspective consciousness, metaphysically speaking, for potential consciousness exists only when actual consciousness might occur. Accordingly, I will mainly focus on actual consciousness in the present work.

There are two varieties of actual introspective consciousness – actual consciousness of mental *occurrences*, and actual consciousness of *enduring* mental states that are stored and static. Actual consciousness of occurrences takes place, for example, when an agent takes note of a passing thought, and also when an agent judges that he is perceiving an object of a certain sort. On the other hand, there is actual consciousness of a stored state when an agent judges that he believes (and has believed) that Albany is the capital of New York. Now it might seem at first that awareness of continuing states is quite different than awareness of occurrent states; but closer consideration shows that there is reason to think that these two forms of awareness are closely related. Thus, it seems likely that it is necessary to activate or "refresh" a continuing state in order to appreciate its existence introspectively. For example, in order to appreciate that one has the given belief about Albany, it seems necessary to activate the belief in some way – perhaps by asking the question, "What is the capital of New York?" Once this state has been activated, one can move from the resulting occurrent manifestation of it (e.g., the answer, "Albany!") to an introspective judgment that acknowledges the continuing state. If this is right, then the present case is similar to cases in which one achieves actual, occurrent awareness of an occurrent state. In the former as in the latter, one moves from an occurrent mental state to an introspective judgment.

In addition to showing that actual introspective consciousness of enduring states is closely related to actual introspective consciousness of mental occurrences, this line of thought shows that the former in fact depends on the latter. Introspective consciousness of occurrences is more fundamental than introspective consciousness of enduring states. Because of this dependency, in the present work I will be concerned principally, though not exclusively, with consciousness of occurrences.

, Introspective awareness of a mental state is independent of information about the external world, and it is also immediate, in the sense that it does not derive from chains of reasoning. If one arrives at a belief about one of one's mental states via inferences from one's behavior, or because a therapist has presented one with a theory of one's states that convincingly explains certain of one's dreams and emotional experiences, the belief does not qualify as introspective. It would probably be a mistake, however, to join various writers in maintaining that introspective beliefs must be entirely non-inferential. Generally speaking, achieving introspective awareness of a mental state is a matter of passing from the state itself to a judgment about the state. It is natural to think of transitions of this sort as inferences.

As we have noted, a state counts as introspectively conscious just in case it is an object of introspective awareness. It follows that questions about introspective consciousness are principally questions about the nature of introspection. One of the main questions about introspection is concerned with the nature of the vehicles of introspective awareness – the meta-cognitive states that represent or register our first order states. A number of contemporary philosophers endorse the view that these vehicles are perceptual in character, or at least quasi-perceptual, while others contend that they involve conceptualization and take the form of judgments. This controversy will receive considerable attention in a later chapter. Another very important question about introspection concerns the processes by which introspective awareness is produced. At first sight, at least, these processes seem to be highly variegated. Consider, for example, a case in which you judge that you are currently perceiving a red square. It is, I think, quite natural to suppose that this introspective judgment is produced by a relatively straightforward inferential process – a process that is similar to the one that produces the non-introspective judgment that there is a red object in front of you. Now consider a case in which I ask you whether you think that the population of London is larger than that of New York. Suppose that an answer to this question is stored somewhere in your memory, and that, once it is activated, the memory leads you to self-ascribe the belief that London is the larger city. How exactly did you arrive at this judgment? Not, it seems, by a direct inference that has roughly the same form as perceptual inferences, but rather by searching various memory files by a Google-like procedure. More particularly, it seems that my question primes a mental search engine with the key words "London," "New York," and "population," and then sets it in motion. These two examples pose the following question: Is introspection highly multiform, in the way that the examples suggest, or do the various introspective processes have a common nature that comes into view when one considers them more closely? As with the question about vehicles of introspection, we will be examining this question about introspective processes at some length.

I conclude this introductory discussion by noting that introspective consciousness is of fundamental scientific importance. This was originally emphasized by Freud. Many components of the Freudian model of the mind are now widely, and correctly, dismissed as pseudoscientific, but the notions of actual and potential introspective consciousness continue to play substantial roles in psychology. The mental states that are accessible to introspection are precisely the ones that can be reported in speech (in subjects with normal linguistic capacities, at any rate), and it is the ability of an agent to report his mental states that provides the principal evidence for scientific theories of consciousness. Moreover, there is reason to think that states that are introspectively conscious are also accessible to a large range of high level cognitive faculties, including those that are responsible for reasoning and for control of behavior. It seems that potential introspective consciousness marks a causal joint in the mind, a locus of causal relevance and authority that is of central importance in cognitive processing.

1.4   EXPERIENTIAL CONSCIOUSNESS

It is important to get a fix on this form of consciousness in the early going, for it turns out to be highly relevant to each of the remaining forms. To understand them, it is necessary to understand their respective relationships to experiential consciousness.

As we saw, experiential mental states fall into one or the other of two large categories – occurrent propositional attitudes and states with a proprietary phenomenology. Thoughts, volitions, and passing wishes count as experiences, but so do perceptual states, experiences of pain, and mental images. Now the members of these two categories are quite different from one another. Thus, occurrent attitudes have propositional objects that have conceptual contents and are individuated by logical forms, but this seems not to be true of states with a proprietary phenomenology (hereafter *P-states*). For example, while it seems to be true that a judgment of the form *if p then q* is different from the corresponding judgment of the form *either not-p or q*, we would not be inclined to say that the contents of perceptual experiences are individuated by logical differences of this sort. Another important difference derives from the phenomenological or qualitative nature of members of the second category. There is reason to doubt that thoughts, volitions, and other occurrent attitudes are individuated phenomenologically. When one is aware of a thought one is necessarily aware of its content, but it seems that one is not aware of any properties like the ones that are usually cited as paradigms of phenomenology – pain, the way it feels to be angry, the way yellow things look, the way oranges taste, and so on. Accordingly, the fact that P-states have a qualitative nature amounts to a metaphysical difference of substantial importance. In view of these differences, it is prima facie quite puzzling that we group members of the two categories together under a single concept, calling them all "experiences." What, if anything, is shared by all of the states that we classify in this way?

There are just three possibilities. It might be that occurrent attitudes and P-states share an intrinsic feature that is revealed by introspection. Perhaps they have a certain halo or phosphorescence. It also might be that we think of them as having similar relationships to the agencies that are responsible for introspective awareness, that we count them all as conscious experiences because we can become conscious *of* them in similar ways, and/or to similar degrees. Finally, it might be that they bear similar relations to a range of high level cognitive faculties – a range that includes the faculties responsible for introspective awareness, but a number of others as well. The thought here is that if a mental state is to count as an experience, it must be available or accessible to several of the faculties in the range, but that it need not be available to all of them. Thus, according to this suggestion, if a mental state occurs in a creature that lacks the capacity for introspective awareness, it can still have experiential status, provided that it is available to other high level faculties, such as the ones responsible for forming beliefs and desires. I will discuss each of these possibilities in turn.[4]

When you consider an experiential state introspectively, are you aware of an intrinsic phosphorescence that the state shares with all other experiences? When you consider a thought introspectively, for example, are you aware of it as having an intrinsic property that it shares with passing wishes, perceptual states, and experiences of pain? My guess is that your answer to these questions will be "no." Certainly that is the right answer in my case. When I attend introspectively to a thought, I am aware of content-related properties that distinguish it from other thoughts, and also of properties, such as the property *being a thought*, that it shares with other thoughts, but I cannot discriminate an intrinsic feature that I can also identify as present when I introspectively consider experiences of quite different kinds, such as a perceptual experience of a green leaf or an experience of pain in my right foot. If there is a phosphorescence that all experiences share, it is invisible, hiding shyly from introspection "behind" the more straightforward properties to which we have access. But no such property could give us a *reason* to group all experiences together under a single concept.

What about the second possibility? Might it be true that all experiences enjoy a special relationship with the agencies that are responsible

---

[4] There are other ways in which one might try to explain experiential consciousness, but I regard them as being significantly less plausible than the three I cite in the text. One alternative that should at least be mentioned is the view that states with experiential consciousness are so endowed because they involve reflexive awareness – that is, the view that each experientially conscious state provides its subject with awareness of that very state. The idea that consciousness is reflexive is currently enjoying a vogue (see, e.g., Uriah Kriegel and Kenneth Williford (eds.), *Self Representational Approaches to Consciousness* (Cambridge, MA: MIT Press, 2006)), but I can see no merit in it, especially when, as is usually the case nowadays, it is explained in terms of self representation. Here is a short argument in support of my view: "Generally speaking, when a mental state *M* represents an item *x,* it is because it is useful for the cognitive agencies that deploy *M* to have information about *x*. Hence, if a mental state *M* represented itself in addition to representing an external state of affairs, it would be because *M* was used by at least two different cognitive agencies – one that performed a world-oriented task (e.g., elaborating plans), and therefore required information about the world, and another that performed a meta-cognitive task (e.g., assessing evidence for judgments), and therefore required information about mental states. We have reason to believe, however, that meta-cognitive agencies have their own proprietary representations – that is, representations that are like *I see a blue sloop* and *I am thinking about New York* in that they have constituents with *explicit* psychological content. (See Chapter 8.) Assuming that this is correct, it is unclear why meta-cognitive agencies should have any use for additional representations of mental states. By the same token, it seems that it would serve no purpose to suppose that the representations that are concerned with the world (that is, representations such as perceptual experiences) also have a second layer of representational content that is self-referential. It seems unlikely that this supposition could do any useful explanatory work."

for introspective awareness? Might it be the case, in particular, that all experiences are alike in that they *would* become objects of introspective awareness if we were to attend to them – or if we were to ask a general question like, "What sorts of mental event are occurring now?" Certainly it seems to be true that experiences are intimately related to introspective agencies in adult human beings. Our introspective grasp of occurrent attitudes and P-states is immediate, effortless, and on the whole quite accurate. Even so, however, the concept of an experience seems not to come to the same thing as the concept of a mental state that is actually or potentially an object of introspective awareness. We are strongly inclined to attribute experiential consciousness to the mental states of small children and higher animals, despite having no reason to credit such beings with introspective capacities. A chimpanzee can consciously perceive the food in his dish, and can consciously judge that a stick would make a good tool, but can a chimp be introspectively aware that he is having a perceptual experience of food, or that he is making a judgment about a stick? We have no reason to think so. Our willingness to attribute experiential consciousness far outruns our evidence concerning introspective capacities.[5]

Moreover, it seems that we would be quite willing to continue to attribute experiential consciousness to other creatures even if we were to acquire evidence that ruled decisively against their being capable of introspective awareness. Suppose for a moment that it has been conclusively established that vervet monkeys lack meta-cognitive faculties.[6] Suppose,

[5] I should stress that I am not claiming that animals lack meta-cognitive faculties, but only that a common sense perspective provides no reason for thinking that they possess them. It remains to be seen whether psychologists will find *scientific* grounds for thinking that animals are capable of meta-cognition. In my view this is possible but unlikely. Dorothy L. Cheney and Robert M. Seyfarth review some of the relevant evidence in *Baboon Metaphysics* (Chicago: University of Chicago Press, 2007), Chapter 9, and eventually settle on the view that it is inconclusive, even with respect to the question of whether higher animals such as chimps and baboons have meta-cognitive states. Peter Carruthers provides another useful review of the literature in "Meta-cognition in Animals," *Mind and Language* 23 (2008), 58–89. He argues persuasively that, so far, anyway, there is no compelling experimental evidence for animal meta-cognition. For an opposing view, see Sara J. Shettleworth and Jennifer E. Sutton, "Do Animals Know What They Know?" in Susan Hurley and Matthew Nudds (eds.), *Rational Animals?* (Oxford: Oxford University Press, 2006), pp. 235–246. (In setting up experiments in this area, and also in interpreting them, it is crucial to keep in mind the distinction between behavior which expresses an animal's *knowledge* that it is in a certain mental state (e.g., a state of uncertainty), and behavior which only expresses *the fact that* an animal is in that mental state. I cannot argue the point here, but my sense is that Shettleworth and Sutton neglect this distinction.)

[6] I am here elaborating a hypothesis that Dorothy L. Cheney and Robert M. Seyfarth tentatively endorse in their classic work, *How Monkeys See the World* (Chicago: University of Chicago Press, 1990). The authors cite several considerations which tend to support the claim that "monkeys do not know what they know and cannot reflect upon their knowledge, their emotions, or their beliefs" (p. 254).

in particular, that we have found neuroanatomical evidence showing that vervets altogether lack the brain mechanisms that are responsible for meta-cognition in humans. Suppose further that it has been established that vervets can think about certain topics, and also that they have perceptual states that are on the whole quite similar to ours. Finally, suppose that it has been established that, apart from their not being objects of introspective awareness, states of these two kinds play roles in the internal economy of vervets that are similar to the roles that they play in us. Is the epistemic state we are imagining here one that contains a commitment to denying that the thoughts and perceptual experiences of vervets are conscious experiences? No. We can easily imagine our being in that state while finding it entirely appropriate to use the notion of experience, and also the notion of consciousness, in characterizing the mental states of vervets.

We must conclude, then, that experiences are mental events that participate in certain distinctive ways in the stream of higher level cognitive activity. But what, specifically, are the forms of participation that secure for them the status of experiences? The answer I wish to propose is that a mental event x is experientially conscious just in case x is, potentially, at least, a maximally proximal causal trigger for several of the high level cognitive agencies that are recognized by folk psychology. These agencies include the ones that are responsible for producing speech, forming beliefs and other propositional attitudes, making choices, elaborating plans, exercising on-line control of intentional actions, creating memories, monitoring mental states, and producing introspective judgments. In saying that a mental event must be a *maximally proximal* causal trigger for the agencies in question, I mean that it must be capable of doing causal work without being retrieved from memory, "refreshed," or converted into a different form. In short, it must be capable of doing causal work without additional processing. Further, in saying that a mental event need only be capable of serving as a causal trigger for *several* of the relevant agencies in order to count as an experience, I mean to allow for the fact that creatures can enjoy conscious experiences even though they lack one or more of them. As we have just seen, while it is true that conscious experiences in adult human beings can easily become objects of introspective awareness, we are prepared to attribute consciousness to states of creatures that have no meta-cognitive capacities. "Several" is meant to accommodate that fact. It is also meant to accommodate the fact that in all creatures, experiences of different types have different forms of causal relevance. An experience of pain, for example, seems not to be immediately relevant to planning and other forms of practical reasoning. Its causal relevance to these activities is indirect, being mediated by the beliefs and desires to which it gives rise. On the other hand, occurrent beliefs and desires are immediately relevant to practical reasoning.

What experiences have in common, then, is an immediate causal relevance to the various forms of high level mental activity.[7] This view has the virtue of predicting and explaining our confident ascriptions of experiential status to mental events, and also the virtue of predicting and explaining our tendencies to waver or feel confused when confronted with abnormal cases.

Consider the familiar example of the truck driver who suddenly realizes that he has absolutely no memory of what has transpired for the last half hour.[8] He knows by inference from his current location that he has negotiated a hilly and well traveled route, requiring frequent changes of gear and also adjustments to changes in the flow of traffic, but he has no memory of the perceptual states that guided him, nor of any of the other mental processes that produced his plastic and adaptive behavior. Did the driver have perceptual *experiences* during the period that is lost to him? Most people who consider the present case find it hard to answer this question. There is an inclination to answer "yes," because it seems that the driver must have had experiences of the road and the other vehicles in order to arrive safely at his destination. A complex series of adaptive actions seems to require guidance by perceptual experiences. At least, that is true in normal cases. But there is also tendency to regard the driver's perceptual states as unconscious. Perhaps the driver was completely absorbed by thoughts of a forthcoming vacation, and by vivid images of

[7] A referee has pointed out that experientially conscious events might not be *causal* triggers of the processes that lead to the formation of beliefs, memories, plans, and so on. They seem to us to be causal triggers when we view them from the perspective of introspection; but work by Benjamin Libet indicates that our commonsense perceptions concerning the causal powers of conscious mental events can sometimes be quite erroneous. (Libet's intriguing research indicates that conscious volitions often follow, rather than precede, the initial stages of the actions that they seem, when they are viewed from the perspective of introspection, to cause. See, e.g., Libet, *Mind Time: The Temporal Factor in Consciousness* (Cambridge, MA: Harvard University Press, 2004).) In response to this point, I will just say these two things: first, in my view Libet's work does not establish that conscious decisions are altogether lacking in causal efficacy with respect to action (they could, for all Libet's work tells us, be causally necessary conditions of the later stages of actions); and second, what is more important for our present concerns, it would be possible to reformulate all that I have said about the constitutive liaisons of conscious experiences in such a way that reference to causation was replaced throughout by reference to counterfactual dependence.

[8] David Armstrong, *The Nature of Mind and Other Essays* (New York: Cornell University Press, 1980), p. 59.

the walks he would take on the beach with his girlfriend. Or perhaps he was consumed by worries about his own health or that of one of his children. If his attention was fully occupied in one of these ways, then he was very likely relying heavily on stored visuomotor routines that do not require consciousness for their execution. Very likely there was no need for fully processed perceptual representations of the road, and therefore no need for perceptual consciousness. Or so it can seem.

The view that experiences necessarily enjoy a broad causal relevance with respect to high level mental activity predicts our ambivalence concerning the truck driver. After all, the driver's perceptual states have a rather low degree of causal relevance. They activate and shape actions that seem to us, due to their plasticity and adaptiveness, to be intentional. Presumably they also activate memories of the route that the driver is following, thereby enabling him to recognize the important landmarks and make the appropriate turns. But they differ from paradigms of experiential consciousness in that they have only these rather limited causal powers. Thus, for example, they are incapable of activating the faculties that produce perceptual judgments and perceptual memories. Because of this, they do not fully satisfy the requirement of broad causal relevance.

In the last section we observed that potential introspective consciousness appears to mark a causal joint in the mind. We have found in this section that the same is true of experiential consciousness. If an event is characterized by experiential consciousness, it enjoys a broad relevance to psychological faculties that are of considerable importance in their own right. In view of this fact, it is reasonable to expect that science will become increasingly interested in experiential consciousness. It has historically been the responsibility of philosophers to chart the domain of experiential consciousness, but in all likelihood they will soon have partners in this endeavor.

I conclude this section by considering an objection to the present account of experiential consciousness. It runs as follows: "According to the account, a mental event counts as a conscious experience in virtue of its causal *powers* – its *potential* for activating various high level cognitive agencies. In effect, then, the account represents experiential consciousness as a dispositional affair. Reflection shows, however, that we do not think of experiential consciousness as dispositional or modal in character. A thought is an experience because of *the way it actually is*, not because of what might happen to it in different circumstances."

This objection is misguided. It is entirely possible to accept the present account while agreeing that experiential consciousness depends on the way an event actually is, for the dispositional properties of a state are properties that it actually possesses. Moreover, while dispositions themselves have a subjunctive or modal character, they are grounded in laws that describe causal relations among actual events. It is the fact that a state actually satisfies certain laws that endows it with its dispositional properties. This is true, in particular, of the dispositions that are invoked in the foregoing account of experiential consciousness. If an event has the potentialities specified in the account, this is because it actually satisfies causal laws that link it to the activity of various high level cognitive faculties – laws which imply that events like the given event always or generally trigger such activity when certain other conditions are satisfied. The reference to potentialities or dispositions could easily be replaced by a list of laws if the exact nature of the laws was known. (The nature of the laws is not known because folk psychology provides us with no real grasp of the "other conditions" that must be fulfilled in order for experiences to do causal work.)

Objections of the present sort are familiar from the literature. It is common to criticize theories that seek to explain consciousness in terms of causal potentialities by saying that consciousness depends only on the actual nature of events. Taken at face value, such objections fall easily to responses like the one I have just given. But it may be that they actually derive from a somewhat more complex intuition – an intuition which can be expressed by saying that consciousness depends on the *actual, manifest* nature of a mental event. That is to say, it may be that those who raise objections like the one we have been considering do so because they feel that dispositions and other modal properties are not manifest. But if this intuition really is the source of the objections, then the objections derive ultimately from the sense that consciousness is an intrinsic property of mental events that is accessible to us via introspection. We have already examined this idea and found it wanting.

1.5 ACCESS CONSCIOUSNESS

The notion of access consciousness has figured prominently in contemporary discussions since the publication, in 1995, of Ned Block's "On a Confusion about a Function of Consciousness." Here is what he says in that paper:

A state is A-conscious if it is poised for direct control of thought and action. To add more detail, a representation is A-conscious if it is poised for free use in reasoning and for direct "rational" control of action and speech. (The "rational" is meant to rule out the kind of control that obtains in blindsight.) An A-state is one that consists in having an A-representation. I see A-consciousness as a cluster concept in which reportability is the element of the cluster that has the smallest weight even though it is often the most practical guide to A-consciousness.[9]

In later writings Block has considered the possibility of changing this definition by replacing the list of specific forms of control with a general reference to *global* control, but he has continued to give preference to his original characterization. He gives his reason for preferring the list-based account in the following passage:

[A definition that explains "A-conscious" as "directly available for global control"] has the advantage of avoiding enumerating the kinds of control. That makes the notion more general, applying to creatures that have kinds of control that differ from ours. But it has the disadvantage of that advantage, counting simple organisms as having A-consciousness if they have representations that are directly available for global control of whatever resources they happen to have.... [I]t would not do to count a slug as having A-conscious states simply because there is some machinery of control of the resources that a slug happens to command.[10]

We do not want to say that the internal states of slugs are conscious, but we do want to say that states are conscious if they share certain of our high level cognitive faculties. According to Block, the only way to honor both of these commitments is to explicitly cite the relevant faculties in defining consciousness.

Now to say that a state is poised to do something is to say that it is disposed to do it. Accordingly, as it is characterized in the foregoing definition, access consciousness depends on dispositions or causal tendencies. Block has come to regret this consequence of his definition. From his current perspective it is a category mistake to think of consciousness as modal or dispositional in character.[11] Instead of saying that a mental state counts as conscious if it is poised to play a certain role in cognition, he now prefers to say that consciousness attaches to mental states that are actually "broadcasting" to, or sending causal signals to, the faculties that are responsible for reasoning and purposive behavior. This is certainly a way of accommodating the view that consciousness is not a dispositional affair, but as we have seen, that view appears to derive from intuitions that

---

[9] Block, "On a Confusion about a Function of Consciousness," p. 382.
[10] Ned Block, "Concepts of Consciousness," in David J. Chalmers (ed.), *Philosophy of Mind: Classical and Contemporary Readings* (Oxford: Oxford University Press, 2002), pp. 206–218. The quotation occurs on p. 208.
[11] *Ibid.*

can appropriately be set aside. Moreover, it seems to be a mistake to think that we classify mental states as conscious because we are aware that they are actually in causal contact with various mental faculties. Consider a case in which you are thinking actively about an interesting topic and are at the same time perceiving the room in which you are located. Do you have any reason to think that your perceptual experience is actively sending causal signals to the faculties that are responsible for reasoning and control of action? No. You know that the perceptual experience is *capable of* sending out such signals, but you have no grounds for thinking that it is actually doing so. Still, you know that your perceptual state is conscious. For these reasons, I propose here to focus on the older version of Block's position, according to which mental states are conscious in virtue of being poised to produce certain effects.

Apart from the new emphasis on causal broadcasting, Block's account of access consciousness is quite similar to the account of experiential consciousness that I offered in the preceding sections. Each account explains a notion of consciousness in causal terms, and each account represents its target notion as a cluster concept. That is to say, each account explains its target notion in terms of a list of causal powers, but requires only that a critical mass or "enough" of these powers be present in order for the notion to be applicable. On the other hand, there are two important differences between the accounts. First, the list of causal powers that I use in characterizing experiential consciousness is much longer than the list that Block uses in his definition of access consciousness. And second, while my definition allows states without representational content to count as having experiential consciousness, Block limits the applicability of access consciousness to states that involve representations and have representational content. This difference is important because it shows that it would be inappropriate to use the notion of access consciousness in explaining experiential consciousness. The notion of experiential consciousness applies to states with a phenomenological dimension as well as to occurrent propositional attitudes. For example, it applies to experiences of pain. But do experiences of pain involve representations? Do they have representational content? I shall answer these questions in the affirmative in later chapters; but it would be wrong to think that affirmative answers are built into folk psychology, and by the same token, it would be wrong to think that the notion of experiential consciousness presupposes that experiences of pain have a representational character. In sum, the notion of access consciousness, as it is defined by Block, carries a presupposition that is not shared by the notion of experiential consciousness. It follows that it would be a mistake to rely on the former notion in attempting to define the latter.

Do we possess a notion of consciousness that we apply only to mental events that we can recognize as having content? More specifically, do we possess a notion that we are willing to apply to other high level mental occurrences but not to experiences of pain? As far as I can tell, the answer is "no." If a notion of consciousness can be applied to occurrent propositional attitudes, perceptual experiences, and to other high level states that we recognize as having content, it can be applied to experiences of pain as well – even though neither introspection nor folk psychology gives us much reason to think that such experiences have representational content. The notion of access consciousness is a reasonably close approximation to a notion that we actually do possess, the notion of experiential consciousness, and in fact, it would not be difficult to transform the former into the latter by liberalizing Block's definition. But as it stands, it does not correspond to anything that we can see at work in our actual practice. Accordingly, I will say no more about it in the present work.

1.6 CONSCIOUSNESS *OF*

Consciousness *of* comes in a variety of forms, but in the interests of definiteness I will focus here on perceptual consciousness *of*. It is an especially fundamental form, and has received much attention from philosophers and scientists.

To be perceptually conscious *of* something is to perceive it consciously, and to perceive something consciously is to be aware of it in virtue of being in a perceptual state that is a *conscious experience*. Accordingly, it is possible to explain what it is to be perceptually conscious *of* something by applying the account of experiential consciousness that is given in Section 1.5. (All of this applies, mutatis mutandis, to other forms of consciousness *of*.)

These observations are perfectly correct, and they are all that we need to keep in mind if we are interested only in the question of what makes it true that a perceptual state is *conscious*, or in other words, the question of what the *consciousness* of a perceptual state consists in. But there are further questions about perceptual consciousness that are worthy of consideration. One of these is the question of whether perceptual awareness is essentially representational, or is best understood as a form of access to objects that does not involve representations. Further, assuming that perceptual awareness is in fact representational, there are questions about the contents of the relevant representations. Is it propositional or more like the content of pictures? Another question concerns the validity of the claim, made by many philosophers and psychologists, that perceptual consciousness of the objective physical properties of objects depends on consciousness of other properties that can appropriately be called *appearances*. Still another question is concerned with what it is that makes a particular object an object of perceptual awareness. What makes it true that a given object is the object that an agent is perceptually conscious *of*?

I will discuss questions about perceptual consciousness *of* in Chapters 5 and 9.

1.7 PHENOMENAL CONSCIOUSNESS

A state possesses phenomenal consciousness if it has a phenomenological dimension, or in other words, if it presents its possessor with a qualitative characteristic, or *quale*. As this definition makes clear, if one wishes to explain phenomenal consciousness, it suffices to explain what it is to be a quale, and what it is for an agent to be presented with a quale.

Before undertaking the task of explaining qualia, which will be a primary concern of later chapters, it is necessary to adopt an initial characterization of qualia as a class, a characterization that specifies all of them, and that brings their common nature to the fore. One approach is to say that qualia are properties that we normally think of as *subjective*, in the sense that it is possible to grasp them fully only from the point of view of an experiencing subject. They are properties which, it is natural to think, are given to us fully when we experience them directly, and only when we experience them directly.

Is this the best way to define qualia? Certainly it has an important virtue: it honors standard views as to which properties are paradigms of the qualitative. The paradigms include the intrinsic characteristics of bodily sensations (e.g., pain), the ways that objects appear to us when we perceive them (e.g., the way yellow things look to normal observers in bright sunlight), the ways that subjects feel when they undergo emotions (e.g., the feelings of listlessness and enervation that accompany depression), and the ways objects are presented to us when we imagine them perceptually (e.g., the colors that are presented to one when one imagines the American flag). Reflection shows that the given definition implies that all such properties are qualitative. This is certainly a point in favor of the definition. Notice, however, that the characterization explains qualia in terms of our tendency to *think of* certain properties as subjective. It does not explain them as properties that genuinely *are* subjective. The reason for this is that there are metaphysical theories of qualia which deny that they can be said to be subjective in the relevant sense. We need an account of qualia that can be accepted by all of those who propose defensible accounts of their metaphysical nature. We don't want a conception which implies that advocates of one or more of these proposals are contradicting themselves. But it would be nice to have a characterization that succeeded in picking qualia out in terms of properties that they actually have, instead of properties that we merely take them to have. Is there a characterization that both meets this condition and is acceptable to occupants of a range of points of view?

Characterizations in terms of subjectivity have a certain currency in the literature, but so do characterizations of several other sorts.

A. According to one such alternative, qualia are intrinsic properties of experiences that are known to us via introspection. This account has a certain intuitive appeal, but it fails to satisfy the criterion of interperspectival acceptability: there are well motivated theories of qualia that are incompatible with it. Thus, there are theorists who reject the idea that qualia are properties of experiences, preferring to maintain that it is experience itself that provides us with access to qualia, not some sort of higher order, introspective awareness that is directed on experience from above. From this perspective, qualia are properties to which subjects have access via a relation of experiential awareness. They are objects of experience, things of which we have experience, not properties of experiences or states of experiential awareness.

To amplify: Consider an agent who is perceiving a red object in broad daylight. The agent is aware of certain distinctive color qualia in virtue of having this perceptual experience. Some theorists maintain that the qualia in question are properties of the experience, and that the agent is aware of them in virtue of a state of introspective awareness that has the experience as its object. Others deny these claims, urging that in a typical case, there is no object of awareness that is internal and mental. Instead, they say, the only object of awareness is the external object that the agent is perceiving – the object that is red. Accordingly, they conclude, the color qualia must somehow be properties of that object. Moreover, the agent's awareness of them should be classified as perceptual rather than introspective.

Both of these views enjoy a certain intuitive plausibility, and have provided motivation for prominent theories of qualia. We should not adopt a definition of qualia that rules either of them out as absurd.

B. Another widely accepted alternative makes use of the notion of what it is like to be in a mental state. Here is an example of this way of explaining them, due to Ned Block: "Qualia include the ways things look, sound, and smell, the way it feels to have a pain, and more generally, what it's like to have experiential mental states." Other authors give essentially the same account.[12]

The trouble with characterizations of this sort is that they are too inclusive. If "what it is like" is used in the way we use it in everyday life, the notion of what it is like to be in a mental state includes many components or dimensions of a mental state other than its qualitative character. What is it like to experience a pain? Surely this includes feeling an aversion, both to the pain itself and whatever is perceived to be its cause, perceiving one's body as it recoils from the perceived cause, wanting the pain to end, feeling anxious about one's body and the future course of the pain, focusing one's attention on the site where the pain is located, and thinking about ways of reducing the pain, or obtaining relief from it. None of these items is exclusively qualitative in character. What is it like to see a pumpkin? Surely this includes an amodal awareness of the various parts of the pumpkin that are not immediately present to the perceiver, aesthetic responses to the shape and color of the pumpkin, and various expectations as to how the pumpkin would respond if it was subjected to certain forces, such as being pushed. Qualia are among the properties that are picked out when we refer to what it is like to be in a mental state of type M, but they are far from being the only properties that are involved in the state. One might hope to avoid this problem by saying (a) that qualia are properties that determine what it is like to be in a state, and (b) that qualia are independent of the thoughts, expectations, preferences, propositional memories, intuitions, and amodal perceptual states that are involved in or accompany the state. But it is clear on reflection that this response is inadequate. Response (b) is largely negative in character. It is not a satisfactory way of identifying what qualia have in common. Moreover, an argument would be needed to show that the list of excluded phenomena (thoughts, expectations, etc.) is complete. Otherwise there is no reason to think that the account succeeds in specifying all qualia and nothing else.

C. Faced with these difficulties, one might try to explain qualia by invoking the fact that qualia appear to give rise to substantial metaphysical

---

[12] Ned Block, "Qualia," in Richard Gregory (ed.), *The Oxford Companion to the Mind*, 2nd edition (Oxford: Oxford University Press, 2004), pp. 785–789. The quoted material occurs on p. 785.

problems. As we will see in the next chapter, there are reasons for thinking that qualia are not reducible to physical properties of any kind, including the neurobiological properties with which they are most strongly correlated. With this fact in hand, we might attempt to characterize qualia by listing the standard paradigms, and then saying that, in general, properties count as qualitative if they give rise to metaphysical problems of the same sort as the ones that the paradigms generate. One would then make the definition more concrete by formulating the standard arguments for property dualism, the view that qualia are ontologically independent of physical properties.

There is something to be said for this approach, but it is not clear that it is superior to the one I cited at the outset, which explains qualia in terms of our sense that they are subjective. For it is not at all clear that arguments for property dualism are independent of our *take* on qualia – that is, of how we think about them and/or experience them. The arguments may not depend, at the deepest level, on the way qualia are in themselves, but rather on certain ways of thinking about them that are encouraged by commonsense psychology, and by the fact that our primary epistemic access to them involves a specific form of awareness (experiential awareness) that may in some ways be misleading. If so, the present characterization resembles the first characterization in that it is based ultimately on how qualia seem to us, rather than how they really are. It appears, however, this fourth characterization is no *less* successful than the initial one, which is based on our impressions concerning the subjectivity of certain properties. Like the initial characterization, the present one implies that all of the paradigms are in fact qualitative. Also, again like the first characterization, it is compatible with a wide range of metaphysical theories of qualia. But more: it is arguable that the fourth characterization arises from intuitions that are closely related to the ones that provide motivation for the first account. Thus, when one considers the standard arguments for property dualism, one appreciates that they tend to depend, at one point or another, on the idea that qualia are subjective, in the sense that our grasp of them derives from taking the point of view of an experiencing subject.

Although the first and fourth characterizations are similar in these ways, I will give preference to the first one in the present work. I find it more illuminating than the second one, largely because it does not presuppose the complex argumentation that is needed to support the idea that qualia at least seem to have a kind of ontological autonomy.

We began this survey of options because the initial characterization of qualia in terms of our *impression* that they are subjective is not entirely satisfactory. We have found, however, that the initial characterization is at least superior to the alternatives. I will therefore adopt it here. It is, after all, meant only to be a preliminary account, adopted because it promises to provide guidance in the early stages of our search for an illuminating *theory* of qualia.

In addition to this preliminary characterization of the class of qualia, we need a preliminary characterization of what it is for a mental state to *present* a qualitative character to a subject. There are just two possible views about this matter. According to one, qualia are properties of experiences, and a quale is presented to a subject when the subject is aware of an experience introspectively. This view implies, for example, that an experience of pain is an experience that has the property *being a pain*, and that a pain is presented to a subject when the subject has a meta-cognitive grasp of an experience that exemplifies this property. According to the other view, qualia are not properties of experiences but rather properties that we are aware of in virtue of having experiences. That is to say, according to the second view, there is a form of awareness, experiential awareness, that has qualia as its objects. We invoke this form of awareness when, for example, we speak of an experience of pain. An experience of pain is not an experience that exemplifies the property *being a pain*, but is rather a form of awareness of pain. This awareness is not meta-cognitive or second order but rather just first order, in the way that perceptual awareness is simply first order. On this view, what it is to be presented with a quale is simply to be experientially aware of the quale, to have experience *of* the quale.

I will proceed on the assumption that the second of these two ways of understanding what it is for a quale to be presented to a subject is correct. I will justify this choice with an extended argument in Chapter 3, but in addition, I will try to make it apparent as we move forward that the second way is much more fruitful than the first.

Returning now to phenomenal consciousness, I wish to suggest that it consists in experiential awareness of (instances of) qualitative characteristics, where qualitative characteristics are characteristics that we find it natural to think of as subjective. Phenomenal consciousness is a form of *consciousness* because the mental states that provide us with awareness of qualitative characteristics are experientially conscious, in the sense explained in Section 1.5. They are mental states that have certain distinctive causal powers.

Phenomenal consciousness is of interest to philosophers because it has proved to be extremely difficult to locate qualia in the physical world.

Consider, for example, the way a light blue object looks to us when we view it in bright sunlight. It has turned out to be very difficult to explain how this quale is related to states of the brain, and also quite difficult to explain how it is related to the physical processes in the external world that are causally responsible for our awareness of the quale. Indeed, as we will see in the next chapter, there are several extremely persuasive arguments which purport to show that the problem of locating the way blue things look in the physical world is intractable – that the quale is not implied or metaphysically determined by any physical property or set of physical properties, and a fortiori, that it is not identical with any physical properties or set of such. One of my principal objectives in the present work is to solve this problem – to show that despite appearances to the contrary, qualia can appropriately be regarded as reducible to physical properties. Most of the ensuing discussion is motivated, either directly or indirectly, by my desire to reach this objective.

1.8 SUMMARY

I have been concerned in this chapter to fix ideas, to introduce a few distinctions, to argue for several foundational claims, and to identify the questions that will be explored at length in future chapters. The list of these questions is as follows:

1. What is the nature of introspection and, correlatively, of introspective consciousness?
2. What is the nature of consciousness *of*? More specifically, what is the nature of perceptual consciousness *of*?
3. What is the nature of phenomenal consciousness, and more particularly, of the qualitative characteristics that serve as its objects? Can these characteristics be located in the physical world?

I will not be able to provide answers that address all aspects of these questions, but I will try to give answers that advance the discussion of the aspects that are most central and have the greatest philosophical significance.

In the case of the first question, as already noted, I will try to resolve the controversy between those who maintain that introspective awareness always involves conceptualization or judgment and those who maintain that it is principally perceptual or quasi-perceptual in character. According to the solution I will propose, introspection properly so called is always conceptual and doxastic. Introspective awareness always takes the form of judgment. To be sure, there is such a thing as perceptual or quasi-perceptual awareness of qualitative states, such as pain and the ways objects appear to us when we encounter them perceptually; but awareness of this sort is not really introspective, because the objects on which it is directed are not really mental. To be aware of a pain is to perceive a disorder of a certain sort in one's body, and to be aware of how yellow things look is to perceive a certain viewpoint-dependent property of an external object. I do not claim any immediate plausibility for these views. Rather, it requires considerable argumentation to bring their merits into view. Presenting the requisite argumentation will be the burden of several later chapters.

I will also maintain that introspection is highly polymorphous, in the sense that the processes responsible for introspective judgments are quite diverse. An introspective judgment to the effect that one is thinking that *p* inevitably has a quite different causal history than an introspective judgment to the effect that one is perceiving that *p*. Further, any judgment about an occurrent state inevitably has a quite different history than any judgment concerning an enduring state that exists in cold storage. The outputs of introspective processes are uniform – they are all higher order judgments. But the inputs are highly heterogeneous, and require highly heterogeneous forms of processing.

It will follow from my account of introspection that the agencies that are responsible for introspective awareness are dissociable from the agencies that produce and make use of first order mental states, and therefore, that introspective consciousness is dissociable from experiential consciousness, consciousness *of*, and phenomenal consciousness.

In the case of the second question, I have already maintained that to be conscious *of* an item is to be aware of the item in virtue of being in a state that is experientially conscious. If this is right, and the account of experiential consciousness in 1.5 is correct, then what remains is to offer a theory of awareness. I will begin this task by arguing that awareness is essentially representational in character. Awareness of an item necessarily involves being in a state that represents it. I will then turn to the specifically perceptual form of awareness. It will follow from my account of awareness that perceptual awareness has a representational structure, and that perceptual experiences have representational contents. I will be concerned to elaborate these points by explaining the more basic forms of perceptual content. More specifically, I will be concerned to explain a form of representational content that endows perceptual experiences with their qualitative dimension (or, in other words, to explain what is involved in being aware of perceptual qualia), and also to explain the form of content that supports perceptual awareness of external *objects*.

With respect to the third question, as already promised, I will maintain that the correct answer is, "Yes, qualia *are* physical in character, in the sense that they are reducible to physical properties." My discussion of qualia will have two parts. The first part, which will occupy Chapter 2 and Chapter 4, will be concerned with the leading contemporary theories of qualia and qualitative awareness. It will be largely negative and critical, and will be designed to set the stage for an alternative theory that I wish to propose. The second part will present this alternative theory – or, more precisely, those portions of it that are concerned with visual qualia, pain and other sensory qualia, and emotional qualia. The theory is broadly representationalist in character, in the sense that it argues for a representational account of awareness of qualia and relies heavily on assumptions about representations in closing the "explanatory gap" between qualia and the physical world, but it diverges sharply from other versions of representationalism at a number of points. It will be presented in Chapters 5, 6, and 7. Chapter 3 will treat foundational issues that are germane both to my objections to current theories and to the new theory that I wish to put in their place.

In sum, the present work is concerned with questions about introspective consciousness, perceptual consciousness *of*, and phenomenal consciousness. I have already said almost all of what I have to say about experiential consciousness. As the reader will recall, Section 1.5 proposes that experiential consciousness be explained in terms of causal relations to high level cognitive agencies, but it provides very little information about matters of detail. In Chapter 9 I will briefly characterize what seem to me to be the most important questions about such matters, but I will not attempt to answer them. In my judgment, they must await progress in the clinic and the laboratory.

Although I will not be explicitly concerned with experiential consciousness again until the very end of the book, I will frequently speak of experience, and will in Chapter 3 describe a form of awareness that I call *experiential awareness*. In interpreting such passages, please keep it in mind that, as I noted at the outset, there appear to be two senses of the term "experience," a broad sense in which it is applicable both to occurrent propositional attitudes and to P-states (states with a phenomenological dimension), and a narrower sense in which it is applicable only to P-states. It is the first sense that we have in mind when we say that thoughts are experiences, or that passing wishes are experiences. We have the second sense in mind when we say such things as "All knowledge of the external world derives from experience" and "Experience is our only source of evidence about the world." I will generally be using "experience" in the narrower sense – the sense in which it applies only to P-states. This is particularly true of those passages in which I speak of experiential awareness. Experiential *consciousness* is a property that is possessed by all occurrent attitudes and all P-states. On the other hand, experiential *awareness* is a form of awareness that has a phenomenological dimension. It is not a property of mental states, but a form of consciousness *of.* It is unfortunate that the English language associates two such different meanings with the same word, but confusion can be avoided by keeping the ambiguity in mind and choosing the sense that is appropriate to the context.

CHAPTER 2

Theories of qualia

This chapter is concerned with four widely discussed theories of the metaphysical nature of qualia – qualia physicalism, qualia functionalism, property dualism, and a view I will call *Harmanian representationalism.* There will be much more discussion of property dualism than of the first two theories, for it is one of my main concerns in the present work to show that property dualism is false. The reader must know how I understand the position, and what I take to be the main motivation for holding it, in order to be able to assess the objections to it that I shall develop. There will also be an extended discussion of Harmanian representationalism. It is a parent of a fifth theory of qualia that I will articulate and defend in later chapters. A discussion of the strengths and weaknesses of Harmanian representationalism will help to set the stage for that fifth account.

2.1 PHYSICALISM

As I will understand it here, *qualia physicalism* (hereafter *physicalism,* for short) is the view that qualia are reducible to physical properties. "Physical" is being used quite broadly in this formulation. It applies to properties of the sort that are in the domain of physics, but it also applies to properties that belong to the domain of biology. Thus, physical properties include the properties that are studied by neuroscience.

In the most demanding sense of the term, a property P_1 is said to be reducible to another property P_2 if P_1 is *identical with P_2.* In a somewhat less demanding sense, a property P is said to be reducible to a set of properties Σ if P is *realized by* the members of Σ – that is, if instantiations of P consist in or are constituted by instantiations of the members of Σ. And in a still less demanding but nonetheless robust sense, P is said to be reducible to the members of Σ if P *supervenes logically* on those other properties, where this means that it is logically impossible for there to be two things that are alike with respect to the members of Σ but that differ with respect to P.

According to *identity physicalism*, it is true in the first sense of "reducible" that qualia are reducible to physical properties. *Realization physicalism* asserts that this is true in the second sense of "reducible," and *supervenience physicalism* asserts that it is true in the third sense.

I will be concerned in this book mainly with identity physicalism, though the other versions of physicalism will also receive some attention. There are three reasons for this focus. First, the notion that identity physicalism uses to define reducibility, the concept of identity, is more basic and better understood than the concepts of realization and supervenience. In effect, it is a logical concept, and we have a very good grasp of the logical principles that govern it. Second, as we will see in a moment, there are several reasons for accepting identity physicalism that seem quite substantial. These reasons are more transparent, and correspondingly more persuasive, than anything that can be said on behalf of the other two forms of physicalism. And finally, as I see it anyway, it is in the end possible to answer the main traditional objections to identity physicalism, though the task of finding answers is not an easy one, and will in fact occupy our attention for much of this book.

One of the considerations favoring identity physicalism is that we obtain a simpler and more fully integrated view of the world if we maintain that qualia are identical with physical properties than if we allow that these two realms are separate. Again, if we suppose that qualia are identical with physical properties, we will easily be able to accommodate the intuition that qualitative states are causally efficacious – that they bring about behavior and other mental states, and that in doing so they do necessary causal work, work that does not merely duplicate work that is being done independently by physical properties. We will be able to accommodate the intuition because, if qualia are *identical* with physical properties, they have exactly the same causal powers as the latter. It follows that they can do causal work without merely duplicating the work of physical properties.[1] A third benefit of identity physicalism is that it provides us with an explanation of why qualitative states are strongly correlated with certain neural states: the correlations exist because qualitative states are *identical with* their neural correlates.[2] (Here I

[1] In its contemporary form, this argument for identity physicalism is due to Jaegwon Kim. See his *Mind in a Physical World* (Cambridge, MA: MIT Press, 1998), pp. 29–47.
[2] This argument was, I believe, first advanced in my book *Sensations: A Defense of Type Materialism* (Cambridge: Cambridge University Press, 1991), pp. 22–26. Incidentally, Chapter 2 of *Sensations* is an extended discussion of the considerations favoring identity physicalism. The reader who would like more information about the motivation for identity physicalism is referred to that chapter.

am just assuming that tight psychoneural correlations obtain. As we will soon see, this assumption can be defended.)[3]

Unfortunately, in addition to possessing these virtues, identity physicalism is also confronted with a number of objections. In the immediately following paragraphs I will consider an objection that is widely regarded as fatal, but is in fact quite misguided. In later sections I will consider the objections arising from property dualism. Every argument for dualism is in effect an argument against physicalism. I will review these arguments and consider how an advocate of physicalism might reply to them.

The *multiple realization argument* denies that qualia are correlated uniquely with physical properties. Instead, the argument maintains, qualia are *multiply realized by* physical properties. Thus, for example, it denies that there is a physical property P such that P is instantiated when and only when pain is instantiated. Rather, it affirms, there is a range of physical properties $P_1, ..., P_n$ such that pain is correlated with P_1 in members of the species S_1, correlated with P_2 in members of the species S_2, ... and correlated with P_n in members of the species S_n. In more concrete terms, the argument continues, the neural property that is correlated with pain in human beings is probably quite different than the one that is correlated with pain in octopuses, and both of these properties are probably quite different than the one that is correlated with pain in rattlesnakes. Accordingly, the strongest claim that we can make about the relationship between pain and the physical world is that it is *realized* by physical properties – and in particular, that it is realized by P_1 in members of S_1, realized by P_2 in members of S_2, and so on. We cannot claim that the relationship involves identity. For it is clear that we cannot say that pain is identical with all of these realizing properties, and it would be arbitrary to pick one of them and say that pain is identical with it. Hence, identity physicalism is false.[4]

---

[3] As I see it, the motivation for realization physicalism is less robust than that for identity physicalism; but realization physicalism receives support from the principle that all else being equal, it is appropriate to give preference to theories that represent their domains as unified and integrated. An account of qualitative facts that represented them as constituted by physical facts would postulate more unity, and a higher degree of integration, than a dualist account that represented them as connected with physical facts only by contingent laws of nature. Accordingly, on the assumption that all else is equal, the given principle authorizes us to prefer realization physicalism to dualist views.

Thus, in my view, anyway, there is something to be said for realization physicalism. On the whole, however, I take a dim view of the prospects of supervenience physicalism. I give a reason for this view in the Appendix.

[4] This argument was devised by Hilary Putnam. See his "Psychological Predicates," in W. H. Capitan and D. D. Merrill (eds.), *Art, Mind, and Religion* (Pittsburgh: University of Pittsburgh Press, 1967), pp. 37–48.

This line of thought has been enormously influential, but in my view it is undercut by the observation that we are guided principally by considerations of similarity in attributing qualitative states to members of other species. Thus, for example, a member of another species – say, a bat – must strike us as relevantly similar in order to count as experiencing pain. Now in everyday life we are aware only of superficial forms of similarity, having to do with overt behavior, and as a result, we are often willing to attribute pain to creatures whose behavior is in fact produced by neural mechanisms that are quite different from the mechanisms that are responsible for human pain-behavior. But the criteria governing our use of the concept of pain are implicitly sensitive to internal microstructural similarities and differences as well as to external macro-similarities and macro-differences, as is shown by the fact that we become increasingly guarded in our attributions of mental states to other creatures as our knowledge of interspecific neural differences increases. We are perhaps willing to attribute forms of pain to certain creatures that we know to lack our highly sophisticated apparatus for processing information about bodily damage, but we tend to be very reluctant to suppose that their experience of pain is at all similar to ours. In general, substantial differences in neural structure seem to us to be grounds either for refraining altogether from attributing qualitative states to other creatures, or for maintaining that the qualitative dimension of their existence is quite remote from ours.[5]

Now of course, if this is true, then it can hardly be the case that considerations having to do with the neural constitution of other creatures provide us with a good reason for rejecting identity physicalism. On the contrary, since our criteria for attributing qualitative states are sensitive to neural differences, we have good reason to suppose that interspecific differences in qualitative states are accompanied by neural differences in a way that advocates of identity physicalism should find entirely congenial.

It should be emphasized that the line of thought does not commit us to denying that members of remote species share highly determinable or generic qualitative properties with human beings. The claim is only that our principles do not require us to say that members of remote species have the highly determinate qualitative properties that we enjoy. It should also be emphasized that the latter claim suffices to defeat the multiple realization argument. An advocate of identity physicalism can allow with

---

[5] This is, in essentials, the line of thought I use against the multiple realization argument in *Sensations*, Chapter 9.

impunity that remote creatures share our highly determinable qualitative properties, provided only that they also share certain of our highly determinable neural properties.

In view of these reflections, it is reasonably clear that one should take identity physicalism seriously if one is inclined to take seriously any of the versions of physicalism that we have distinguished. But actually, there is reason to think that we should narrow the scope of our attention still further, and focus on a specific form of identity physicalism that is sometimes called *central state physicalism*. CS physicalism is the following doctrine:

Qualia are identical with neural properties that are instantiated by events in the central nervous system – more particularly, by events in the cerebral cortex.

Prima facie, at least, qualia are more tightly correlated with neural properties of cortical events than with any other physical properties. If this is right, CS physicalism is the most viable form of identity physicalism.[6]

Because of its virtues, identity physicalism will continue to play a prominent role in the present chapter. More specifically, we will be concerned, in most of the chapter, with the opposition between CS physicalism and the dualistic view that qualia are independent of physical properties. There will, however, be a short discussion of realization physicalism in Section 2.3, and a more elaborate discussion of supervenience physicalism in the Appendix.

2.2   FUNCTIONALISM

A property P is a *causal* property just in case the objects that possess P do so in virtue of their actual and potential causal relations. Thus, for example, the property of being a can opener is a causal property because the things that possess it do so in virtue of having a causal power – the ability to open cans. The property of being a pocket calculator is a causal property because it can be analyzed in terms of two causal powers – it has the ability to calculate values of simple functions, and it can be carried in one's pocket. A third example is the property C, which is explained by the following definition: an internal state of an agent has C just in case (i) the state is normally caused by damage to the body, and (ii) it normally has effects that include withdrawal from the damage-causing stimulus, nursing a damaged body part, wincing, and crying out. Notice that C is possessed by pains.

---

[6] CS physicalism was originally proposed in U. T. Place, "Is Consciousness a Brain Process?" *British Journal of Psychology* 47 (1956), 44–50, and in J. J. C. Smart, "Sensations and Brain Processes," *Philosophical Review* 68 (1959), 141–56. My *Sensations* is a defense of the view.

A *functional* property is a causal property of a particular sort. More specifically, a property is a functional property if it is a property that mental states of agents have in virtue of their actual and potential causal relations to environmental stimuli, to behavior, and to various other mental states. Thus, for example, the property C^* is a functional property: an internal state of an agent has C^* just in case (i) the state is normally caused by damage to the body; (ii) it normally has effects that include withdrawal from the damage-causing stimulus, nursing a damaged body part, wincing, and crying out; and (iii) it normally causes distress and a lasting aversion to the cause of the damage. Both C and C^* are possessed by pains, but the definition of C^* seems to do a better job of capturing what is distinctive about pains than the definition of C. Thus, for example, it seems that a comparatively simple robot could be in a state that possesses C, but nothing could be in a state that possesses C^* unless it was capable of experiencing distress and aversion. Of course, distress and aversion are mental states.

Functionalism is the view that every mental property is identical with a functional property.[7] Thus, for example, a version of functionalism might claim that pain is identical with the functional property C^*. In general, functionalism conceives of mental states "as nodes in a complex causal network that engages in causal transactions with the outside world by receiving sensory inputs and emitting behavioral outputs."[8]

Qualia functionalism is the view that qualia are identical with functional properties. It is this restricted form of functionalism that I will be considering here.

Qualia functionalists generally prefer their theory to qualia physicalism because they believe that their theory does a better job of accommodating the alleged multiple realizability of qualitative states. Since functionalists explain mental states in terms of abstract causal roles, they can say that qualitative states are shared by creatures with very different types of brain. To see why this might be so, consider a simple example of a causal property – say, the property of being a can opener. Things with very different structures can serve as can openers. Also, while almost all can openers are made out of metal, it is possible to use many different types of metal in the manufacture of can openers. Can openers can differ from one another radically in material composition. Thus, the property of

---

[7] Functionalism was born in Putnam's "Psychological Predicates." Jaegwon Kim's *Philosophy of Mind*, 2nd edition (Cambridge, MA: Westview Press, 2006), Chapters 5 and 6, provides an excellent exposition and examination of the view.

[8] Kim, *Philosophy of Mind*, p. 104.

being a can opener is multiply realizable. In general, causal properties are multiply realizable by physical properties.

As we have seen, while many people have found the multiple realizability argument persuasive, it seems to have a disabling flaw – at least for the special case of qualia. Accordingly, the advantage that is usually claimed for qualia functionalism is illusory. Moreover, qualia functionalism has a very serious disadvantage. On reflection, we find that it is quite implausible that qualia can be analyzed *exhaustively* in terms of actual and potential causal relations. Consider a mild bodily sensation like a tingle. Generally, when one is aware of a tingle, one is not aware of any causal interactions between it and other items. Nor is one aware of a *tendency* to bring about various effects. A tingle does not, for example, make one want to scratch the part of the body where it occurs. Nor does it have much of a tendency to cause one to continue to attend to it – tingles are not especially interesting. Accordingly, it would be very counter-intuitive to say that *all there is to the tingle* is causal relations. Moreover, reflection shows that the same is true even of much more puissant qualitative states like pains. To be sure, when one is aware of a pain one is aware that it has various effects and also various causal tendencies – for example, it causes you to wish that it would cease. But is it at all plausible that *all there is to the pain* is effects and tendencies? To me, at any rate, it is obvious that the answer should be "no." (Interestingly, this answer is ratified by the testimony of patients with pain asymbolia and other disorders that decouple pains from their normal effects. Despite no longer finding pains terrible or even bothersome, patients of this sort continue to call certain sensations "pains," and to maintain that these sensations have the same sensory or qualitative character as they did before the decoupling occurred.[9]) In general, qualitative states seem at least to have aspects or components that can be identified independently of their causal roles. Central state physicalism, which identifies qualia with neural properties rather than causal roles, is in a much better position to accommodate these aspects than functionalism.

It is clear, then, that introspection provides grounds for rejecting qualia functionalism. Now it might be countered that introspection should not be the final arbiter of metaphysical accounts of qualia. Perhaps there are theoretical grounds for identifying qualia with functional properties. And perhaps introspection is simply too myopic to register the functional character of qualia. I am on the whole sympathetic with observations of

---

[9] See, e.g., Nikola Grahek, *Feeling Pain and Being in Pain* (Oldenburg: Bibliotheks- und Informationssystem der Universität Oldenburg, 2001).

this sort. There is reason to think that introspection is a highly fallible instrument. Accordingly, *if* it is true in a given case there are theoretical grounds for supposing that a characteristic is different than introspection represents it as being, *then* it can be appropriate to discount the testimony of introspection. In the present case, however, I do not see any theoretical grounds for an across the board identification of qualia with functional properties. The only fully general argument for such an identification is the multiple realization argument, which we have found to be deeply flawed.

I should emphasize that the foregoing objection is directed only against *qualia* functionalism. The point of the objection is that qualitative states have aspects or dimensions that can be identified independently of causal relations to inputs, outputs, and other mental states. There are mental phenomena that lack such dimensions. Functionalist treatments of such phenomena are immune to the objection.

2.3   PROPERTY DUALISM, PART I

The central tenet of property dualism is that qualia are sui generis. Qualia are not reducible to physical properties of any sort, nor are they reducible to functional properties. There are three main forms of this view: *identity dualism* denies that qualia are identical with physical or functional properties; *realization dualism* denies that qualia are realized by properties of either of these other two kinds; and *supervenience dualism* denies that qualia supervene on properties of either of the other kinds.

None of the versions of property dualism deny that there are laws of nature linking qualia to states of other kinds. On the contrary, they are perfectly content to recognize that there are rigid laws linking pain and other qualia to various forms of cortical activity. They claim only that any such laws must be metaphysically contingent – that they do not involve relations of logical necessity. Pain may be linked to a certain type of brain activity, B, by laws of nature, but it is not reducible to B.

I will be principally concerned with identity dualism, largely because it is diametrically opposed to identity physicalism. As indicated earlier, identity physicalism is more transparent than other forms of physicalism, and is also, prima facie, at any rate, supported by a larger and more persuasive array of considerations. Another reason for considering identity dualism is that it receives especially strong support from intuitions and arguments. I will, however, consider an especially engaging argument for realization dualism at some length, and will discuss supervenience dualism in an appendix. Each of the forms of property dualism has a certain appeal, and contributes its appeal to the overarching general doctrine that qualia are sui generis. Any attempt to evaluate the overarching doctrine must make contact with all of its concrete embodiments.

The present section is concerned exclusively with arguments for property dualism – there will be six in all. The next section will discuss some replies to the arguments, and will also compare the merits of property dualism with those of physicalism.

The Cartesian modal argument

The modal argument that I wish to consider here is intended to establish property dualism, but it derives from an argument for substance dualism that Descartes presents in the *Sixth Meditation*. Substance dualism is the view that the mind, considered as a mental substance, is distinct from the physical body, and also from all of the parts of the body, including the brain. In arguing for this view, Descartes begins by endorsing the following Conceivability/Possibility Principle:

Everything which I clearly and distinctly understand is capable of being created by God so as to correspond exactly with my understanding of it.[10]

He then infers this Separation Principle:

The fact that I can clearly and distinctly understand one thing apart from another is enough to make me certain that the two things are distinct, since they are capable of being separated, at least by God.

In arriving at the Separation Principle, he is evidently presupposing a second premise that he does not explicitly state. This additional premise must look something like this:

If it is possible for two things to exist apart from one another, then those things are distinct.

The remaining premise is a proposition to the effect that Descartes is able to understand mind existing apart from body and body existing apart from mind:

I have a clear and distinct sense of myself, insofar as I am simply a thinking, non-extended thing; and on the other hand I have a distinct idea of body, insofar as this is simply an extended, non-thinking thing.

---

[10] All quotations from Descartes are taken from John Cottingham, Robert Stoothoff, and Dugald Murdoch, *The Philosophical Writings of Descartes*, Volume II (Cambridge: Cambridge University Press, 1984), p. 14.

Combining the Separation Principle with this claim about his understanding of mind and body, Descartes arrives at an endorsement of substance dualism:

> It is certain that I am really distinct from my body, and can exist without it.

What is distinctive about this argument is that it makes a case for a form of dualism by appealing to the Conceivability/Possibility Principle.

Descartes's argument has a presupposition that nowadays many people question – the doctrine that the conscious mind is a substance. From a contemporary perspective, the conscious mind is not a continuing object that satisfies certain criteria of unity and persistence, and that exists independently of particular mental states and processes, but is rather best seen as a kind of logical construction, the set or totality of states and processes that count as conscious, or as a mode of functioning of a substance that also has a number of *un*conscious modes of functioning. There are, however, certain related arguments that are not called into question by doubts about the substantiality of the conscious mind. One of these is an argument that uses the Conceivability/Possibility Principle to justify *property dualism*. It is this argument that I wish to focus on here.

Before we proceed, however, we should take note of an objection that Arnauld raised against Descartes's argument for substance dualism.[11] Arnauld began by pointing out that it is possible for someone to conceive of an item without conceiving of it as having certain of its essential properties. In particular, he observed, it is possible to conceive of a right triangle without conceiving of it as having the Pythagorean property (that is, without conceiving of it as satisfying the condition that the square of the hypotenuse is equal to the sum of the squares of the sides). "How can you be sure," Arnauld then asked Descartes, "that something like this is not happening when you conceive of your mind without conceiving of it as being accompanied by the body? Perhaps in conceiving of the mind you are failing to conceive of all of its essential properties, and perhaps some of these properties are physical in character. What guarantees do you have that this is not the case?" As I read Descartes, he never fully appreciated the force of this objection, though he did try to meet it in various ways. I will not review his response here. Instead I will just note that he needs an additional premise to the effect that when he conceives of his mind clearly and distinctly, he also conceives of it *completely*, in the

[11] Antoine Arnauld, *Sixth Set of Objections*, in Cottingham, Stoothoff, and Murdoch, *The Philosophical Writings of Descartes*, pp. 278–284.

sense that he conceives of it as having all of the essential properties that it in fact possesses.

If we reconfigure Descartes's argument so that it is concerned with our present topic, qualia, and in the interests of definiteness we focus on the special case of pain, we obtain a line of thought that runs as follows:

First premise: We are able to conceive clearly and distinctly of situations in which pain exists without being accompanied by φ-activity. (I here use the expression "φ-activity" to stand for a certain neurobiological property – the neurobiological property that will in fact turn out to be correlated most intimately with pain.)

Second premise: When we conceive of pain, we conceive of it completely, in the sense that in conceiving of it we do justice to all of its essential properties.

Third premise: If it is within our power to conceive of its being the case that *p* clearly, distinctly, and completely, then it is genuinely possible that *p*.

Lemma: By the first, second, and third premises, it is genuinely possible for pain to exist without being accompanied by φ-activity.

Fourth premise: If it is genuinely possible for *x* to exist without being accompanied by *y*, then *x* is not identical with *y*.

Conclusion: Pain is not identical with φ-activity.

We can use a similar argument to show that any quale is distinct from the neural property with which it is most closely associated in the actual world.

Now the first, third, and fourth premises of this argument all have a certain intuitive appeal, but the second premise needs a defense. Is it true that we can conceive of pain completely? Prima facie, at least, the answer is "yes." Let us assume that we are conceiving of it from a first person perspective, and that this is the way of conceiving of pain with which the argument is concerned. Now when we conceive of pain from the first person perspective, our conception is determined by our experience of pain. Is it possible that our experience of pain fails to reveal the full essential nature of pain? It seems that the answer should be "no." After all, when we experience pains our awareness of them is *direct*, in the sense that there is no mediating appearance or mode of presentation. Pains are *self presenting*, not presented to us by something else, which might occlude their essential natures. Moreover, pains are not given to us perspectivally: it makes no sense to speak of experiencing pains from different points of view. But this means that it makes no sense to ask how pains might appear to us if we could experience their "backsides" or their "insides." Hence, it cannot be the case that pains have parts or aspects that experience fails to register. How then could it be the case that pains have a hidden dimension? More specifically, how could they have a hidden dimension that includes properties such as *involving the firing of thousands of neurons* or the property *involving the release of neurotransmitters*? It seems that our normal models of how dimensions can be hidden have no application in this case.

As is often noted, it is possible to construct similar arguments to show that qualia are distinct from functional properties as well as physical properties. (I will henceforth use "physical property" in a broadly inclusive sense, according to which it stands for both physical and functional properties.)

The knowledge argument

Although it is possible to find precursors of the knowledge argument in various earlier texts, it seems to have been first stated explicitly in papers that Frank Jackson wrote in the 1980s. Here is Jackson's first formulation of the argument:

Mary is a brilliant scientist who is, for whatever reasons, forced to investigate the world from a black and white room *via* a black and white television monitor. She specializes in the neurophysiology of vision and acquires, let us suppose, all of the physical information there is to obtain about what goes on when we see ripe tomatoes, or the sky, and use terms like "red" and "blue" and so on. She discovers, for example, just which wave-length combinations from the sky stimulate the retina, and how exactly this produces *via* the central nervous system the contraction of the vocal cords and the expulsion of air from the lungs that results in the uttering of the sentence "The sky is blue." … What will happen when Mary is released from her black and white room or is given a colour television monitor? Will she *learn* anything or not? It seems just obvious that she will learn something about the world and our visual experience of it. But then it is inescapable that her previous knowledge was incomplete. But she had *all* the physical information. Ergo there is more to have than that, and physicalism is false.[12]

Elsewhere Jackson tells us exactly what it is that Mary will learn: "For when she is let out of the black-and-white room or given a color television, she will learn what it is like to see something red, say."[13] Another way to put this is to say that she will learn how red things look, and still

---

[12] Frank Jackson, "Epiphenomenal Qualia," *Philosophical Quarterly* 32 (1982), 127–136. The paper is reprinted in David J. Chalmers (ed.), *Philosophy of Mind: Classical and Contemporary Readings* (Oxford: Oxford University Press, 2002), pp. 273–280. The quoted passage occurs on p. 275.
[13] Jackson, "What Mary Didn't Know," *Journal of Philosophy* 83 (1986), 291–295, reprinted in Ned Block, Owen Flanagan, and Güven Güzeldere (eds.), *The Nature of Consciousness* (Cambridge, MA: MIT Press, 1997), pp. 567–570. The quoted passage occurs on p. 567.

another is to say that she will become acquainted with the appearance that red things present to normal observers.

Jackson's line of thought can be recast as a formal argument as follows:

First premise: Before Mary left her black and white room, she knew all of the physical facts about color and color perception.

Second premise: Yet there was a fact about color that she didn't know – the fact that red things look a certain way.

Third premise: If it is possible to know all of the members of a certain set Σ of facts without being in a position to know a given fact, f, f is not identical with any of the members of Σ.

Conclusion: The fact that red things look a certain way is not identical with any of the physical facts about color and color vision.

This line of thought is concerned only with a particular color quale. As Jackson points out however, it can easily be generalized: "Clearly the same style of Knowledge argument could be deployed for taste, hearing, the bodily sensations and generally speaking for the various mental states which are said to have (as it is variously put) raw feels, phenomenal features, or qualia."[14]

Nagel's argument

Thomas Nagel's wonderful paper "What is it Like to be a Bat?" presents a critique of reductionist theories of qualia and phenomenal consciousness that even now, more than thirty years later, continues to be broadly influential.[15] Nagel tells us that it is not his intention to promote property dualism. Rather, he is concerned to show that the discussion of qualia needs to be reframed in ways that would carry it beyond the conflicts between physicalism, property dualism, and the other standard positions. Reflection shows, however, that his line of thought can easily be adapted so as to yield an argument for property dualism. Moreover, it has seemed to many readers that this argument is not undercut by Nagel's concerns about the merits of standard positions. The argument has a direct and immediate appeal that earns it independent consideration.

Nagel begins his discussion by maintaining that the specific qualitative character of an experience is subjective, in the sense that it can be fully

---

[14] Jackson, "Epiphenomenal Qualia," in Chalmers, *Philosophy of Mind*, p. 275.
[15] Nagel, "What is it Like to be a Bat?" *Philosophical Review* 83 (1974), 435–50, reprinted in Chalmers, *Philosophy of Mind*, pp. 219–226.

appreciated only from the point of view of the subject of the experience. In the case of a bat, for example,

we may ascribe general *types* of experience on the basis of the animal's structure and behavior. Thus we describe bat sonar as a form of three-dimensional forward perception; we believe that bats feel some versions of pain, fear, hunger, and lust, and that they have other, more familiar types of perception besides sonar. But we believe that these experiences also have in each case a specific subjective character, which it is beyond our ability to conceive.[16]

Nagel explains the key notion of subjectivity in the following passage:

There is a sense in which phenomenological facts are perfectly objective: one person can know or say of another what the quality of the other's experience is. They are subjective, however, in the sense that even this objective ascription of experience is possible only for someone sufficiently similar to the object of ascription to be able to adopt his point of view – to understand the ascription in the first person as well as in the third, so to speak. The more different from oneself the other experiencer is, the less success one can expect with this enterprise.[17]

In combination, these two passages present us with the following doctrine, which I will eventually take as the initial premise of an argument for property dualism:

First premise: Facts about the qualitative character of an experience are fully accessible only from the point of view of the being who is the subject of the experience.

In Chapter 1 I defined qualia as characteristics that we *suppose* to be fully accessible only from the point of view of the experiencing subject. In effect, this first doctrine of Nagel's asserts that we are *right* to suppose that certain characteristics have only this very limited sort of accessibility. The characteristics that we *suppose* to have only the limited form *really do* have only the limited form.

After making a case for the first doctrine, Nagel goes on to reason as follows:

This bears directly on the mind-body problem. For if the facts of experience – facts about what it is like *for* the experiencing organism – are accessible only from one point of view, then it is a mystery how the true character of experiences could be revealed in the physical operation of that organism. The latter is a domain of objective facts *par excellence* – the kind that can be observed and understood from many points of view and by differing perceptual systems. There are no comparable imaginative obstacles to the acquisition of bat neurophysiology by

---

[16] *Ibid.*, p. 221.   [17] *Ibid.*, p. 222.

human scientists, and intelligent bats or Martians might learn more about the human brain than we ever will.[18]

As I understand it, the main point of this passage is the following doctrine about the physical character of an experiencing subject:

Second premise: The facts about the physical constitution of a subject are fully accessible from the third person point of view, and also from a variety of other points of view, that are occupied by members of other species.

Like the first doctrine, this second one is extremely plausible.

Now let us add the following truism to the two doctrines we have already flagged:

Third premise: If facts about the qualitative character of the experiences of a subject are fully available only from the point of view of the experiencing subject, and facts about the physical constitution of a subject are available from a variety of points of view, then the former facts are not identical with any subset of the latter.

In combination with the first two premises, this new one yields a conclusion that looks like this:

Conclusion: Facts about the qualitative character of the experiences of a subject are not identical with any set of facts about the physical constitution of the subject.

This is of course a version of property dualism.

As noted, the present conclusion is not the one that Nagel himself recommends. Instead, he prefers to think of the first and second premises as undercutting the motivation for views like physicalism and property dualism, and as even challenging their meaningfulness. In fact, however, if we grant that the first and second premises are meaningful and well motivated, as it seems we must, then we must adopt a similar attitude towards the conclusion. Thus, given that the terminology in the third premise also figures in the first and second premises, we must hold that the third premise is fully meaningful if the others are. Further, given that we grant meaningfulness of the third premise, we must also grant its truth, for it is an instance of a principle of logic (Leibniz's Law). Thus, contrary to what Nagel himself says, there is a strong argument that easily and naturally transmits the intuitive appeal of the first and second premises to property dualism.

---

[18] *Ibid.*, p. 222.

The explanatory gap argument

Joseph Levine is primarily responsible for articulating the intuition that there is an explanatory gap separating processes in the brain from the qualitative dimension of a subject's experience, and for emphasizing its importance for the debate between physicalists and advocates of property dualism. In particular, he was the first to see that this gap might provide the basis for an argument that provides dualism with additional support.

The argument begins with the following observation:

> [I]f materialism is true, there ought to be an explanation of how the mental arises from the physical. … If nature is one large, lawful, orderly system, as the materialist (or naturalist) insists that it is, then it should be possible to explain the occurrence of any part of that system in terms of the basic principles that govern nature as a whole.[19]

The second step points out that it seems impossible to explain the existence of qualia in terms of brain processes – or physical occurrences of any other kind.

The problem, however, is that there are good reasons for thinking that, unlike other macro domains, when it comes to qualia, we are not lacking merely enough detail to provide the requisite explanation, but any idea of how such a theory might go. That is, there is an explanatory gap between the physical and the mental (at least when it comes to qualia).[20]

Levine develops this view as follows:

> As I now look at my red diskette case, I'm having a visual experience that is reddish in character. Light of a particular composition is bouncing off the diskette case and stimulating my retina in a particular way. That retinal stimulation now causes further impulses down the optic nerve, eventually causing various neural events in the visual cortex. Where in all of this can we see the events that explain my having a reddish experience? There seems to be no discernible connection between the physical description and the mental one, and thus no explanation of the latter in terms of the former.[21]

Together, the first two passages entail the falsity of materialism, and the third passage helps us to see that the main contention of the second passage is really quite plausible.

---

[19] Joseph Levine, *Purple Haze* (Oxford: Oxford University Press, 2001), p. 69. I should mention that Levine does not see his argument as a refutation of physicalism, but rather as a powerful argument for dualism that physicalists have not yet been able to answer.
[20] *Ibid.*, p. 69.   [21] *Ibid.*, p. 77.

The quoted passages provide the gist of the explanatory gap argument, but they prescind from a couple of important details. One is the idea that a full and final explanation of the facts involving a property *P1* in terms of facts involving a property *P2* should make it inconceivable that the latter facts might have occurred without being accompanied by the former. Levine illustrates this idea by appealing to the standard explanation of what happens at the macro level when water boils in terms of the kinetic energy of H_2O molecules:

Molecules of H_2O move about at various speeds. Some fast-moving molecules that happen to be near the surface of the liquid have sufficient kinetic energy to escape the intermolecular attractive forces that keep the liquid intact. These molecules enter the atmosphere. That's evaporation. The precise value of the intermolecular attractive forces of H_2O molecules determines the vapor pressure of liquid masses of H_2O, the pressure exerted by the molecules attempting to escape into saturated air. As the average kinetic energy of the molecules increases, so does the vapor pressure. When the vapor pressure reaches the point at which it is equal to atmospheric pressure, large bubbles form within the liquid and burst forth at the liquid's surface. The water boils.[22]

Levine then makes the following claim: "[G]iven a sufficiently rich elaboration of the story above, it is *inconceivable* that H_2O should not boil at 212° sea level ... ."[23] The other additional idea is the claim, familiar from the Cartesian modal argument, that where *S* is any set of facts involving physical properties of the brain, it is easy to conceive of the members of *S* existing without being accompanied by any qualitative facts. Here is a passage in which Levine gives expression to this point:

No matter how rich the neurophysiological story gets, it still seems quite coherent to imagine that all that should be going on without there being anything it is like to undergo the states in question. Yet, if the physical story really explained the qualitative character, it would not be so clearly imaginable that the qualia should be missing.[24]

Given that Levine relies so heavily at this point on the conceivability of situations involving neurophysiological facts but no qualitative facts, there is a temptation to suppose that his reasoning is just a variant of the Cartesian reasoning we considered earlier – that the explanatory gap argument collapses into the Cartesian modal argument. But this would be a mistake. The Cartesian modal argument exploits intuitions about the relationship between conceivability and possibility; the gap argument

---

[22] *Ibid.*, p. 79.   [23] *Ibid.*, p. 79; my emphasis.   [24] *Ibid.*, p. 79.

relies on intuitions about the relationship between conceivability and explanation.

Pulling the various ideas we have been reviewing into a formal argument, we wind up with a line of thought that looks something like this:

First premise: If materialism is true, then there exists a full and final explanation of facts involving qualitative properties in terms of facts involving physical properties.

Second premise: If there is a full and final explanation of qualitative facts in terms of certain physical facts, then it should be inconceivable that the latter facts might occur without being accompanied by the former.

Third premise: Where Σ is any set of physical facts, it is possible to conceive of the members of Σ existing without being accompanied by any qualitative facts.

Conclusion: Materialism is false.

As we have seen, Levine argues persuasively for his premises. Prima facie, at least, the argument is successful.

But what exactly does the conclusion mean? What are the defining properties of the view that Levine calls "materialism"? The answer is that, as Levine conceives of the view, materialism asserts that every property that is not itself a basic physical property is realized by basic physical properties.[25] Thus, when it is restricted to the properties that are of special interest to us, materialism is roughly equivalent to the doctrine I earlier called "realization physicalism" – the doctrine that every qualitative property is realized by physical properties. To the extent that it is successful, Levine's argument counts against this doctrine, and also promotes its opposite, realization dualism.

We may wonder whether considerations having to do with the explanatory gap can be used to call other forms of physicalism into question as well. In particular, can such considerations be used to call identity physicalism into question? To ask this question is to ask whether the following variant of the first premise is correct:

(*) If identity physicalism is true, then there exists a full and final explanation of facts involving qualitative properties in terms of facts involving physical properties.

The answer seems to be "yes," for it is plausible that it is possible to explain a fact involving a qualitative property P_1 by showing it follows from a set of facts involving a physical property P_2 and a claim to the effect that P_1 is identical with P_2. What about the doctrine that many people

---

[25] *Ibid.*, p. 21.

think of as *minimal* or *basic physicalism* – the doctrine that all properties supervene on physical properties? Is it challenged by considerations having to do with the gap? To ask this second question is to ask whether (**) is correct:

(**) If supervenience physicalism is true, then there exists a full and final explanation of facts involving qualitative properties in terms of facts involving physical properties.

Here the answer seems to be "no." Roughly speaking, one property supervenes on another if the latter property entails the former property: supervenience boils down to entailment. Thus, in effect, (**) claims that if qualia are entailed by physical properties, then it is possible to explain facts involving qualia in terms of facts involving physical properties. It does not take much reflection to see that this claim is false: there is clearly more to explanation than entailment. (Thus, for example, facts involving the property of being a prime number are entailed by facts involving the property of being a Gothic cathedral, since the former facts are necessary. But no one thinks that facts involving prime numbers can be explained by facts involving cathedrals.) It turns out, then, that there is at least one important form of physicalism that is not called into question by a gap argument.

The appearance/reality argument

I turn now to an argument that cannot be attributed to any specific individual, and that is rarely made fully explicit, but that seems to lie just beneath the surface of a great many discussions. It begins with the observation that it is inappropriate to distinguish between the appearance of a quale and the corresponding reality. Generally speaking, if it seems to one that one is experiencing a certain quale, then one *is* experiencing it. Having made this initial observation, the argument goes on to point out that physical properties do not enjoy this sort of immunity to illusion and hallucination: it is always possible that what seems to be an instance of a given physical property is actually an instance of a property of a quite different sort. Indeed, what seems to be an instance of a given physical property may fail to exist altogether. But if this is the case, the argument continues, then physical properties have a characteristic that qualia lack – they admit of an appearance/reality distinction. It follows by Leibniz's Law that qualia are distinct from physical properties.

Is it true that qualia are immune to illusions and hallucinations? To appreciate the plausibility of this claim, consider a case in which you have an experience that makes it appropriate to judge that you are in pain. Might the judgment be false despite being appropriately grounded in this way in an actual experience? Might the experience somehow fail to reveal the true nature of its object? Might it be that the sensation you are experiencing is actually quite different than your experience of it suggests, or that it does not exist at all? Prima facie, at least, the answer to all of these questions is "no." A situation in which it seems to you experientially that you are in pain is a situation in which you really are in pain. (It is essential in considering the questions that you focus on a situation in which you actually have an experiential ground for judging that you are in pain, or in other words, a situation in which you are having an experience of the sort that you have when you really are in pain. A situation in which you simply judge that you are in pain, without your judgment being appropriately grounded in an experience, will not serve our present purpose. (It is possible to judge that one is in pain without having an experiential ground for so judging. This can happen, in particular, when one's concept of pain has been primed by an earlier threat or warning. Priming increases the chance that a concept will be applied inappropriately.)) Alternatively, consider a situation in which an object presents a certain color appearance to you – perhaps it appears to be red. Could it be the case that the object is only *appearing to appear* red, and that it is actually appearing some quite different way? No. There is no distinction to be drawn between the way an object appears to appear and the way it really appears. In the case both of pain and the appearance of red, appearance and reality come to the same thing.

Perhaps it will be useful to reconfigure the appearance/reality argument a bit, using terminology that highlights its connection with certain areas of the literature:

First premise: Pains are self presenting. In other words, there is no difference between its seeming to one that one is experiencing a quale and its being the case that one is experiencing a quale. (In still other words, qualia do not admit of an appearance/reality distinction.)

Second premise: Brain states are not self presenting. In other words, where B is any brain state, there is a difference between its seeming to one that a brain is in B and its being the case that a brain is in B. The same is true of all other physical properties.

Lemma: Qualia have a characteristic that brain states lack – the characteristic *being self presenting*.

Third premise: If x has a property that y does not have, then x is not identical with y.

Conclusion: Qualia are not identical with brain states, nor with physical properties of any other sort.

Perhaps the reader shares my sense that this argument has had, and continues to have, a considerable subterranean influence.

The introspection argument

Like the appearance/reality argument, the introspection argument has no locus classicus or paramount defender. It too tends to lie beneath the surface of discussions. There is, however, an explicit and highly prominent argument with which it enjoys a certain kinship – Wilfrid Sellars's grain argument, which maintains that the "grain" or degree of complexity of a qualitative state is quite different than that of any of the physical states with which it is correlated.[26] It is conceivable that Sellars intended to give a version of the introspection argument, but his formulation of the grain argument admits of a variety of interpretations, and anyway, it appears to lack a component that is crucial to the introspection argument, as I shall present it here.

The argument has two main premises. One is the claim that introspection can provide us with no grounds for attributing the sort of mereological and causal complexity to an instance of a qualitative state that is possessed by instances of neural states. Compared to neural states, qualitative states are quite simple. Indeed, their smallest discriminable components seem to be perfectly simple. The other key premise is the view that introspection provides the subject of a qualitative state with full cognitive access to its essential nature. It follows from this view that if a qualitative state Q is identical with a neural state N, and x is the subject of an instance of N, then introspection should provide x with access to the mereological and causal complexity of N. Our subject x should be able to just *see* that the instance of Q involves an immense number of interacting neurons. Together, these two premises imply that qualitative states are not identical with physical states.

To amplify: When I am attending introspectively to a pain, I am aware of something that appears to resist characterization in terms of neuroscientific concepts. To apply neuroscientific concepts to it would be like

---

[26] Wilfrid Sellars, "Philosophy and the Scientific Image of Man," in R. Colodny (ed.), *Frontiers of Science and Philosophy* (Pittsburgh: University of Pittsburgh Press, 1967), pp. 35–78. This paper is reprinted in Sellars, *Science, Perception and Reality* (Atascadero, CA: Ridgeview Publishing Company, 1991), pp. 1–40. The central idea of the grain argument appears on p. 26.

applying them to a patch of blue sky. Is it possible to account for this resistance to neuroscientific description by appealing to the difference between
appearance and reality? Can we say that pains really do admit of neuroscientific descriptions, but appear not to do so because introspective awareness provides us only with appearances of pains, appearances that fail to
attest to their essential natures? Apparently not. For it seems impossible
to draw a distinction between the appearance of a pain and the underlying reality. In the case of pains, it seems, the appearance *is* the reality.
Is it possible to account for the resistance to neuroscientific description
by pointing out that neuroscientific concepts, like all material concepts,
are schematized perceptually – that the rules governing their use prevent
us from applying them unless we have a *perceptual* ground for doing so?
It seems that it is possible to account for some of the resistance in this
way, but not all of it. Thus, there are concepts that apply to neural states
whose content appears to be largely independent of perception – mereological concepts, for example, and purely structural concepts of other
kinds. If the property of being a pain *just is* a certain property of brain
states, shouldn't it be possible, when one is aware of a pain introspectively,
to find some basis for a mereological description of the pain that parallels
the mereological description of the corresponding brain state? It is quite
tempting to respond affirmatively here. (Here I am assuming that mereological concepts are governed by a logic that is operative in all of their
deployments, and that makes it possible for us to grasp mereological relationships in a variety of domains. It is a mistake to think of mereological
concepts as restricted in their use to perceptible phenomena.)

In full dress regalia, the introspection argument comes to this:

First premise: Introspection provides no basis for applying neural concepts to
qualitative states. On the contrary, when we are introspectively aware of qualitative states, it seems to us that the objects of awareness have properties, such as
the property of being resolvable into minimally discriminable components that
are absolutely simple, that preclude the application of neural concepts.

Second premise: Because there is no appearance/reality distinction for qualitative states, introspection provides us with full cognitive access to the essential
natures of such states.

Lemma: Accordingly, qualitative states lack the properties that are expressed
by neural concepts, and possess positive properties that are incompatible with
neural properties.

Third premise: If x has a property that y does not have, then x is not identical
with y.

Conclusion: Qualitative states are not identical with neural states (nor, since
the argument can be generalized, with physical states of any other kind).

This line of thought shares a crucial premise with the appearance/reality argument, but the arguments are sufficiently different in other respects to warrant our viewing them as distinct.

This completes my catalog of arguments for property dualism. In the next section I will make a case for their resilience by showing that they can withstand a prima facie promising strategy for doing away with them.

2.4 PROPERTY DUALISM, PART 2

In the 1980s and 1990s advocates of central state physicalism developed a position that has come to be known as *conceptual dualism*.[27] This view, which continues to enjoy a currency in the literature, is composed of the following three doctrines: (i) all awareness of qualia involves conceptualization, (ii) our concepts of qualitative states differ in kind from all of the concepts that count intuitively as standing for physical properties, and (iii) it is possible to exploit this difference in explaining the intuitions that seem prima facie to call central state physicalism into question. Different philosophers have propounded somewhat different versions of conceptual dualism, but they all endorse the doctrine that simple introspective judgments involving qualitative concepts are non-inferential and require neither theoretical knowledge nor perceptual information about the external world for their justification. A qualitative concept carries no presuppositions about the metaphysical nature of the quality that it represents, nor does it interpret the quality in any way or attribute any causal powers to it. The concept is used only to register the comings and goings of the quality. The idea is that any such concept differs markedly from the concepts that play a role in neuroscience, and that it also differs from the perceptual concepts that we use to record the observations that provide support for neuroscientific theories. Moreover, there are no a priori ties linking it to concepts of either of these two kinds.

---

[27] Conceptual dualism seems to have made its first appearance in my "In Defense of Type Materialism," *Synthese* LIX (1984), 295–320. Another early source is Brian Loar, "Phenomenal States," in James J. Tomberlin (ed.), *Philosophical Perspectives*, Volume 4 (Atascadero, CA: Ridgeview Publishing Company, 1990), pp. 81–108. It figures prominently in three other works by me: *Sensations*; "Imaginability, Conceivability, Possibility, and the Mind-Body Problem," *Philosophical Studies* 87 (1997), 61–85; and "There are Fewer Things in Reality than are Dreamt of in Chalmers's Philosophy," co-authored with Brian McLaughlin, *Philosophy and Phenomenological Research* LIX (1999), 445–454. It is also featured in a book by David Papineau (*Thinking about Consciousness* (Oxford: Oxford University Press, 2002)), in several papers by Brian McLaughlin (e.g., "Color, Consciousness, and Color Consciousness," in Quentin Smith and Aleksander Jokic (eds.), *Consciousness: New Essays* (Oxford: Oxford University Press, 2003), pp. 97–154), in a paper by Janet Levin ("What Is a Phenomenal Concept?" in Torin Alter and Sven Walter (eds.), *Phenomenal Concepts and Phenomenal Knowledge* (New York, NY: Oxford University Press, 2007)), and in unpublished work by Katalin Balog.

Unlike property dualism, which commits us to a complex ontology that includes irreducible qualitative properties along with physical and functional properties, conceptual dualism carries no commitment to an expanded ontology. We are independently committed to concepts, and we know independently that concepts come in a number of different varieties. We can acknowledge the existence and independence of qualitative concepts without adding in any significant way to the complexity or magnitude of our picture of the world.

How exactly might one use conceptual dualism to respond to the arguments for property dualism? I will give four examples. In each case, the point is that conceptual dualism can provide full explanations of intuitions that at first sight seem to favor property dualism, and can thereby establish that the existence of these intuitions is fully compatible with central state physicalism.

First, a conceptual dualist might respond to the Cartesian modal argument by maintaining that it is possible to explain why it seems to us that qualitative states can exist independently of the neural states that normally accompany them by appealing to the fact that our concepts of qualitative states are logically independent of our concepts of neural states. Since it is logically coherent to form conceptual representations of situations in which qualitative states are not accompanied by neural states, and since we normally determine whether a situation is logically possible by checking to see whether we can conceive of it coherently, we naturally have vivid intuitions to the effect that it is genuinely possible for qualitative states to exist independently of neural states.

Second, a conceptual dualist can reply to the knowledge argument as follows: Instead of saying that the superscientist Mary acquires knowledge of a new property when she experiences a red object for the first time, we should say that Mary comes to know an old property in a new way. More specifically, we should say that she acquires a new *concept* of a familiar property. This concept stands for a physical property, P, but it differs from her earlier concepts in that it is a qualitative concept. That is, it is a concept that can be applied to brain states on the basis of introspection. Her earlier concept of P could not be applied on the basis of introspection. Rather, it could be applied only on the basis of external perception and/or inference from neuroscientific theories. Now states of knowledge are individuated by the concepts that serve as their constituents, so the states of knowledge involving Mary's new qualitative concept count as new relative to her scientific knowledge, which by hypothesis she has had for some time. They count as new even though the facts they represent were also represented by components of Mary's scientific knowledge. Accordingly, it is possible to accept them as new without supposing that qualitative facts are distinct from physical facts.

Third, an advocate of conceptual dualism can respond to the explanatory gap argument by saying that whether a given theory explains a fact depends on how the fact is conceptualized. This point is in effect conceded by Levine, who takes the relation between an explanatory theory and the items it explains as deductive:

> [I]n a good scientific explanation, the explanans either entails the explanandum, or it entails a probability distribution over a range of alternatives, among which the explanandum resides. In other words, I take explanation to essentially involve deduction.[28]

It follows from this view that explanation is a relation between sentences or propositions, not a relation between extra-linguistic and extra-conceptual facts, for items that are extra-linguistic and extra-conceptual cannot stand in relations of deducibility. But this means that it might well be possible to explain a fact when it is characterized in terms of neural concepts, but impossible to explain it when it is characterized in terms of qualitative concepts. By the same token, it follows that it is a mistake to infer that there is an explanatory gap just because one finds it impossible to explain a fact when it is construed in qualitative terms, at least if the existence of such a gap is thought to have ontological significance. The gap may only be a conceptual gap, and therefore of no importance for metaphysics.

Fourth, a conceptual dualist can object to the appearance/reality argument by saying (i) that introspection necessarily involves conceptualization, and (ii) that the concepts involved in introspective awareness of qualia inevitably fail to do justice to the organizational complexity and internal causal dynamics of the associated neural states. In other words, it can be maintained that it is after all possible to draw an appearance/reality distinction with respect to qualitative states – that is, a distinction between reality as conceptualized and reality as it is in itself. This distinction is not the same as the familiar distinction between reality as it is presented to us perceptually and reality as it is in itself, but it seems that it would do the necessary work in this context. For example, it seems that we could use it to explain why certain qualitative states seem to us to be simple. Insofar as our concepts of such states lack internal structure,

---

[28] Levine, *Purple Haze*, p. 74.

they fail to reflect the internal organization of the corresponding neural structures.

These objections are too short and sketchy to secure deep conviction, but they would at least succeed in shifting the burden of proof to the shoulders of an advocate of property dualism if their common presupposition, the contention that all awareness of qualia involves conceptualization, could be shown to be correct. Reflection shows that this is a very strong claim – one that clearly requires a substantial defense. Surprisingly, however, as far as I know, advocates of conceptual dualism have never attempted to defend it. Moreover, what is much more important, there are strong reasons for doubting in advance that any such effort would be successful. Indeed, to say this is to understate the matter. There are two very good reasons for thinking that the claim is false.

One of these reasons is that awareness of qualitative states generally reveals a complexity that cannot easily be captured in conceptual terms. Any complex array of qualia would serve to illustrate this point. In the interests of definiteness, let us agree to focus on the array of qualia that is presented by Vermeer's *View of Delft* as an example. It would take literally hours to describe even a small corner of this painting fully in conceptual terms, and by then, of course, various external and internal conditions would have changed in ways that would make it necessary to rely heavily on memory in characterizing the qualia that the rest of the canvas had originally presented. Which of us is capable of feats of memory of that magnitude? But anyway, it would clearly be absurd to say that our apprehension of the qualia presented by the painting involves laborious framings of descriptions and heroic searches of memory. In grasping the qualia that are presented by the painting, we just open our eyes and take them in.

To be sure, there is a way of capturing these qualia conceptually. One can do so by making use of a demonstrative concept such as ***this** array of color and shape qualia*. But awareness that involves demonstrative concepts presupposes subconceptual awareness, for it is impossible to secure a referent for a demonstrative concept unless one independently *attends to* the item one wishes to demonstrate. Thus, for example, I must normally be attending visually to a particular object in order to secure a referent for *that house*, or even for *that pink house over there on the corner*.

In view of these considerations, it seems that one must either fall short of doing justice to the complexity of arrays of qualia in conceptual terms, or do justice to them by using concepts which presuppose that there is a form of access to qualia that is independent of conceptualization. On either scenario, there is a problem for the view that we must conceptualize qualia to be aware of them.

This brings us to the second reason for rejecting this view. When one is aware of a qualitative property, one is always aware of a highly determinate form of it. For example, when one is aware of an instance of pain, one is always aware of it as being a pain of a particular level of intensity. And when one is aware of an object as presenting a reddish appearance, one is always aware of it as presenting an appearance of a particular shade of red. Because of this, it is generally impossible to do full justice to the distinctive nature of a qualitative state by representing it conceptually – unless one makes use of a demonstrative concept, thereby relying on a form of awareness that cannot be explained in conceptual terms. Our general concepts tend to stand for generic or determinable properties, as is entirely natural, given that the cognitive functions of general concepts include classification of particulars and enabling thoughts about regularities, trends, and patterns. We have a general concept that stands for pains, but not one that stands for pains of precisely *this* level of intensity. Also, while we have a concept that stands for the quality that is presented by red objects generally, and several concepts that stand for more determinate forms of this quale, we have no concepts that stand for maximally determinate forms of it.

Together, the considerations we have been reviewing amount to a decisive objection to the central contention of conceptual dualism. It is just not true that awareness of qualia always involves conceptualization. On the contrary, conceptually informed awareness of qualia is a superstructure that requires an entirely independent form of awareness for its support. This more fundamental form of awareness, which I will eventually call *experiential awareness*, will receive considerable attention in later chapters. (We will also revisit the present considerations concerning the complexity and determinacy of qualia in later chapters. In each case, these topics will receive somewhat different treatment than they have received here. The alternative formulations will clarify and strengthen the case I have just now been constructing.)

There is a version of conceptual dualism that might be thought to be immune to the objections we have been considering. According to this view, which has been championed in recent years by David Papineau, qualitative concepts literally *incorporate* the qualitative states to which they refer.[29] Thus, for example, the qualitative concept that I am currently

---

[29] Papineau, *Thinking about Consciousness*, Chapter 4.

using to refer to pain literally has the current pain in my foot as a constituent. Papineau's idea is that we form qualitative concepts by combining concrete qualitative states with a concept-building operator. This operator is meant to be a counterpart of quotation marks. One forms a quotation name for an expression E by combining quotation marks with E. So also, according to Papineau, we form qualitative concepts by combining concrete qualitative states with the operator *the experience: …* Now if one has this view in mind, it might seem that there is no problem about forming conceptual representations that capture the complexity of qualitative arrays and the determinacy of individual qualia. To represent an array A or an individual quale Q, one simply has to combine *the experience: …* with A or Q.

Unfortunately, while Papineau's view has a certain initial appeal, reflection shows that it has substantial liabilities. Thus, in the first place, as Papineau points out, it follows from his characterization of phenomenal concepts that judgments that classify current sensations in terms of phenomenal concepts are incorrigible. It seems, however, that it is possible to make experiential judgments about qualitative states that misclassify them. Thus, to borrow an example that Rogers Albritton once used in a seminar, suppose that I have been primed to expect a pain but that I instead experience a sensation of intense cold. Might not the priming lead me to judge erroneously, at least for an instant, that I am in pain? And isn't it plausible that in making this judgment, I would be deploying the very same concept of pain that I use in making experiential classifications that are correct? Second, it appears to follow from Papineau's proposal that experiential thoughts about pains must change in character as the intensities of their referents diminish, fading into nothingness when their referents cease to exist. By the same token, it seems to follow that if one is to continue thinking about a pain after it has ceased to exist, one must do so by changing the concept in terms of which the thoughts are couched. Neither of these consequences seems to me to be in keeping with the data of introspection. Third, it seems that thoughts about pains have different phenomenal locations than the pains to which they refer: thoughts about pains are in the head, while pains themselves are normally in the body. How then can it be true that thoughts about pains have the phenomenal characters of their constituents?

As I see it, these consequences of Papineau's view count as a *reductio*. But anyway, there is reason to doubt that the view can provide support for the claim that all awareness of qualia involves conceptualization. This is because one generally experiences more than one quale at any given time. Which state is the one to which the operator *the experience:* ... should be applied? Surely that depends on one's interests and concerns. But it is impossible to be interested in a quale unless one is aware of it in some way. More specifically, it seems that one must be attending to it, at least to some degree. But this attentive awareness must be a subconceptual affair. It appears, then, that it is impossible to develop Papineau's theory adequately, in such a way as to explain how one goes about forming a qualitative concept in a particular case, unless we allow that there is a more basic form of awareness of qualia.[30]

For a period of seventeen years, beginning in 1984, I was confident that conceptual dualism could be used to undercut the arguments for property dualism.[31] Other people shared this confidence. With regret, however, I have come to see that the foundations of conceptual dualism were never subjected to a thorough examination. The emphasis was always on showing how to apply conceptual dualism in criticizing property dualism. As soon as one turns one's attention to the foundations, it becomes clear that the motivation is quite poor. By the same token, one appreciates that the motivation for property dualism is quite substantial.

2.5   HARMANIAN REPRESENTATIONALISM

"Harmanian representationalism" is my term for a family of views about perception and perceptual qualia that Gilbert Harman put forward in 1990.[32] The paper in which they appeared has deservedly had an immense influence.

Harman makes the following two claims about perceptual experience:

a. Perceptual awareness of the world is not mediated in any way by awareness of intrinsic features of experience. In other words, when you perceive the world, you are aware only of external objects and the properties and relations of external objects. In still other words, "[W]hen you see a tree, you do not experience any features as intrinsic features of your experience. Look at a tree and try to turn your attention to the

---

[30] This paragraph and its predecessor are borrowed from my "Remarks on David Papineau's *Thinking about Consciousness*," *Philosophy and Phenomenological Research* 71 (2005), 147–154.

[31] Hill, "In Defense of Type Materialism."

[32] Gilbert Harman, "The Intrinsic Quality of Experience," in James J. Tomberlin (ed.), *Philosophical Perspectives*, Volume IV (Atascadero, CA: Ridgeview Publishing Company, 1990), pp. 31–52. The paper is reprinted in Ned Block, Owen Flanagan, and Güven Güzeldere (eds.), *The Nature of Consciousness* (Cambridge, MA: MIT Press, 1997), pp. 663–675. All of my page references will be to this reprinted version.

intrinsic features of your visual experience. I predict you will find that
the only features there to turn your attention to will be features of the
presented tree... ."[33]

b. When you are introspectively aware of a perceptual experience, you are
   aware only of representational features of your experience; you are not
   aware of intrinsic features.

Here is how Harman expresses the point:

In the case of a painting, Eloise can be aware of those features of the painting that are responsible for its being a painting of a unicorn. That is, she can
turn her attention to the pattern of the paint on the canvas by virtue of which
the painting represents a unicorn. But in the case of her visual experience of a
tree, I want to say that she is not aware of, as it were, the mental paint by virtue
of which her experience is experience of seeing a tree. She is aware only of the
intentional or relational features of her experience, not of its intrinsic nonintentional features.[34]

The first claim is equivalent to *direct realism*, the idea that perceptual
experience provides us with direct, unmediated access to external phenomena. The second claim can be expressed by saying that perceptual
experience is *transparent to introspection*. When one tries to attend introspectively to a perceptual experience, the thesis maintains, one is aware
only of what it is an experience *of*, where this means that one is aware
only of what the experience represents or signifies. Suppose, for example,
that you are perceptually aware of a blue expanse, and that you decide to
examine this experience introspectively. According to Harman, you will
be aware *only* that it is an experience *of blue*. The experience may have
other, intrinsic features, but introspection does not disclose them.

The term "transparency thesis" is sometimes applied to Harman's first
doctrine, sometimes to his second doctrine, and sometimes also to the
combination of the two. I will use "direct realism" to refer to the first
doctrine, "Harman's transparency thesis" to refer to the second doctrine,
and "Harman's position" to refer to the combination.

In addition to initiating the contemporary discussion of perceptual transparency, Harman's paper also fundamentally transformed the
contemporary discussion of perceptual qualia. In fact, however, there is
no one theory of perceptual qualia that is mandated by Harman's position – the implications of his position for perceptual qualia depend very
much on one's views as to what qualia are.

[33] *Ibid.*, p. 667.   [34] *Ibid.*, p. 667.

If by "perceptual qualia" one means something like "the intrinsic features of perceptual experiences that are given in introspection,"
then Harman must be understood as proposing an *elimination* of perceptual qualia. His position entails that there are no intrinsic properties
of perceptual experience that are accessible to introspection, so, on the
given account of qualia, his position entails that perceptual qualia do
not exist.

On the other hand, if by "perceptual qualia" one means something like
"the ways things look, feel, smell, and so on," then Harman should be
read as proposing a *reduction* of perceptual qualia to the representational
contents of perceptual experiences. But there are two forms that such a
reduction might take. (i) One might claim that each perceptual quale Q
is identical with a representational property P – a property like *being an
experience as of red*, or *being an experience that represents red*. On this view,
qualia are properties of experiences. (ii) Alternatively, instead of claiming
that Q is identical with the representational property P, one might claim
that Q is identical with the external, physical property that experiences
with P represent. On this view, perceptual qualia are not properties of
experiences, but rather properties of things like walls and cars. The view
implies that perceptual qualia are either properties like *red* or properties
like *presenting a red appearance*.

Harman is usually interpreted as proposing either (i) or (ii), and is
therefore generally taken to be advocating a version of *representationalism*.
The term "representationalism" stands for a family of theories of qualia
that emphasize the role that representations play in visual perception and
other forms of experiential awareness. To be more specific, they all maintain that the qualitative character of experience can in one way or another
be explained in terms of the representational content of experience. After
this point of agreement, however, versions of representationalism diverge
sharply from one another. Thus, it is clear that (i) and (ii) are quite different views.

As far as I can tell, it is not at all clear which of (i) and (ii) Harman prefers, if indeed he has a preference. Perhaps he is best understood as asserting only the following disjunctive thesis: if perceptual qualia exist at all,
then they are *either* representational properties of perceptual experiences
or properties that are represented by perceptual experiences.

As the foregoing quotations from Harman suggest, he maintains that
his two central doctrines receive strong support from introspection.
Indeed, this is the only type of direct support that he claims for them.
It is introspection which shows that our awareness of external objects is

not mediated by awareness of internal phenomena, and it is introspection which shows that introspection reveals only the representational properties of experiences.

Harman's position has a strong intuitive appeal, but it also faces some very substantial objections. I will mention three of these. One calls attention to the fact that perceptual experience is complex in a way that neither direct realism nor Harman's transparency thesis acknowledges. This omission provides advocates of "mental paint" with an opening. It may be possible to develop Harman's position in such a way as to close this lacuna, but he has not provided us with a promising strategy for doing so. The second objection points out that it is not at all clear how to extend Harman's theory of perceptual qualia so as to yield an account of qualia of other kinds, such as the qualia associated with experiences of pain. The third objection maintains that there are possible cases in which creatures possess qualia, and in fact the same qualia as we possess, but in which the relevant mental states have no representational content. If this is right, then the project of explaining phenomenology in terms of representational content must fail.

1. Harman's transparency thesis claims that introspection discloses only the intentional or representational properties of experience – that is, what a perceptual experience is an experience *of.* But it seems that in addition introspection reveals how external objects *look* to us. Suppose, for example, that you are looking at an SUV far ahead of you on the road. Suppose also that you consider your current visual experience introspectively. It seems that you will become aware of two facts about it: first, you will become aware that it is an experience *of* an object that is rather large; and second, you will become aware that it is an experience of something that *looks* rather small. Now suppose that you are looking at a tan wall that is partly well illuminated and partly cloaked in shadow. Suppose that you consider this second experience introspectively. It seems that you will become aware of two facts about it: first, you will become aware that it is an experience *of* a wall that is uniformly tan in color; and second, you will become aware that it is an experience of a wall that *looks* light tan in some places and *looks* chocolate-brown in others. In general, it seems that experiences both *represent* the objective physical properties of objects and *present* the appearances of objects. But if this is true, then, prima facie, anyway, Harman's position is wrong. I will call this *the problem of appearances.*

Peacocke was the first to raise an objection of this sort. (The objection was presented in his *Sense and Content*, which appeared several years before Harman's paper.[35] Thus, Peacocke's line of thought was in effect a preemptive strike against a view that had not yet found a champion.)

Peacocke maintained that there is a range of characteristics that are possessed by experiences but that seem to be independent of representational properties. He called them "sensational properties," and described them as intrinsic properties of "regions of the visual field." He also maintained that we become aware of them when we reflect introspectively on experience. In combination, these claims imply that there are intrinsic properties of experiences that we are directly aware of in introspection. This contradicts Harman's transparency thesis.

Peacocke began by calling attention to cases in which (i) experiences represent objects as having the same objective property, but (ii) the objects nonetheless look different to the observer. He observed, for example, that when your experience represents two trees as being the same in size, it can still be true that the nearer tree looks larger to you. The fact that the nearer tree looks larger to you is clearly a fact about your experience, but how can it be a fact about the representational properties of your experience? By hypothesis your experience represents the objects as being the same in size. So, Peacocke concluded, the fact that the nearer tree looks larger to you must be a fact about the non-representational properties of your experience. ("Yet there is some sense in which the nearer tree occupies more of your visual field than the further tree."[36])

Note that Peacocke is in effect making the following three claims.

(i)   The representational content of a visual experience has to do with the objective, physical properties of external objects.
(ii) When an observer has a visual experience of a certain sort, the object of awareness looks a certain way to the observer in virtue of his having that experience. The object presents a certain appearance to the observer.
(iii) When an object looks a certain way to one, one is aware of a *sensational property* that is exemplified somewhere in one's *visual field*.

As far as I can tell, Peacocke uses "visual field" to stand for an internal mental entity of some sort. Thus, unlike his first two claims, Peacocke's third claim is a substantive metaphysical thesis. He is proposing a

[35] Christopher Peacocke, *Sense and Content* (Oxford: The Clarendon Press, 1983). The relevant portions of this book are reprinted in Ned Block, Owen Flanagan, and Güven Güzeldere (eds.), *The Nature of Consciousness* (Cambridge, MA: MIT Press, 1997), pp. 351–354. All of my references will be to this reprinted version.
[36] *Ibid.*, p. 345.

mentalistic account of the nature of the appearances that objects present to us.

There are similar cases involving color, sound, and motion. Peacocke writes:

> Imagine you are in a room looking at a corner formed by two of its walls. The walls are covered with paper of uniform hue, brightness and saturation. But one wall is more brightly illuminated than the other. In these circumstances, your experience can represent both walls as being the same color: it does not look to you as if one of the walls is painted with brighter paint than the other. Yet it is equally an aspect of your visual experience itself that the region of the visual field in which one wall is presented is brighter than that in which the other is presented.[37]

In order to counter this objection Harman must do two things. First, he must claim that in addition to their objective physical properties, objects possess a range of relational, viewpoint-dependent properties that can appropriately be regarded as appearances or ways of looking. Second, he must change his transparency thesis so that it implies that introspection reveals two types of representational content – one that is concerned with the objective physical properties of objects, and another that is concerned with their relational, viewpoint-dependent properties. By making these changes in his position, he would be complicating his transparency doctrine, but he would at least preserve the claim that introspection reveals no properties of experiences other than representational properties. And he would effectively block Peacocke's version of the objection, for the second change would give him an account of the nature of appearances that is incompatible with Peacocke's third claim (i.e., with (iii)).

There is a passage in which Harman acknowledges the problem of appearances, and also the desirability of making the indicated changes. Here is what he says:

> Another point is that Eloise's visual experience does not just present a tree. It presents a tree as viewed from a certain place. Various features that the tree is presented as having are presented as relations between the viewer and the tree, for example, features that the tree has from here. The tree is presented as "in front of" and as "hiding" certain other trees. It is presented as fuller "on the right." It is presented as the same size "from here" as a closer smaller tree, which is not to say that it really looks the same in size, only that it is presented as subtending the same angle from here as the smaller tree. To be presented as the same in size from here is not to be presented as the same in size, period… . [T]his

---

[37] *Ibid.*, p. 345.

feature of the tree from here is an objective feature of the tree in relation to here, a feature to which perceivers are sensitive and which their visual experience can somehow represent things as having from here.[38]

As this passage shows, Harman thinks that external objects have *appearance properties* in addition to their objective physical properties. He holds, for example, that an object's looking small consists in its subtending a comparatively small visual angle with respect to *here* – that is, the place that is occupied by the eye of the observer.

Clearly, this is the kind of thing that Harman needs to say. As we will see in a later chapter, however, it is very difficult to work out the details of a position of this sort. It appears, for example, that it is quite wrong to identify looking small with subtending a small visual angle. Thus, the quoted passage is not an answer to Peacocke. It is at best a gesture in the direction of an answer.

I conclude this description of the problem of appearances by emphasizing that the problem is one involving the ways objects *look* to us. When we introspectively examine our perceptual experiences, we become aware of what they are experiences *of*, and we also become aware of how objects *look* to us in virtue of our having the experiences. Peacocke proposes to *interpret* facts of the form *x looks F to me* in terms of awareness of sensational properties of a visual field, and Harman proposes to *interpret* them in terms of representational content that is concerned with relational, viewpoint-dependent properties of external objects. These are both *interpretations* of a set of facts that can actually be interpreted in still other ways. (A so-called adverbialist would take them to be facts involving adverbial determinations of mental processes.) In order to deal with the problem in a satisfactory way, Harman must do two things: (i) develop his interpretation of facts of the given form, providing us with details that are adequate to the phenomenological and scientific facts, and (ii) show that his interpretation is superior to alternatives. As things now stand he has fulfilled neither of these obligations.

2. Although it seems right to say that introspection reveals no internal mental objects when we use it to examine visual and auditory experiences, the *internal objects objection* points out that it also seems right to say that we can be aware of internal mental objects when we introspectively consider experiences of occurrences like pains and itches. There is a powerful intuition to the effect that pains and other "bodily" sensations are purely mental or at least mind dependent. But pain and other

---

[38] Harman, "The Intrinsic Quality of Experience," pp. 666–667.

sensory characteristics are qualia. Hence, it appears that there are qualia that Harmanian representationalism cannot explain.

Further, it seems right to say that there are internal sensory objects associated with touch, taste, and smell. In the case of touch, for example, if one turns one's attention to what is happening inside one's fingers when one is running them along the surface of an object, it seems that one is thereby made aware of *touch sensations* of various kinds. This is not to say that one is always aware of touch sensations when one is tactually examining an object. One can be – and perhaps usually is – aware of the texture and temperature of the surface of the object rather than the sensations in one's fingers. In general, it seems that what one is aware of when one is touching something depends on the direction of one's attention. When one attends to what is happening inside one's fingers one is aware of sensations; and when one attends to the surface of the object one is touching one is aware of properties of the surface. (Note that the fact that the sensations occur when one attends to what is happening "inside one's fingers" does not undercut the intuition that the sensations are mind dependent. In general, bodily sensations seem to us to depend for their existence on our being aware of them despite having locations. This paradox is one of the problems that a theory of qualia must solve.)

Like the observations about pains and itches, these observations challenge Harman's transparency thesis. It is not at all clear how Harman should respond to them.

3. The *Swampman objection* begins by observing that we can imagine a creature, Swampman, who is brought into existence by a quantum fluctuation in a swamp gas of some sort.[39] We can also imagine that Swampman's nervous system is a neuron-for-neuron duplicate of yours. This is immensely unlikely, of course, but it seems to be possible, and possibility is all that the objection requires. Now if Swampman's nervous system is a perfect duplicate of yours, then, since it is of course true that you are continuously aware of qualia, it is natural to think that Swampman is continuously aware of qualia too. Indeed, it is natural to think that he enjoys exactly the same qualia that you enjoy. But it is also natural to think that the representational contents of perceptual experiences depend in one way or another on the evolutionary history of the species of the individual who has the experiences (that is, on historical facts of

---

[39] Swampman made his first appearance in the literature in Donald Davidson, "Knowing One's Own Mind," *Proceedings and Addresses of the American Philosophical Association* 60 (1987), 441–458.

the form *experiences of type E were selected during the development of the species because they encoded information about property P*).[40] If this is so, then, since Swampman has no personal history and belongs to no species, his experiences are devoid of representational content. Thus, Swampman seems to be a creature who satisfies two conditions: his phenomenology is just like yours, but he has no states with the same representational contents as your perceptual experiences. Assuming that this is correct, Swampman shows that it is possible to hold phenomenology fixed while allowing representational content to vary.

There are a number of other objections to Harmanian representationalism that we could consider, but perhaps enough has been said to show that it does not by itself provide an adequate account of qualia, nor even a satisfactory basis for responding to the arguments for property dualism. Still, the idea that experience is essentially representational is very appealing, and one has the sense that it might well be useful to keep the notion of representation in play in developing a theory of the qualitative dimension of experience. Harman deserves immense credit for securing a place for the notion in the contemporary literature about this topic. I will attempt to build on his insights in later chapters. I hope to convince the reader that a representationalist account of qualia is fully defensible, and that objections like the ones that we have been considering can be met.

APPENDIX

The discussion of physicalism in earlier sections is concerned primarily with identity physicalism. Very little has been said about supervenience physicalism – the doctrine that qualia supervene logically on physical properties. This appendix is concerned with this alternate form of physicalism. I will begin by pointing out that it seems impossible to reformulate the Cartesian modal argument in such a way as to provide a persuasive objection to supervenience physicalism. The situation here is typical: in general, it is impossible to restate the arguments against identity physicalism and realization physicalism in such a way that they apply to

---

[40] The idea that the representational content of perceptual experiences is biologically determined is not inevitable, but it is widely regarded as highly plausible, and there is much that can be said in its defense. It would take us too far afield to review the relevant arguments here. For discussion see Ruth Millikan, *Language, Thought and Other Biological Categories* (Cambridge, MA: MIT Press, 1984); David Papineau, *Reality and Representation* (Oxford: Blackwell, 1987) and *Philosophical Naturalism* (Oxford: Blackwell, 1993); and Fred Dretske, *Explaining Behavior: Reasons in a World of Causes* (Cambridge, MA: MIT Press, 1988).

supervenience physicalism. There is, however, a rather different sort of argument that calls supervenience physicalism into question. I will present this different argument, and will also buttress it with some supporting considerations.

When we attempt to transform the foregoing Cartesian argument into an argument against supervenience physicalism, we wind up with a line of thought that looks like this:

First premise: We are able to conceive clearly and distinctly of zombies. Hence, we are able to conceive clearly and distinctly of situations in which φ-activity exists without being accompanied by pain.

Second premise: When we conceive of φ-activity, we conceive of it completely, in the sense that in conceiving of it we do justice to all of its essential properties.

Third premise: If it is within our power to conceive of its being the case that p clearly, distinctly, and completely, then it is genuinely possible that p.

Lemma: By the first, second, and third premises, it is genuinely possible for φ-activity to exist without being accompanied by pain.

Fourth premise: If it is genuinely possible for x to exist without being accompanied by y, then x does not supervene logically on y.

Conclusion: Pain does not supervene logically on φ-activity.

Arguments of roughly this sort have enjoyed considerable popularity in recent years. One reason is of course that their conclusions have a broad significance. Both identity physicalism and realization physicalism entail supervenience physicalism. Accordingly, if arguments like the present one are correct, they do away with all three forms of physicalism with a single stroke. The other reason for the popularity of these arguments is that they are regarded as quite strong.

Reflection shows, however, that the second premise of the present argument is much less plausible than the second premise of the Cartesian argument against identity physicalism that we considered in Section 3.3. Prima facie, at least, it is highly plausible to claim, as that earlier argument does, that pain is self presenting. Accordingly, it is highly plausible to claim that our grasp of the essential nature of pain is complete. But it would be absurd to say that φ-activity is self presenting. Our grasp of φ-activity is grounded in a theory and mediated by experimental data. Accordingly, there can be no guarantee that we have succeeded in identifying all of its essential properties. It could have a dimension that experience does not reveal, a dimension that is hidden from us when we approach it from the third person perspective. In view of this fact, it is clear that the present argument fails.

In my judgment, what we see here is typical: as a rule, it is impossible to restate arguments against identity physicalism and realization physicalism in such a way that they apply to supervenience physicalism.[41] Supervenience physicalism makes a much weaker claim than either of the other main forms of physicalism, and as a result, it is much more difficult to refute. (Recall that we found in Section 3.3 that the explanatory gap argument fails when it is reconfigured as an argument against supervenience physicalism.)

As far as I know, there is only one truly persuasive objection to supervenience physicalism – namely, that it posits relations of logical necessitation that are sui generis and quite mysterious. Suppose for reductio that supervenience physicalism is true. Reflection shows that this commits us to saying that qualitative facts are entailed, or logically necessitated, by physical facts. But also, it commits us to giving an account of *why* this relation of necessitation obtains. What explains it? We could answer this question in a fully intelligible way by saying that qualitative properties are identical with physical properties; but if we said that, we would have explained supervenience physicalism by assuming the truth of identity physicalism. In effect, we would have collapsed the distinction between supervenience physicalism and identity physicalism. We could also answer the question in an intelligible way by saying that qualitative properties are realized by physical properties. (To see this, consider the functional property C^* of pains that was discussed in Section 2.2. This property is realized in the human brain by the neural properties in a certain set Σ. Reflection shows that the facts involving C^* are exhaustively constituted by facts involving the members of Σ, provided that the latter are taken to include the laws of nature in which the members of Σ are involved. Given that the C^*-facts are exhaustively constituted by the Σ-facts, it is clear that the former must be necessitated by the latter. What we see in this case holds generally: realization involves exhaustive constitution, and exhaustive constitution entails necessitation.) It is clear, however, that this second way of answering the question causes supervenience physicalism to collapse into realization physicalism. Like the first way of answering the question, it deprives supervenience physicalism of independent interest.

What else could explain the posited necessitation of qualitative facts by physical facts? We cannot say that this relationship is grounded either in formal logic or in conceptual truths, because there are neither laws of logic nor conceptual truths that link qualitative facts to physical facts. But this means that the relationship is a mystery. All familiar and well understood relations of logical necessitation arise either from identities,

[41] For a quite different assessment, see David J. Chalmers's brave and brilliant book *The Conscious Mind* (Oxford: Oxford University Press, 1996).

or from relations of realization, or from formal logic, or from conceptual truths. Hence, if we cannot explain the posited necessitation in one of these ways, we cannot explain it at all. It would have to be accepted as a separate, sui generic form of necessitation – a form for which there is no independent motivation. Accordingly, considerations of simplicity counsel against recognizing it. (I am indebted here to Kevin Morris.)[42]

I can see only one objection to this line of thought. Suppose it is true, as Kripke has argued, that one's actual ancestry is part of one's essence.[43] Then it is necessary that George W. Bush is the son of George H. Bush and Barbara Bush. It might be maintained that this necessity is not grounded either in property identities, or in constitution relations, or in formal logic, or in conceptual truths. But it gives rise to a relation of logical necessitation: given that it is necessary that George W. Bush is the son of George H. Bush and Barbara Bush, the state of affairs *George W. Bush exists* logically necessitates the state of affairs *George H. Bush and Barbara Bush have a son*. Hence, there are relations of necessitation that are not grounded in any of the four ways enumerated above.

The answer to this objection is that there are good grounds for thinking that Kripkean a posteriori necessities are grounded in conceptual truths. Certainly it was never part of Kripke's intention to deny this. Consider, for example, the following passage: [44]

So we have to say that although we cannot know a priori whether this table was made of ice or not, given that it is not made of ice, it is *necessarily* not made of ice. In other words, if P is the statement that the lectern is not made of ice, one knows by a priori philosophical analysis, some conditional of the form "If P, then necessarily P." If the table is not made of ice, it is necessarily not made of ice. On the other hand, then, we know by empirical investigation that P, the antecedent of the conditional, is true – that this table is not made of ice. We can conclude by *modus ponens*:

$$P \supset \Box P$$
$$P$$
$$\overline{}$$
$$\Box P$$

[42] For a discussion of the requirement that relations of supervenience be explainable, see Terry Horgan, "From Supervenience to Superdupervenience: Meeting the Demands of a Material World," *Mind* 102 (1993), 555–586.

[43] Saul A. Kripke, *Naming and Necessity* (Cambridge, MA: Harvard University Press, 1979).

[44] Saul Kripke, "Identity and Necessity," in Stephen P. Schwartz (ed.), *Naming, Necessity, and Natural Kinds* (Ithaca, NY: Cornell University Press, 1977), pp. 66–101. The quoted passage occurs on p. 88.

Evidently, Kripke thought that his a posteriori necessities derive from conditionals that can be seen to be true on the basis of "a priori philosophical analysis." Such conditionals would of course count as conceptual truths.[45]

To summarize: It appears that supervenience physicalism cannot be refuted by adapting the arguments that call identity physicalism and realization physicalism into question. But there is an independent reason to think that supervenience physicalism is misguided. Thus, if supervenience physicalism is seen as independent of identity physicalism and realization physicalism, then it must also be seen as postulating relations of logical necessitation that are unique, unexplained, and mysterious. No one could love a creature with these deformities.

---

[45] For further discussion of these issuses, see Christopher S. Hill, "Modality, Modal Epistemology, and the Metaphysics of Consciousness," in Shaun Nichols (ed.), *The Architecture of the Imagination: New Essays on Pretence, Possibility, and Fiction* (Oxford University Press, 2006), pp. 205–236.

CHAPTER 3

Awareness, representation, and experience

In this chapter I will have three main concerns. First, I will propose a principle about awareness that takes it to be essentially representational in character. Second, I will take the first steps toward making a case for this principle. Later chapters will complete the case by showing that the theory is epistemologically and metaphysically fruitful. Finally, I will introduce and attempt to explain a form of awareness that I call *purely experiential awareness*. It stands opposed to all forms of awareness that involve conceptualization, and a fortiori, to all forms that involve judgment. It will play a large role in later chapters.

3.1 THE NATURE OF AWARENESS

Whatever else may be true of awareness, it is clear to all of us that it is a cognitive relation. It is also reasonably clear that it can link agents to entities of four types – objects, properties, events, and facts. Thus, it is perfectly natural, and also perfectly appropriate, to say that Jones is aware of the table in front of him, that he is aware of the pattern of the oriental carpet he is standing on, that he is aware of the double play that is currently in progress, and that he is aware of the fact that the refrigerator is empty. Unfortunately, beyond these easy, rather superficial observations, the nature of awareness is highly controversial. It is not at all clear what it consists in. Indeed, as we will see, there are some who would deny that it can be said to "consist in" anything. On the contrary, these authors maintain, it is necessary to view it as conceptually and metaphysically primitive.

I wish to suggest, however, that awareness actually has a complex internal structure, and that part of that structure is captured by the following principle:

(P) If an agent is aware of *x*, then the agent is in a mental state that represents *x*.

69

According to (P), at least one representation is constitutively involved in every state of awareness.

The primary argument for (P) comes from contemporary cognitive science. As is well known, cognitive science has enjoyed immense explanatory success in recent years, both with respect to high level cognitive phenomena and with respect to lower level perceptual phenomena. Among other benefits, these explanatory achievements have extended and enhanced our understanding of a broad range of forms of awareness. We can now see much more deeply into conceptually grounded awareness and also into vision and the other forms of perceptual awareness. In addition, as we will observe at some length in a later chapter, cognitive science has improved our grasp of awareness of pain and other bodily sensations. Now, as is also well known, the theories that are responsible for these accomplishments all presuppose that the mind is essentially representational in character – that mental states are generally endowed with representational contents, and that mental processes are generally either in the business of producing new representational states or in the business of modifying old ones. This is no less true of the parts of cognitive science that have implications for awareness than of other parts. Accordingly, we must recognize that our newly achieved understanding of the various forms of awareness crucially depends on the assumption that awareness is essentially representational. But this means that it involves a commitment to (P).

I will not attempt a general review of the ways in which cognitive science has enhanced our understanding of awareness. This is likely to be familiar territory for most readers, for the literature contains a number of brilliant expositions of these achievements by people who have contributed to them.[1] We will have occasion to take note of a number of sample achievements in later chapters, but there is no need for a systematic survey.

I will, however, provide an argument for (P) that is meant to supplement the primary argument that I have just sketched. Although representationalist theories of awareness are universally accepted in cognitive science, they do not enjoy the same popularity among philosophers.

---

[1] Readers who wish to review representationalist theories in cognitive science are encouraged to look at Stephen Palmer's magnificent *Vision Science* (Cambridge, MA: MIT Press, 1999). Since it focuses on perception, Palmer's text is especially pertinent to the themes of the present work. Another useful text is Randolph Blake and Robert Sekuler, *Perception*, 5th edition (New York: McGraw-Hill, 2005), and a third is Jeremy Wolfe, Keith R. Kluender, Dennis M. Levi, Linda M. Bartoshuk, Rachel S. Herz, Roberta L. Klatsky, and Susan J. Lederman, *Sensation and Perception* (Sunderland, MA: Sinauer Associates, 2006). These two books offer less detailed coverage of visual perception than Palmer's massive volume, but they cover other perceptual modalities as well as vision.

Historically speaking, many philosophers have preferred to develop non-representationalist theories of certain forms of awareness, including especially perceptual awareness and introspective awareness of sensations; and this preference is shared by a number of contemporary philosophers. Accordingly, it seems wise to supplement the primary argument for (P) by scrutinizing some of the competing proposals. This effort will occupy the next three sections. I will focus there on the competitors of (P) that seem to command the most respect at present – Bertrand Russell's view that *acquaintance* is metaphysically primitive, and therefore has no representational structure, G. E. Moore's closely related idea that perceptual consciousness is *diaphanous* or *transparent*, and C. J. Ducasse's notion that awareness of a sensory quality is not a fact involving a cognitive relation, but is rather a fact involving an adverbially qualified monadic property, a property that can be called a *mode of awareness* or a *form of experience*. I will try to show that each of these accounts has serious liabilities that are not shared by representationalist theories.

3.2   RUSSELLIAN ACQUAINTANCE

Russell developed his views about acquaintance in the early years of the twentieth century.[2] These views underwent significant changes, but early and late, he held that facts involving acquaintance provide the foundation for the edifice of knowledge. He also subscribed to the following four doctrines: (i) Acquaintance connects subjects that are essentially mental to objects and universals, and also to facts, where facts are taken to be complexes consisting of objects and relations. (ii) Acquaintance comes in a variety of forms: for example, the relation of acquaintance that we bear to currently existing objects is somewhat different in character than the relation that we bear to objects that existed in the past. (iii) Unlike belief and judgment, acquaintance does not involve conceptualization or interpretation of the items to which it gives us access. (iv) More generally speaking, acquaintance is metaphysically primitive: once one has distinguished the different forms of acquaintance, and described the items in each of their domains, one has said all there is to say about it. Acquaintance does not admit of any sort of analysis into simpler elements. In particular, it would be a mistake to suppose that acquaintance with x constitutively involves a representation of x. (In Russell's phrase, it would be a mistake to suppose

[2] See, e.g., Bertrand Russell, "On the Nature of Acquaintance," in Robert Charles Marsh (ed.), *Logic and Knowledge: Essays 1901–1950* (London: George Allen and Unwin, 1956), pp. 127–174.

that acquaintance involves "mental modifications called 'contents', having a diversity which reproduces that of objects."[3])

There continues to be considerable interest in acquaintance in contemporary philosophy, especially among philosophers who are epistemological foundationalists. Moreover, portrayals of acquaintance tend to be fundamentally Russellian in character. Here, for example, is what Richard Fumerton says about it:

> Acquaintance is a sui generis *relation* that holds between a self and a thing, property, or fact. To be acquainted with a fact is not *by itself* to have any kind of propositional knowledge or justified belief, and for that reason, I would prefer not to use the old terminology of knowledge by acquaintance. One can be acquainted with a property or fact without even possessing the conceptual resources to *represent* that fact in thought, and certainly without possessing the ability to linguistically express that fact.[4]

> Because acquaintance is not like any other relation, there is no useful genus under which to subsume it. One can give examples of facts with which one is acquainted and in this way present a kind of "ostensive" definition of acquaintance, but philosophers who think the concept is gibberish are unlikely to find themselves acquainted with their being acquainted with various facts. When one is acquainted with a fact, the fact is *there* before consciousness. Nothing stands "between" the self and the fact. But these are metaphors and in the end are as likely to be misleading as helpful.[5]

Other contemporary foundationalists tend to share these views, or hold closely related ones, but there is one aspect of the contemporary picture

---

[3] *Ibid.*, p. 174. The quoted passage summarizes Russell's discussion of Meinong's view that acquaintance with objects involves "contents." According to Meinong, as Russell interprets him, when one is acquainted with an object *x*, there is a modification of the mind that explains why one is acquainted with *x* rather than some other object *y*. Russell thinks that no such explanation is needed: "At first sight, it seems obvious that my mind is in different 'states' when I am thinking of one thing and when I am thinking of another. *But in fact, the difference of object supplies all the difference required.* There seems to be, in the hypothesis of 'states' of mind, an operation (generally unconscious) of the 'internal' theory of relations: it is thought that some intrinsic difference in the subject must correspond to the difference in the objects to which it has the relation of presentation. I have argued this question at length elsewhere, and shall therefore now assume the 'external' theory of relations, according to which difference of relations affords no evidence for difference of intrinsic predicates. It follows that, from the fact that the complex 'my awareness of *A*' is different than the complex 'my awareness of *B*', it does not follow that when I am aware of *A* I have some intrinsic quality which I do not have when I am aware of *B* but not of *A*. There is therefore no reason for assuming a difference in the subject corresponding to the difference between two presented subjects." (*Ibid.*, pp. 171–172; my italics.)
    This is one of a number of passages which show that Russell was committed to the metaphysical simplicity of acquaintance.
[4] Richard Fumerton, "Classical Foundationalism," in Michael R. DePaul (ed.), *Resurrecting Old-Fashioned Foundationalism* (Lanham, MD: Rowman and Littlefield Publishers, Inc., 2001), pp. 3–20. The quoted passage occurs on p. 14.
[5] *Ibid.*, p. 14.

of acquaintance that Fumerton's account fails to make fully explicit. He says that states of acquaintance do not involve conceptual representations, but that is only part of the story. To complete the picture, it is necessary to add that acquaintance is innocent of *all* forms of representation. If acquaintance involved representation, it could be infected by vagueness and distortion. Moreover, it could contain interpretive elements that were essentially free creations of the subject, and therefore had no basis in the properties of the represented object. Any of these flaws would prevent acquaintance from providing a satisfactory foundation of knowledge. Or at least, this is how things would appear from the perspective of the foundationalist epistemology I mean to be characterizing. From that perspective, a satisfactory foundation for knowledge must provide an ideally trustworthy platform for inference. If there was any chance that acquaintance fails to put one in touch with the real natures of its objects, due to its having a representational structure, then, to obtain knowledge from acquaintance, it would be necessary to know that the relevant representations have an appropriate degree of determinacy of content, and also an appropriate degree of fidelity. And where would such vindicating knowledge come from? It would have to come out of the blue.

Despite its noble lineage, and its roots in vivid epistemological intuitions, I think we can see that the Russellian view of acquaintance encounters insurmountable problems.

In the first place, Russellian theories have very substantial ontological commitments – commitments that are unnecessary and therefore unsustainable. As we have seen, such theories maintain that facts involving acquaintance are metaphysically primitive – they cannot be reduced to facts that are in some sense more basic. Russellian theories contrast sharply in this respect with representationalist theories, for the latter are compatible with reductive accounts of acquaintance, and indeed identify crucial components of such accounts. If a representationalist theory is accepted, we can talk freely of acquaintance without automatically incurring additional ontological commitments. It follows that the ontological burdens of Russellian theories may be unnecessary. It seems possible, and even likely, that we can live without them. But this means that we should not accept a Russellian theory unless the motivation for it is extremely strong. Is this condition satisfied? To see that it isn't, consider the chaotic state of contemporary epistemology. If we had been given a compelling argument for Russellian foundationalism, we would observe order and consensus instead of chaos and competition.

Russellian theories also have explanatory shortcomings. When we are acquainted with an object, our cognitive grasp of the object is characterized by *directedness* (it is concerned with *that* object), *scope* (it is not concerned with various other objects that are in the environment of the given object), *perspective* (it affords access to one side or aspect of the given object in preference to others), and *resolution* (it affords access to some levels of the mereological structure of the object but not to all). Now if we allow ourselves to say that acquaintance with an object involves a representation of it, then all of these features of acquaintance can be explained. Thus, if acquaintance is directed on a certain object x on a particular occasion, we can explain that directedness by saying that x is included in the content of the relevant representation. Equally, if the scope of acquaintance includes certain objects y and z that are in the vicinity of x, but not certain other neighboring objects u and w, we can explain this fact by an appeal to the content of the representation. Generally speaking, the more inclusive the content of a representation, the broader the scope of the state of awareness in which that representation is involved. And so on. On the other hand, if we join Russell and contemporary foundationalists in supposing that acquaintance is metaphysically primitive, and therefore in denying that it has a representational structure, we will forgo all of these explanations, and have no others – that is, no others of the same quality – with which to replace them. No one could welcome such a result. Absent an argument of a sort that we have never been given, an argument which makes it extremely plausible that Russellian acquaintance must be embraced if we are to have a satisfactory epistemology, the result is a sufficient reason for rejecting the Russellian picture.

In claiming that a Russellian theory of acquaintance must deny that facts about the scope, etc. of acquaintance can be explained, I mean to be claiming that Russellians must forgo *reductive* explanations of such facts, not that they are precluded from giving *causal* explanations. Suppose, for example, that I am currently acquainted with a red object, which is located directly in front of me, but that I am not acquainted with a green object that is located in the next room. I recognize, of course, that a Russellian theory can explain this fact. What I wish to claim is that a Russellian is precluded from giving an explanation of the sort that a representationalist can give. A representationalist can explain the fact by saying that it is *constituted*, in part, by a fact involving my current perceptual representations, but a Russellian theory can only explain it by saying that it is *caused by* this representational fact.

To amplify: suppose that we are concerned to explain the scope of my current state of acquaintance – that is, the fact that the scope includes the red object but not the green one. A representationalist can explain this by saying that my state of acquaintance is constituted, in part, by a representation whose content includes the red object but not the green object. (This fact about content can in turn be explained in terms of laws governing the acquisition of representational content. In my view, these laws will refer to the ways in which genes for states that covary with external objects of various types are selected by evolutionary pressures.) This would be a fully reductive explanation of the given fact about the scope of my state. On the other hand, if the Russellian is to explain the given fact, he must appeal to a causal law that links ontologically irreducible facts of acquaintance to facts of other kinds, including, no doubt, facts involving representations. (The law would presumably have something like the following form: If x is currently tokening a perceptual representation of a red object, and certain other conditions are satisfied, then x is perceptually acquainted with a red object.) This law would be an irreducible posit, and would therefore swell the Russellian's already unsustainable burden of ontological commitments. It follows that the representationalist's explanation of my state of acquaintance is superior to the Russellian's explanation. More specifically, it is superior because it commits us to fewer irreducible laws. But this means that we should give preference to the representationalist's explanation, for there is a general principle to the effect that better explanations are more worthy of our belief than poorer ones.

Before concluding this section on the Russellian theory, I should acknowledge a way of developing the theory that somewhat reduces its exposure to the present objection.

Russell sympathetically entertained a number of different views concerning the nature of the objects of acquaintance, but he was strongly drawn to the idea that they are *mental* entities that are *fully* revealed to us when we are acquainted with them. A number of contemporary defenders of Russellian theories of acquaintance are also inclined to embrace this idea. In a phrase, Russellians are often inclined to think that the objects of acquaintance are *sense data*.[6] Now if one holds this view, one will be prepared to deny that it is possible to adopt different perspectives or viewpoints with respect to the objects of acquaintance. It is impossible to view a sense datum from more than one perspective. Moreover, if one embraces sense data, one will deny that objects of acquaintance have layers of grain, or different levels of mereological structure, that are successively revealed

---

[6] See, e.g., Bertrand Russell, *Mysticism and Logic* (London: George Allen and Unwin, 1917), Chapter 10.

as the resolution of acquaintance increases. A sense datum has only a single layer of grain: when grain changes, it does so because one sense datum has been replaced by others, not because one has acquired more detailed knowledge of the original sense datum. It follows that the sense datum gambit significantly reduces the explanatory obligations of Russellian theories. Clearly, if one denies that acquaintance has a perspectival character, and also that it has different degrees of resolution, then one will have no obligation to explain alleged facts involving the perspectival character and resolution of acquaintance. One need not explain what doesn't exist.

Although there are significant costs associated with accepting sense data, this way of developing the Russellian theory of acquaintance does at least diminish the force of the second of the two objections I have presented above. But it leaves part of the problem untouched. There is still a need to explain the direction and scope of particular instances of acquaintance. Suppose I am now acquainted with a reddish circular sense datum. Why am I aware of that sense datum rather than another one? A Russellian theory cannot answer this question by giving a reductive explanation. Unlike a representationalist account, which can explain why acquaintance has a particular object in terms of the content of its constituent representation, a Russellian account must take facts of this sort as primitive, and therefore as requiring explanation in terms of causal laws. As we observed earlier, laws of this sort increase the Russellian's ontological burden. Moreover, Russellians will need to appeal to additional irreducible laws in explaining why my state of awareness has the scope it has. Let us suppose that I am presently aware *only* of a reddish circular sense datum. In particular, I am not aware of the greenish triangular sense datum that has claimed your attention. Why is this? Why am I not aware of both sense data? A representationalist would find it easy to answer this, if he could be moved to countenance sense data at all. But a Russellian can only explain it if he is prepared to embrace an even more inflated ontology.

To summarize: Russellian theories of acquaintance carry ontological commitments, both to particular facts and to causal laws, that representationalist theories avoid. In view of this fact, we are well advised to prefer the latter to the former.

3.3   MOOREAN TRANSPARENCY

At roughly the same time as Russell was developing his theory of acquaintance, G. E. Moore was arguing for a closely related account of perceptual consciousness. At the most basic level, he maintained, perceptual consciousness involves two components, an act (a state of being aware) and an object. The act and the object are causally independent. One does not influence an object of consciousness by becoming conscious of it. Conversely, consciousness is not affected by its object. Indeed, there is nothing about consciousness of any one object that distinguishes it from consciousness of any other object, save only the differences between the objects themselves. It follows that consciousness does not have a representational structure: if consciousness of x is the same as consciousness of y, save for the differences between x and y, then it cannot be true that consciousness of x involves a different representation than consciousness of y. But more: Moore did not just deny that consciousness has a representational structure; he denied that it has an internal organization of any kind. According to Moore, consciousness is featureless. His reason for this extraordinary view was that introspection does not disclose any features when it is turned in the direction of consciousness. When we introspectively attend to perceptual consciousness, Moore claimed, all we encounter are features of whatever object consciousness is directed on.

To illustrate these doctrines, Moore invited his readers to consider two sensations, a sensation of blue and a sensation of green. Each of the sensations has two components, he maintained, an act and an object. The first component is the same in both cases; it is the second component that accounts for the unique nature of each sensation. But mustn't there be something about the act component of the first sensation that explains why it is focused on blue rather than green? Must there not be some sort of modification of consciousness that brings it into rapport with blue? Moore answered "no." Thus, like Russell, he was committed to the view that perceptual consciousness is metaphysically simple and therefore primitive. His grounds for this commitment seem to have been quite different, however, for it seems that he was not moved by primarily epistemological considerations. He was not trying to identify a type of cognitive contact with the world that is innocent of vagueness, distortion, and free interpretation. Rather, his motivation seems to have been entirely introspective. We must take consciousness to be simple and primitive, he seems to have thought, because introspection provides no grounds for attributing either representational or intrinsic properties to it. Perceptual consciousness is transparent to introspection, so it must be metaphysically transparent – the mental equivalent of glass.

These views are set forth in the following passages:

The term "blue" is easy enough to distinguish, but the other element which I have called "consciousness" – that which sensation of blue has in common with sensation of green – is extremely difficult to fix. … [T]hat which makes the sensation of blue a mental fact seems to escape us: it seems, if I may use a metaphor, to be transparent – we look through it and see nothing but the blue.[7]

[T]he moment we try to fix our attention upon consciousness and to see *what*, distinctly, it is, it seems to vanish: it seems as if we had before us a mere emptiness. When we try to introspect the sensation of blue, all we can see is the blue: the other element is as if it were diaphanous.[8]

In addition to stating Moore's position in a particularly compelling way, these passages show that his reason for holding the position was indeed introspective. According to Moore, consciousness must be regarded as transparent or diaphanous because introspection provides no grounds for attributing either intrinsic or representational features to it. Another author, such as myself, might grant that introspection is limited in this way, but wish to explain the limitation by claiming that the internal nature of perceptual consciousness is not in the domain of introspection. We know that there are innumerable states, features, and activities of mind to which introspection gives us no access – for which, as it were, it is not defined. Indeed, we know that there are many introspectible items that have non-introspectible components or aspects. To my mind, there is no obvious reason why the internal nature of perceptual consciousness should be one of the introspectible items rather than one of the items that fall outside the scope of introspection. But Moore saw things differently. In effect, he started with an epistemological premise – the proposition that introspection provides no grounds for ascribing properties to consciousness. As the foregoing passages show, he found it entirely natural to move from that premise to a metaphysical conclusion – the proposition that consciousness is metaphysically transparent. Evidently, there is a missing premise here: he is presupposing the claim that what is transparent to introspection is metaphysically transparent. This claim seems to

---

[7] G. E. Moore, "The Refutation of Idealism," in *Philosophical Studies* (London: Kegan Paul, 1922), pp. 1–30. The quoted passage appears on p. 20.

My interpretation of Moore is based largely on the one that James Van Cleve sketches in "Troubles for Radical Transparency," in Terry Horgan, Marcello Sebatés, and David Sosa (eds.), *Supervenience in Mind: A* Festschrift *for Jaegwon Kim* (Cambridge, MA: MIT Press, forthcoming). The reader is referred to Van Cleve's paper for supporting arguments. For my purposes, however, it does not matter too much whether the picture presented in the text matches Moore's views. I am more interested in the position itself than in the question of what Moore actually held.

For further discussion of Moore's position, see Benj Hellie, "That Which Makes the Sensation of Blue a Mental Fact: Moore on Phenomenal Relationism," *European Journal of Philosophy* 15:3 (2007), 334–366. Hellie's interpretation is quite different than Van Cleve's.

[8] Moore, "The Refutation of Idealism," p. 25.

me to have very little to recommend it, but Moore seems to have regarded it as obvious.

James Van Cleve has usefully distinguished the sort of transparency that figures in Moore's theory of perceptual consciousness from the sort to which Gilbert Harman appeals in arguing that we have no introspective access to qualia.[9] On the most natural interpretation of the relevant passages, while Harman is concerned to deny that we have no access to the intrinsic properties of experience, he allows that we have access to its representational properties. That is, when we consider an experience introspectively, we are aware of it only as representing an object or situation in the world. This positive claim is brought to the fore in the following passage, which we originally encountered in Chapter 2:

In the case of a painting, Eloise can be aware of those features of the painting that are responsible for its being a painting of a unicorn. That is, she can turn her attention to the pattern of the paint on the canvas by virtue of which the painting represents a unicorn. But in the case of her visual experience of a tree, I want to say that she is not aware of, as it were, the mental paint by virtue of which her experience is experience of seeing a tree. She is aware only of the intentional or relational features of her experience, not of its intrinsic nonintentional features.[10]

In view of remarks of this sort, we must conclude that Harmanian transparency is very different than Moorean transparency. As Van Cleve observes, Moore's doctrine is much more radical. First, in addition to denying that introspection provides grounds for attributing an intrinsic nature to states of consciousness, Moore denies that it provides grounds for attributing representational properties to them. And second, as we have just seen, Moore is prepared to infer metaphysical conclusions from his negative epistemological claims. His position differs from Harman's in both of these respects.

It is worth dwelling for a moment on the contrast between these conceptions of introspection and transparency, for we can extract a valuable lesson from it. Suppose you have an experience that it is natural to describe as an experience of blue. It seems clear that you can become apprised of this fact by introspection. Harman and Moore will both accept this

---

[9] James Van Cleve, "Troubles for Radical Transparency."
[10] Gilbert Harman, "The Intrinsic Quality of Experience," in James J. Tomberlin (ed.), *Philosophical Perspectives*, Volume 4 (Atascadero, CA: Ridgeview Publishing Company, 1990), pp. 31–52. The paper is reprinted in Ned Block, Owen Flanagan, and Güven Güzeldere (eds.), *The Nature of Consciousness* (Cambridge, MA: MIT Press, 1997), pp. 663–675. The quoted passage occurs on p. 667 of that volume.

intuition. Indeed, they will insist on its validity. But what exactly is it that introspection reveals? What exactly is it that you are aware of when you are aware of the experience as an experience of blue? Here Harman and Moore will part company. Harman will say that you are aware of it as an experience that can be said to be *of* blue in a sense of "of" that expresses intentionality. That is, he will claim that you are aware of the experience as one that represents blue. Moore, on the other hand, will prefer to say that you are aware of the experience as an experience that can be said to be *of* blue in a sense of "of" that expresses relationality. That is, he will claim that you are aware of a relational fact – a fact involving a cogniz-ing agent, a cognitive relation that is metaphysically simple, the relation of perceptual consciousness, and an object that differentiates between the given relational fact and all other such facts involving the same agent. (It is the object of consciousness that accounts for the distinctive nature of the fact.) What is important for present purposes is that Moore joins Harman in recognizing that the given experience is an experience *of* blue, but that he interprets the *of*-ness of the experience in an altogether different way, seeing it as constituted by an extensional relation rather than representa-tional content.

Now let us ask: Does introspection itself give us any reason to pre-fer either Harman's interpretation of *of*-ness to Moore's interpretation or Moore's interpretation to Harman's? As far as I can see, the answer is "no." There are other, non-introspective reasons for accepting Harman's view that perceptual consciousness has a representational structure, some of which we observed in the foregoing section on Russell's theory of acquaintance. But as far as I can determine, introspection cannot by itself settle this disagreement between Harman and Moore.

If it seems otherwise, this is no doubt because Harman can try to sup-port his position by saying that it is possible to have an experience of something that does not exist, such as Macbeth's dagger, and by urg-ing that this would not be possible unless perceptual consciousness was intentional. This is initially plausible, but someone with a relational view of consciousness can reply in several ways. Thus, for example, the rela-tionalist can offer a disjunctive interpretation of perceptual experience, maintaining that non-hallucinatory experiences are to be explained in terms of a simple, Moorean relation of awareness, and that hallucinatory experiences like Macbeth's are to be explained in terms of representations of intentional objects.[11] On this view, it is impossible to tell on the basis

---

[11] For discussions of disjunctivism, see M. G. F. Martin, "The Transparency of Experience," *Mind and Language* 17 (2002), 376–425, John McDowell, "Criteria, Defeasibility, and Knowledge,"

of introspection alone whether one is enjoying a veridical experience of a
real object, and one's experience is to be interpreted in relational terms,
or one is instead undergoing an hallucination, and one's experience is to
be understood in representational terms. These metaphysical differences
are not within the domain of introspection. As I see it, this reply to the
point about Macbeth's dagger is decisive. It allows that there are grounds
for thinking that *some* perceptual experiences should be seen as representational, but points out that it does not follow from this that *all* perceptual experience is representational. As a matter of pure logic, this point
is perfectly correct. Moreover, disjunctivism shows how to combine an
acknowledgment of the existence of hallucinations with a relational conception of veridical experiences.

This is not to say that the disjunctivist's account of these matters is
correct. I myself think it is badly misguided, because it commits us to
giving a complex, disjunctive explanation of the fact that hallucinatory
perceptions and their veridical counterparts have identical psychological
and behavioral consequences. When an agent is hallucinating that *p*, he
will respond in the same way as he would if he were actually seeing that *p*
(unless, of course, he has some reason to believe that he is hallucinating).
Representationalism can explain this fact by saying that hallucinating
that *p* and seeing that *p* are fundamentally akin – they both involve a
representation of the state of affairs that *p*. Representationalism is different in this respect than disjunctivism: since disjunctivism views hallucinating that *p* as having nothing in common with seeing that *p*, it is obliged
to give an explanation of the agent's response to hallucinating that *p* that
is different than its explanation of the agent's response to seeing that *p*.
Thus, disjunctivism is more complex than representationalism. This is a
strong reason for preferring the latter view. But the fact that there is a case
of this sort for the superiority of representationalism does not affect the
point that I wish to make here – which, to repeat, is that it is impossible
to rule disjunctivism out on the basis of introspection alone.

In view of this point, the disagreement between Harman and Moore
seems to be a standoff, at least insofar as introspection is taken to be the
arbiter. It seems that the deliverances of introspection are neutral between
the two positions. I stress the contrast between the views, and the apparent
neutrality of introspection, because there is an important methodological
moral here. Contrary to what seems to be the currently received view, it
is impossible to establish a representationalist theory of awareness just by

appealing to introspection. Introspection can reveal that an experience is an experience *of* blue, but the relevant "of" is not self-interpreting. It can be construed as an indicator of intentionality and also as an indicator of relationality. We cannot choose between these construals on the basis of introspection alone. Philosophical argument is needed.

Although the motivation for Moore's views about perceptual consciousness is different from the motivation for Russell's account of acquaintance, in other respects the two positions are quite similar. Most importantly, they both assert that the ground floor facts of awareness involve a cognitive relation that has no internal organization, and that must therefore be taken as a metaphysical primitive. Because of this commonality, Moore's account is vulnerable to the same objections as Russell's: it commits us to a realm of irreducible particular facts, and it is constitutionally incapable of giving a deep, reductive explanation of such features of awareness as directedness and scope. Indeed, it must deny that such an explanation is possible. This is a clear case of philosophical myopia: representational theories of awareness are epistemically available, and they offer deeply satisfying explanations of the given features of awareness, explanations that unify and simplify our theoretical commitments.

In addition to these metaphysical objections to Moore's account of perceptual consciousness, there is also the logical objection that I noted above: Moore has no right to infer a metaphysical conclusion from the essentially epistemological observation that perceptual consciousness is transparent to introspection. To say that perceptual consciousness is transparent to introspection is to make a claim about the limits of introspection: it is to say that introspection does not by itself establish that perceptual consciousness has a representational structure. This claim is quite weak: it comes to the same thing as saying that introspection *leaves it open* whether perceptual consciousness is representational. A claim of this sort is not a promising beginning for an argument that seeks to establish a very substantial metaphysical conclusion.

As we have seen, Moore's theory claims that the differentiae of any fact of perceptual consciousness are due entirely to the distinguishing features of the object of consciousness. This view lives on in several influential contemporary accounts of perception. We encounter it, for example, under the name "Relational View" in John Campbell's *Reference and Consciousness*. Campbell explains the Relational View in the following way:

On [the] Relational View, the phenomenal character of your experience, as you look around the room, is constituted by the actual layout of the room itself: which particular objects are there, their intrinsic properties, such as colour and shape, and how they are arranged in relation to one another and to you. On this Relational View, two ordinary observers standing in roughly the same place, looking at the same scene, are bound to have experiences with the same phenomenal character. For the phenomenal character of the experience is constituted by the layout and characteristics of the very same external objects. We have the ordinary notion of a "view", as when you drag someone up a mountain trail, insisting that he will "enjoy the view". In this sense, thousands of people might visit the very same spot and enjoy the very same view. You characterize the experiences they are having by saying which view they are enjoying. On the Relational picture, this is the same thing as describing the phenomenal character of their experiences.[12]

In saying that the phenomenal character of experience is determined by the object of experience, the scene before one's eyes, Campbell is in effect saying that the distinctive nature of any fact of experiential awareness derives entirely from the object of awareness. Of course, the view that Campbell is characterizing diverges from the view that Moore came eventually to hold in one very important respect: while in his mature work Moore took the immediate objects of perceptual consciousness to be sense data, Campbell takes them to be external physical substances and situations involving such substances. But otherwise the views seem to be similar. This interpretation is confirmed when we find Campbell contrasting the Relational View of perceptual consciousness with what he calls the Representational View. The Representational View attributes a complex internal organization to consciousness – specifically, a representational organization. Campbell explicitly rejects the Representational View. To be sure, he is fully committed to the existence of perceptual representations; but he takes them to be subpersonal, and to be metaphysically external to consciousness. Facts involving perceptual consciousness are metaphysically primitive. It is possible to explain such facts but these explanations are necessarily causal, not reductive.

   With the Relational View before us, we can more easily appreciate a fourth problem with Moore's transparency doctrine – a problem that can also be seen to afflict Russell's theory of acquaintance. It seems wrong to attribute *all* of the distinguishing features of *every* fact of perceptual consciousness to the entities that count as objects of consciousness. How an object of consciousness appears to us sometimes depends, at least in part, on factors that lie on the subject side of the subject/object divide. Thus, for example, an object of consciousness can appear to have a yellowish aspect,

---

[12] John Campbell, *Reference and Consciousness* (Oxford: Oxford University Press, 2002), p. 116.

not because it is yellow or bathed in yellow light, but rather because the subject has an internal malady that influences his experience. That is to say, the phenomenal character of a perceptual experience can be influenced by factors that are independent both of the distal stimulus and of the proximal stimulus. Moreover, this remains true even if "proximal stimulus" is understood to include activity in the retina – and indeed, even if it is understood to include activity in the early processing centers of the brain. More generally, let the boundary between subject and object be drawn in any way one likes. Even if the boundary leaves practically nothing on the side of the subject, as long as the subject is allowed to be capable of being in a range of different internal states, and the way an object looks to the subject is allowed to depend *causally* on the internal states of the subject, there will be a foothold for the view that the way an object appears to a subject can be at least partially independent of properties of the object. This poses a problem for both Moore and Campbell, and for Russell as well, for they are all committed to denying that any such foothold exists. For them, it is *necessarily* true that how an object appears to a subject is determined by the nature of the object. One can read phenomenal character off from the properties of the object of awareness.[13]

Unlike Moore's theory, representationalist theories of awareness have the resources to explain the contributions of the subject. According to them, the phenomenal character of an experience is not determined by the object of awareness. Rather, it is determined by how the subject represents the object. In most cases, perhaps, it will be possible to explain why a subject deploys a certain representation purely in terms of the flow of information from the object, but it will happen on occasion that the internal determinants of representation operate independently of external influences. For instance, it may happen that a light is represented as yellowish green, despite the fact that it is emitting only green light, because the upper reaches of the subject's visual system are affected by a high level visual disorder. In these circumstances, the object of awareness will look yellowish green to the subject. But this means that the phenomenal character of the subject's experience will not be determined by the object.

---

[13] Campbell can try to defend against this objection by invoking disjunctivism, maintaining that if, e.g., my experience has a yellowish cast due to internal factors, this is because it has a quite different metaphysical nature than experiences that are fully veridical. But this response is blocked if, as I have maintained above, disjunctivism can be rejected on methodological grounds. (To repeat, those grounds include the fact that disjunctivism forces us to give ugly, complex explanations of the fact that hallucinations (and illusions) have the same psychological and behavioral consequences as veridical perceptual experiences.)

To summarize: Moore claimed that perceptual consciousness is transparent to introspection – or, in other words, that introspection reveals what perceptual consciousness is directed on (or is *of*), and *only* what perceptual consciousness is directed on. This seems right: it seems that introspection does not attribute a representational structure, or an internal organization of any kind, to perceptual consciousness. It would be wrong, however, to infer from this fact that perceptual consciousness *lacks* a representational structure. There is no reason to think, and in fact much reason to doubt, that introspection is capable of plumbing the depths of consciousness.

3.4   THE ADVERBIAL THEORY

The adverbial theory of awareness was proposed by C. J. Ducasse in 1942. Here is Ducasse's original formulation of the theory:

> The hypothesis, then, which I present as an alternative to Professor Moore's is that "blue," "bitter," "sweet," etc., are names not of objects of experience nor of species of objects of experience but of *species of experience itself.* What this means is perhaps made clearest by saying that to sense blue is then to sense *bluely*, just as to dance the waltz is to dance "waltzily."[14]

In view of this passage, it seems fair to summarize adverbialism by saying that it represents statements of the form "*x* is aware of an instance of the property *Q*," where *Q* is a qualitative property, as standing for facts of the form *x is in a Q-ish state of awareness.* In other words, adverbialism claims that the truth-maker for a statement of the given form is a fact involving *x* and a monadic property, a property that is a *mode* or form of experience, a *way* of experiencing the world.

Why should we believe this astonishing view? Ducasse and its other defenders saw it as presenting an attractive alternative to the sense datum theory. As we have been noticing, Russell and Moore believed that at the most fundamental level, perceptual consciousness involves immediate acquaintance with mental particulars. Qualia were regarded as characteristics of such particulars. Now there is reason to hope that the sense datum theory is false. Sense data pose metaphysical problems because it is not clear how to accommodate them within a physicalist world view. And they pose epistemological problems because, if we are immediately

---

[14] C. J. Ducasse, "Moore's 'The Refutation of Idealism'," in Paul Arthur Schilpp (ed.), *The Philosophy of G. E. Moore* (Lasalle, IL: Open Court Publishing Co., 1942), pp. 225–251. The quoted passage occurs on pp. 232–233.

aware of them rather than physical objects, they are in effect a screen between us and the external world, making any claim to acquire knowledge of the external world from perception problematic. The adverbial theory gives us relief from problems of both kinds, for it enables us to acknowledge the existence of qualia without having to accept the accompanying baggage of mental particulars that instantiate them. This simplifies the obligations facing the physicalist, and clears the way for the epistemologist to work out a theory of direct perceptual access to the external world.

If there were no other alternative to the sense datum theory, these advantages of adverbialism would provide reasonably strong motivation for accepting it. In fact, however, there is at least one other theory that has the same metaphysical and epistemological advantages – the theory of perceptual consciousness that is presented in Chapter 5 and Chapter 9 of the present work. Accordingly, the case for the adverbial theory is fairly weak. It also suffers from some internal problems. I will mention three.

First, it is undeniable that we have *knowledge* of qualia, and this implies that we have some sort of cognitive access to them. But we cannot be said to have access to qualia simply in virtue of being *in* mental states that are adverbially qualified by them. Being *in* a state does not by itself give one cognitive access to that state. Hence, if adverbialism is true, the fact that we have knowledge of qualia implies that there are second order introspective states that are directed on first order adverbially qualified states. It is these second order states that give us our cognitive appreciation of qualia. But now we must notice that *every* perceptual or sensory experience involves an appreciation of qualia. Thus, every perceptual or sensory experience has a phenomenological dimension, and we must appreciate phenomenology in order for there to *be* phenomenology. That is to say, an experience has a phenomenological dimension only if we have access to the phenomenology in virtue of having the experience. It follows that, if adverbialism is true, we must always be introspectively aware of the first order states that are adverbially qualified by qualia. But this is an extravagant view. It would be very expensive for the mind to generate a second order state to accompany every perceptual or sensory state. Since there is no independent reason to suppose that it incurs this expense, we should reject the claim that it does.

Second, it seems to us that the qualitative characteristics that constitute phenomenology are characteristics of the *objects* of perceptual and sensory awareness, not of the mental states by which we are aware of such objects. Suppose you are aware of an object as presenting a blue appearance. The fact that it presents this appearance is a qualitative fact.

But it is a fact about the object. It is not a fact about your experience, for you are not aware of the experience in appreciating the blue appearance of the object. You are aware only of the object. This was the lesson of Harman's transparency thesis. The same is true of awareness of pain. It is not the case that you are aware of *two* things in being aware of the pain – the pain itself and your experience of the pain. You are only aware of one thing – the pain. And the quality *pain* is experienced as a characteristic of that one thing. Adverbialism cannot accommodate this simple fact.

This brings us to the third problem. To state it, it is necessary to distinguish between two senses of the expression "aware of." When "aware of" is used in its *extensional sense*, a statement of the form "*S* is aware of an *F*" entails an existential claim of the form "There is an *F*." This is the sense that we rely on most frequently in everyday discourse. But "aware of" also has an *intensional sense*. When the expression is used in this second sense, a statement of the form "*S* is aware of an *F*" does not have an existential consequence. Consider, for example, a case in which a subject says, "I suddenly became aware of a magnificent unicorn," intending thereby to describe an experience that the subject now recognizes as hallucinatory. In this case, the subject is using "aware of" with its intensional sense. The statement can count as true even though there are no unicorns.

Now it is clear that it would be entirely inappropriate to offer adverbial truth conditions for statements involving the extensional sense of "aware of," for no adverbial theory could explain why such statements have the relevant existential entailments. Consider the statement "I am aware of a green square." It implies that a green square exists. Because of this, we cannot say that it is made true by a sensory state that is qualified by the adverbial properties *green-ishly* and *square-ishly*, for one could be in a state of this sort in a situation in which no green square was present. (To say that one is sensing green-ishly and square-ishly is just to say that one is in a sensory state with a certain intrinsic nature. Nothing follows from this claim about the existence of physical objects that have the properties *green* and *square*.) Moreover, it would be quite implausible to claim that statements involving the intensional sense of "aware of" have adverbial truth conditions. As with other intensional verbs that are used to characterize mental states, such as "believe," "imagine," and "dream about," it is very plausible that the truth conditions for statements involving the intensional sense of "aware of" are concerned with representations and representational contents. Reflection shows that this provides the most comprehensive and most unified explanation of the fact that such statements lack existential entailments. (Since statements about representational contents lack existential entailments, we can explain why statements about awareness lack existential entailments by saying that they are implicitly concerned with representations.) It follows that it would be a mistake to characterize the truth conditions of statements involving the intensional sense of "aware of" in purely adverbial terms. Claiming that an agent is in a state with a certain representational content is quite different from claiming that he is in a state with a certain intrinsic nature.[15]

We have found that the motivation for adverbialism is weak, and that it suffers from several serious problems. Any one of these problems is sufficient to discredit the theory. Indeed, in view of the problems, it is surprising that people have thought that the theory might be correct.

3.5   LOOKING BACKWARDS

In the last three sections I have been concerned to establish the superiority of representationalist accounts of awareness to accounts that seek to explain awareness without supposing that representations are constitutively involved in it. I have not compared these alternative theories to a specific representationalist proposal, but rather to the family of proposals that incorporate (P) or some closely related doctrine:

(P) If an agent is aware of x, then the agent is in a mental state that represents x.

This completes the comparative portion of my defense of (P). As noted earlier, these comparative arguments are not meant to serve as the primary motivation for (P). The primary argument is based on an appeal to the explanatory successes of contemporary cognitive science. That argument was sketched in Section 3.1. Later chapters will illustrate this primary argument by citing illustrative explanatory achievements. For instance, Chapter 6 will review some of the ways in which cognitive science has used representationalist theories to enhance our understanding of awareness of pain.

---

[15] I should add that there is a substantial difference between the view I am primarily concerned to defend in this chapter, the claim that *all* facts of awareness are ultimately representational, and the much weaker claim that I mean to be making here – the claim that representations figure in the truth conditions of statements involving the intensional sense of "aware of." It does not beg any questions to put forward this much weaker claim, for it can be established independently of the stronger one. Indeed, I take it that it can be established by a comparatively simple and straightforward argument. It suffices to appeal, as I have done in the text, to the fact that we can explain how it is possible to be aware of non-existing things in terms of the fact that it is possible to represent non-existing things.

3.6   EXPERIENTIAL AWARENESS

I would like to turn now to a task of a rather different sort. There is a range of different forms of awareness. I would like to single out a form that will be of considerable utility in our later discussions, and to characterize it in a way that is more or less free of obscure and controversial concepts. The form that I have in mind is *purely experiential awareness.* Very roughly speaking, this form of awareness is distinguished from others by the fact that it has a proprietary phenomenological dimension and no conceptual dimension. Awareness of pain is a relatively clear example, as are the most basic types of perceptual awareness. On the other hand, all forms of awareness that involve or presuppose propositional knowledge count as supra-experiential, even if they have an experiential dimension. Suppose, for example, that I perceive a passing airplane by virtue of perceiving its sound. My awareness of the plane has an experiential dimension, but it is not a case of purely experiential awareness because it presupposes the concept of an airplane and the belief that planes are likely to make sounds like the one I am experiencing. It may be, however, that my awareness of the sound of the plane is purely experiential.

I have characterized purely experiential awareness as awareness that involves phenomenology but not conceptualization. This description is unfortunate for several reasons. In the first place, the notion of phenomenology is too vague, and too enmeshed in metaphysical controversies, to be seen as a satisfactory anchor for our future discussions. Second, as we will observe at some length later on, it seems that the notion of experiential awareness plays a fairly large role in our intuitive conception of phenomenology. That is, it seems that we think of qualitative characteristics as characteristics that are presented by experiential awareness. It follows that if we are to understand the notion of phenomenology, we must have available an account of experiential awareness that frees it from dependence on that notion. Finally, since there are many philosophers and scientists who think that all forms of awareness involve conceptualization, it would hinder communication to adopt a definition of experiential awareness that flatly insists on its non-conceptual character. It should be explained in such a way as to remind readers of the motivation for supposing that there can be non-conceptual awareness.

In view of these considerations, it is highly desirable to find a different way of distinguishing purely experiential awareness from other forms of awareness. I will now give a more complicated account that is based on eight features of this form of awareness. One of these features is consciousness – all states of experiential awareness are conscious. Another has to do with the fact that experiential awareness is unmediated, and a third has to do with the fact that our introspective grasp of the internal organization of experiential awareness is quite limited. Three additional features are concerned with the types of information about the world that experiential awareness provides. As I shall explain, this form of awareness gives us access to information that is characterized by a remarkable degree of complexity or density, with information that is highly determinate, in the sense of being concerned with properties that have a high degree of specificity or determinateness, and with information that is abundantly particularized, in the sense of being centered on specific objects and events. Conceptually informed awareness is different in these respects, at least in the sense that it is under no obligation to provide us with information that is complex, determinate, and particularized. The seventh feature has to do with attention. The form of attention that governs experiential awareness is quite distinctive. Finally, purely experiential awareness differs from other forms of awareness in that its deliverances are in no sense up to us – objects and facts are *given* to us in experiential awareness.

The resulting account of experiential awareness will make no use of the notion of phenomenology. I should stress that it is not my intention to deny that experiential awareness has a phenomenological dimension, or to use the account as a basis for explaining phenomenology away. The point of the account is not to eliminate the notion of phenomenology, but rather to make available an instrument that will facilitate our future discussions of it. Questions about the nature of phenomenology will continue to occupy our attention for some time to come.

To begin, then, I observe that purely experiential awareness differs from blindsight and other forms of tacit, implicit awareness in that it is conscious. More specifically, states of experiential awareness have the causal powers that we took to be constitutive of *experiential consciousness* in Chapter 1. Here, as a reminder, is our working definition of this form of consciousness: "A mental event x is experientially conscious just in case x is, potentially, at least, a maximally proximal causal trigger for several of the high level cognitive agencies that are recognized by folk psychology. These agencies include the ones that are responsible for producing speech, forming beliefs and other propositional attitudes, making choices, elaborating plans, exercising on-line control of intentional actions, creating memories, monitoring mental states, and producing introspective judgments." If a subject is experientially aware of an item x, then the subject must be aware of x in virtue of being in a state that has this form of consciousness.

The second distinguishing feature of experiential awareness is that it is direct or immediate: if an agent is aware of an item *x* in virtue of being aware of something else, then it would be wrong to say that the agent is experientially aware of *x*. It follows from this that it is possible to be perceptually aware of something without being experientially aware of it, for we can be said to be perceptually aware of things that we do not perceive directly. (Thus, for example, someone can be said to be perceptually aware of rain in virtue of being aware of a certain pattern of sounds on the roof.) Only direct perceptual awareness counts as experiential.

Third, experiential awareness is transparent to introspection, in the sense that introspection fails to establish, or even to selectively confirm, the view that experiential awareness has a representational structure. Introspective consciousness of experiential awareness of blue can of course reveal that it is awareness *of blue*, and this fact may ultimately be representational in character, but introspection does not reveal it as representational. It is perfectly appropriate for someone who is introspectively aware of experiential awareness of blue to favor the Moorean view that there is nothing distinctive about this form of awareness other than its object.

Now of course, Moore would have thought it appropriate to move from this epistemological observation to a metaphysical conclusion – to infer metaphysical transparency from introspective transparency. But there is no need to follow Moore here, and I prefer not to do so. The claim that experiential awareness is transparent to introspection seems quite right to me, but I see no reason to think that introspection provides full access to the characteristics of mental states, even in those cases in which mental states are comparatively simple and vibrantly conscious. On the contrary, since I hold that all forms of awareness are representational in character, I think that the essential nature of experiential awareness is largely hidden from introspection.

Experiential awareness contrasts with judgment in this respect, for introspection gives us access to the representational contents of our judgments. Thus, if I judge that *p*, then I can come to know introspectively that my judgment is the judgment *that p* – or in other words, that it has the proposition that *p* as its representational content.

The fourth distinguishing feature of experiential awareness is that it gives us condensed and ready access to objects, events, and properties that are extremely complex. I can take in many of the details of a Pollock canvass at a glance, at least if I am being attentive, and I can grasp all of the opposing interactions on a soccer field simultaneously. Perception works miracles of compression and cohesion, in that all of the components of a perceptual representation of a complex item can exist concurrently, in a way that does justice to the relationships among the components of the item. Moreover, experiential awareness of sensations and emotions works similar miracles. As we will observe at some length in a later chapter, experiential awareness can represent pains as having complex internal organizations. And emotions are famous for their dazzling intricacy.

It is quite otherwise in the case of conceptually informed awareness. It is, of course, possible to represent complex entities conceptually, but when one does this, one rarely if ever does full justice to their complexity. Moreover, to the extent that the representation is successful, it tends to be parasitic on experiential awareness. Thus, for example, in order to represent a complex pattern by a demonstrative concept, such as *the shape of that cloud*, I must be attending to the pattern perceptually. Equally, if I am to formulate a description of a complex pattern, I must rely on continued observation of the pattern or hold it in experiential memory, for the components of the description will have to be constructed sequentially. Unlike perceptual experiences, descriptions are not produced by parallel processing. Moreover, the individual components of a long description have to be *entertained* sequentially. It is possible for all of the constituents of a short thought to exist more or less concurrently, but short thoughts cannot do justice to complexity.

In sum, perceptual awareness of complexity is effortless, and satisfies the principle that the components of a complex entity are represented concurrently. It is very difficult to do justice to the complex entities that experience reveals conceptually. Moreover, insofar as one succeeds in doing so, experiential awareness is an essential enabling factor: experiential awareness precedes and sustains the conceptual representation, and is therefore in no sense constituted by it. Finally, conceptual representation of complexity is sequential and therefore fails to satisfy the principle of concurrent representation of components.

Fifth, if one is experientially aware of an abstract, determinable property, one is generally aware of it in virtue of being aware of a highly determinate form of that property. Thus, for example, if one is experientially aware of an object as blue, this is because one is aware of it as navy blue, or as some other highly determinate shade of blue. It is quite different with doxastic awareness. One can judge that an object is blue without judging that it has a more determinate shade of that characteristic.

Sixth, objects of experiential awareness are highly particularized. To have an experience of mountains, it is necessary to have an experience of certain specific mountains; to have an experience of books, it is necessary to have an experience of certain specific books. Again, doxastic awareness is different. I can judge that there are mountains in the distance without forming a judgment about any particular mountains, and I can judge that there are books on the shelf without forming an opinion about any particular books.

Seventh, attention works differently in the case of experiential awareness than in the case of doxastic awareness. When I attend to an object perceptually, my experience of the object will change in accordance with fixed rules. Specifically, the resolution of my awareness will be enhanced and figure/ground contrast will be intensified.[16] When I attend to an object in thought, however, I will no doubt be led thereby to think *more* thoughts about it, but the nature of my additional thoughts will depend very much on contextual factors, such as my current interests, the history of my involvement with the object of awareness, and my general knowledge of the world. There aren't fixed, context-independent rules governing the results of attending to objects in thought. Moreover, when one attends to an object in thought, it is not appropriate to describe the results in terms of an increase in resolution or figure/ground contrast. The import of these notions is largely experiential, at least insofar as they are used literally.

Eighth, experiential awareness is a form of receptivity, but doxastic awareness is in the domain of spontaneity.

The direction of perceptual attention is up to us, but once we have decided to bestow our attention on a particular object, or a particular location, the nature of our perceptual experience is independent of our will. It is *given* to us, in the sense that it is independent of our desires, interests, and choices. On the other hand, even though perceptual *judgments* tend normally to derive directly from experience, it is always in principle possible for us to subject them to reflective assessment. Is that Tom whom I see across the street? Probably, but am I sure that Tom is at all likely to be in this part of town so early in the morning? Is this scarf really yellowish in color? Perhaps, but haven't I heard that the macula tends to yellow as one ages, thereby adding a yellowish cast to other colors? Is this a Saguaro I see before me? Almost certainly, but before

---

[16] These judgments are warranted by introspection, but they have also been confirmed by experiment. See Yaffa Yeshuran and Marissa Currasco, "Attention Improves Performance in Spatial Resolution Tasks," *Vision Research* 39 (1999), 293–305; and Marissa Currasco, Cigdem Penpeci-Talgar, and Miguel Eckstein, "Spatial Covert Attention Increases Contrast Sensitivity across the CSF: Support for Signal Enhancement," *Vision Research* 40 (2000), 1203–1215.

I allow myself to feel absolutely confident that I see a Saguaro, I should perhaps consider whether my current experience has any of the characteristic marks of dreaming. In all these cases, I am exercising my epistemic right to reflect critically on the credentials of my perceptual beliefs. It is always in principle possible for me to proceed in this way, and on some occasions, my assessment will have the effect of reducing my confidence in a perceptual judgment. Indeed, it will sometimes happen that reflective assessment overturns a judgment altogether. Because perceptual judgments are always subject to this sort of reflective evaluation, it is appropriate to join Kant and John McDowell in saying that they are within the realm of spontaneity – that is, of endogenous, rational control.[17] Unlike perceptual experiences, they are not simply given to us. They are not the products of pure receptivity.

We have now found eight features that are characteristic of purely experiential awareness. In the order in which we have considered them, they are consciousness, immediacy, transparency to introspection, complexity of what is revealed by awareness, determinacy of what is revealed, specificity of what is revealed, rigidity of response to attention, and receptivity. When they are properly understood, these characteristics can be seen to distinguish experiential awareness from forms of awareness that involve conceptualization and judgment.

It can be tempting to extend this list of eight characteristics by invoking a ninth. Specifically, it can be tempting to extend it by citing *presentational immediacy*. Objects of experiential awareness are not inferred or posited. They are *presented* to us. They are simply *there*. I acknowledge that this aspect of experiential awareness is of fundamental importance, but I have not included it in my list because I doubt that it is independent of immediacy, Moorean transparency, and receptivity. Yes, the objects of experiential awareness are presented to us. But when we say this, are we saying more than that experiential awareness is direct or immediate, that introspective examination of experiential awareness fails to reveal anything about it other than its objects, and that the objects of experiential awareness are given to us, in the sense that our awareness of them is not controlled or modulated by endogenous, voluntary factors (other than attention)? As far as I can tell, the answer to this question is "no." Even so, however, it is worth noting that presentational immediacy is a feature of experiential awareness, for this is a way of making the implications of immediacy, Moorean transparency and receptivity explicit.

---

[17] John McDowell, *Mind and World* (Cambridge, MA: Harvard University Press, 1994), Lectures I and II.

As noted at the beginning of this section, my goal in citing the foregoing eight features has been to make it plausible that it is possible to single out the form of awareness that provides us with our cognitive access
to qualia without mentioning that it has this particular role. That is, I
have wanted to make it plausible that it need not be part of the *definition*
of this form of awareness that it is the form that puts us in touch with
qualia. I have not tried to *prove* that experiential awareness has the eight
features we have been considering. It is perhaps reasonably clear that all
the determinate forms of experiential awareness that count as perceptual
modalities have the eight features, and I hope it is plausible that other
determinate forms, such as awareness of pain, have at least some of the
features. But I acknowledge that it cannot be fully plausible that all of
the determinate forms of experiential awareness have all of the features
until we have examined several of those forms individually. My hope at
present is just that enough has been said to make it seem reasonable for
me to take the idea that experiential awareness can be singled out without
invoking qualia as a tentative working hypothesis.

I have not cited principle (P) in explaining purely experiential awareness, nor have I presupposed that it has a representational structure at
any point. That it does in fact have such a structure is established by the
arguments given in preceding sections. But it is not part of our intuitive
conception of experiential awareness that it is representational in character, and I have tried to stay fairly close to that conception here. That is
to say, I have tried to base the present account on considerations that are
available from the perspectives of introspection and folk psychology. The
representational nature of awareness is not apparent from those perspectives. It can be glimpsed from them but it is not in full view. To appreciate it, we need to occupy the perspective of philosophy, as enlightened by
cognitive science.

If (P) is correct, then presumably there is a special category of representations that subserve experiential awareness. Call these *experiential
representations*. It would of course be highly desirable to have an account
of experiential representations – of their differentiae, and of how these
differentiae enable them to play a special role in the acquisition of knowledge. There is a range of claims concerning this topic in the literature.
It is sometimes maintained that experiential representations are iconic,
in the sense that they have internal structures that are isomorphic to the
items that they represent. They are also said to be analog, or at least to
have analog components. (The elements of an analog system of representation need have little or no semantically relevant structure of their own,

but the system as a whole will have a structure that is imposed by an ordering relation, and in virtue of having this structure, the system will be isomorphic to the domain that is represented.) A third view is that despite initial appearances to the contrary, experiential representations turn out to be a species of conceptual representations. I think that the last view is too poorly motivated to warrant consideration, but neither introspection nor folk psychology seems to speak with a clear voice about the first and second views. Are there *theoretical* considerations that speak with a clear voice about them? I believe that there are, and we will in fact encounter some of them in later chapters. I will not attempt, however, to construct a detailed account of experiential representation. A detailed elucidation must await progress in cognitive science.

3.7   SUMMARY

In this chapter I have argued for the view that awareness is essentially representational in character, in the sense that representations are constitutively involved in it. I have also identified and tried to explain a form of awareness that will play an important role in our future reflections. This form of awareness, purely experiential awareness, has a phenomenological dimension, but I have tried to show that it can be distinguished from other forms of awareness without mentioning that fact.

APPENDIX

Let us agree to say that an experience *has a phenomenological dimension*, or that it *has phenomenal character*, if it *seems* to the agent who is undergoing the experience that he is aware of one or more qualia. Given this convention, when a mental state involves experiential awareness of qualia, it is always true that the state has a phenomenological dimension. But is it always true that when a mental state has a phenomenological dimension, there is experiential awareness of qualia? No. Consider, for example, a case in which an agent is subject to an hallucination. Always, in a case of this sort, it seems to the agent that he is aware of qualia, but it is not true that there are qualia of which the agent is experientially aware. That is, the agent does not stand in an experiential cognitive relation to an object that actually exemplifies qualia. Rather, in a case of hallucination, the agent *represents qualia as instantiated*. There is representation of qualia in such cases, but no awareness of them. Or so I wish to maintain.

More particularly, I wish to maintain that in a case of illusion or hallucination, an agent has an experience that satisfies the following conditions:

(1) The experience has a phenomenological dimension: it *seems* to the agent that he is aware of one or more qualia.
(2) The experience represents qualia as instantiated.
(3) It seems to the agent that he is aware of qualia *because* the experience represents the qualia in question as instantiated.
(4) The qualia are perceptual qualia; they could be presented in a veridical perceptual experience.
(5) The experience does not provide the agent with *awareness* of qualia. There is no actual instance of qualia of which the agent is experientially aware.

I will not argue for these claims about illusion and hallucination here. They cohere fully with the picture of qualia and qualitative awareness that will be developed in later chapters. They suggest that picture and are suggested by it. Accordingly, insofar as later chapters succeed in making the picture plausible, the claims will share in that plausibility. They will be confirmed by the success of their partner.

(An aside: There is reason to think that there is an *intensional* sense of the verb "aware" – that is, a sense in which it can be true to say that an agent is aware of something of kind K, even though there is no actual instance of K to which the agent bears a cognitive relation. Assuming that there is such a sense, it can of course be correct to say that a victim of an hallucination is aware of qualia. The point of thesis (5) is that an agent of this sort cannot be said to be aware of qualia in an *extensional* sense of "aware" – a sense which meets the condition that an agent cannot be said to be aware of something of kind K unless there is an actual K to which the agent is related. As it is explained in Section 3.6, the expression "experientially aware" is meant to have an extensional meaning.)

As I understand them, then, cases of illusion and hallucination show that a mental state can have a phenomenological dimension without involving awareness of qualia. There is also a third type of case that belongs to this category, though it is somewhat different than the others and requires separate treatment. When an agent imagines an object or a situation, it seems to him that he is aware of qualia, so his experience has phenomenal character. In fact, however, there is good reason to doubt that he is aware of anything that actually exemplifies qualia. If, for example, an agent is imagining a red octopus, it seems to him that he is experiencing reddish qualia; but of course there is no actual octopus that is presenting a red appearance. Moreover, it seems wrong to say that he is aware of an internal, mental simulacrum of a red octopus. The only "object" that is before his mind is an *intensional* object – the imagined octopus. In general, the imagination is no less transparent to introspection than is perception.

If imagining does not involve awareness of qualia, how are we to explain the fact that it *seems* to involve such awareness? It will come as no surprise that I wish to propose the following rough and schematic answer: imagining seems to provide awareness of qualia because it *represents* qualia. Thus, for example, to imagine an octopus is to represent an octopus, and to imagine that the octopus is red is, in part, at least, to imagine it as presenting a red appearance. It is this last fact, the fact that one is representing the octopus as presenting a red appearance, that is responsible for the impression that one is experiencing reddish qualia.

What more can be said about the nature of qualia that are represented by the imagination? Part of the story is that imagined qualia are similar to the qualia that we encounter in perception. It is reasonably clear, for example, that when one imagines a red octopus, and thereby represents the octopus as presenting a red appearance, the appearance property one represents is qualitatively similar to the appearance property one experiences when one actually sees a red object. This *similarity thesis* receives strong support from introspection, and also from Kosslyn's pioneering empirical work on the imagination, which provides many reasons for thinking that the mechanisms and representational codes that support the imagination overlap significantly with the mechanisms and codes that support perception.[18] But the similarity thesis is far from being the whole truth about the matter. In addition to the similarities linking imagined qualia to perceptual qualia, there are also a number of differences. Thus, among other things, the color qualia that are associated with the imagination tend to be less vivid or robust than the corresponding perceptual qualia, the shape qualia tend to be less determinate (more schematic), and the qualia that are determined by textures tend to be less distinct. How are we to account for these significant differences?

---

[18] See, e.g., Stephen M. Kosslyn, William L. Thompson, and Giorgio Ganis, *The Case for Mental Imagery* (Oxford: Oxford University Press, 2006).

I will not address this question in the present work. It has a substantial empirical dimension, and as far as I can determine, there is no body of empirical research that supplies a definite answer. Thus, with respect to imagined qualia, I will here claim only (i) that they are properties that are represented by the experiences that occur when we imagine things, (ii) that representing does not in this case provide us with awareness, (iii) that the similarity thesis is true, and (iv) that there are considerations which prevent us from saying that imagined qualia are exactly the same as perceptual qualia.

CHAPTER 4

The refutation of dualism

4.1 INTRODUCTION

I will begin this chapter by formulating and assessing five views about awareness of qualia that are often in play, either explicitly or implicitly, in discussions of property dualism. Then, after discussing this family of views about awareness of qualia, I will consider several dualism-promoting intuitions about qualia themselves. My third and last topic will be the six arguments for property dualism that we encountered in Chapter 2.

Although I make no claim to completeness, it seems fair to say that the considerations I will be reviewing provide most of the motivation for property dualism. By the same token, it seems fair to say that property dualism should be set aside as a metaphysical extravagance if these considerations can be effectively criticized. As the title of the chapter indicates, it is my goal here to formulate objections that are decisive.

4.2 AWARENESS OF QUALIA

What is involved in being aware of a pain? What is involved in being aware of how an object looks to one? More generally, what is involved in being aware of a quale? There is no well worked out answer to these questions in the literature on qualia. When one explores that literature, however, one finds that there are five views about awareness of qualia that enjoy wide acceptance. Two of these views appear to be presupposed in most discussions of qualia, including discussions by reductionists. The other three views weigh heavily in favor of property dualism. Like the first two views, however, they have strong intuitive appeal. Thus, interestingly, even though reductionists are well advised to reject them, there is little systematic criticism of them in the literature. A fortiori, there is no received opinion as to exactly what might be wrong with them. Even in those quarters in which they do not command acceptance, they are found sufficiently beguiling that they neutralize opposition.

The first of the five views is the claim that we are aware of qualia in virtue of being directly acquainted with them. Our awareness of them is independent of inference, and does not presuppose any sort of general or theoretical knowledge. Qualia are *presented* to us.[1]

The second view is that our awareness of qualia is not intellectual or intuitive. It is experiential. We are aware of qualia by experiencing them.

I suggest that we all find these two views to be quite plausible. There are of course questions about how they should be interpreted, but it is natural, I think, to feel confident that they admit of interpretations on which they count as both substantial and true.

A third widely held view about awareness of qualia is the claim that this form of awareness is not governed by an appearance/reality distinction. There is no difference between how qualia are in themselves and how they are revealed to us by experience.

This view about awareness of qualia is an essential component of dualistic theories, as we will see at some length later on, but the grounds for accepting it are not theoretical. It has an immense intuitive appeal – an appeal that is felt by opponents of property dualism as well as its adherents. Consider the case of awareness of pain. We do not allow that our experience of pain is perspectival – that pains may have sides or facets that our experience of them does not reveal, or that pains may be too distant from us for experience to take their true measure. Nor do we allow that our access to pain may be impaired by counterparts of myopia or color blindness. Nor do we allow that there may be cases in which an experience of pain is illusory or hallucinatory – when an agent has an experience of pain, then, necessarily, he really is in pain. Nor do we allow that there may be cases in which an individual is in pain but has no experience of pain. Thus, for example, even if a soldier is badly injured, we will deny that he is in pain unless we have reason to believe that he is aware of a pain. In brief, we hold that experiences of pain are always veridical, and that pain is always experienced. Much the same is true of other forms of qualitative awareness. Thus, to choose an example involving a perceptual quale, we feel that there is no distinction to be drawn between experiencing an appearance of blue and seeming to experience

---

[1] Here and elsewhere in this chapter, I use "acquaintance" in its ordinary sense, according to which it stands simply for direct awareness. I do not mean to presuppose any of the metaphysical doctrines about the nature of acquaintance that we considered in the preceding chapter.

such an appearance. In other words, if it seems to one that he is enjoying an experience *as of* blue, he really is enjoying such an experience; and if one really is enjoying an experience as of blue, that is how things seem to him. There is no such thing as an appearance of an appearance. Equally, to switch examples again, there is no difference between experiencing the feelings that are characteristic of being afraid and seeming to experience them.

I pause here to guard against a possible misunderstanding. What I mean to be arguing is that, from the perspective of folk psychology, at least, it is impossible to draw an appearance/reality distinction with respect to our *experiential* access to qualia. In urging this view, I do not mean to deny that it is possible to have false *beliefs* about qualia, or even that it is possible for our experience of qualia to encourage such beliefs. It is natural to distinguish between two types of awareness of qualia: experiential awareness, and awareness that involves conceptualization and belief. It is only the former sort of awareness that resists an appearance/reality distinction. There is no problem with drawing such a distinction with respect to the latter sort of awareness.

The fourth of our five views is that the distinctive natures of qualia, the features that distinguish them from each other and also from characteristics of other kinds, can *only* be grasped by experiential awareness. One can of course gain knowledge of contingent features of qualia in other ways. Thus, for example, their causal powers can be grasped independently of experiential acquaintance. But one must be experientially acquainted with a quale in order to appreciate its intrinsic nature.

Like the preceding views, this one has enormous intuitive appeal. Can a person who is color blind grasp what it is for an object to look red? Of course not. Can those rare individuals who are constitutionally incapable of feeling pain grasp the nature of pain? Of course not. Can a human being grasp the qualia that accompany the use of sonar in bats? Of course not. Qualia must be experienced in order to be known.

Although standard expositions of this fourth view do not do so, it is probably best to formulate it in such a way as to allow for the possibility of acquiring an adequate conception of a quale by imagining it. Thus, for example, as Hume pointed out, it seems possible to grasp the distinctive nature of a shade of blue even if one has never experienced that shade. How do we come to appreciate qualia in such cases? The answer, I think, is that we come to appreciate them by imagining them. This answer is consistent with the spirit of the fourth view, for it is natural to think of imagining as a form of experience.

The fifth view is that the essential natures of qualia are *fully* revealed to us via experiential acquaintance. This view is not always made explicit in discussions of qualia, but as we will see in the next section, it is presupposed by many so-called modal arguments for property dualism.

The fifth view has a certain intuitive resonance, but what exactly is the source of its appeal? The answer, I think, is that it is perceived to follow from the first, second, and third of the foregoing views. The first two views claim that it is experiential awareness that gives us access to qualia, and the third view maintains that that experiential awareness does not admit of an appearance/reality distinction. Together, the views imply that we have direct access to the way qualia are in themselves. But this is not all: they seem to imply, in addition, that we have *full* access to how they are in themselves. If there was some part or aspect of how qualia are that is not revealed by experience, then that part or aspect would have failed to appear to us, and it would therefore be possible to draw an appearance/reality distinction with respect to experiential acquaintance. But this means that we have full access to the essential natures of qualia, for the essential properties of a quale are included in how it is in itself.

We have been reviewing a family of five views about awareness of qualia that figures either explicitly or implicitly in large stretches of the literature. As I have been emphasizing, all of the members of the family have a powerful intuitive appeal. This is so even though three of them play a crucial role in arguments for property dualism. This is why reductionists have generally felt the arguments for property dualism to be troubling, and why they have found it difficult to produce decisive refutations of the arguments.

4.3   METAPHYSICAL IMPLICATIONS
OF THE FIVE VIEWS

I will take up the task of evaluating the five views in the next section, but before I turn to that responsibility, it will be useful to consider their implications for questions about the metaphysical nature of qualia. Neither of the first two views has such implications, but as we will now see, the third, fourth, and fifth views play important roles in producing and sustaining the perception that qualia are special properties that cannot easily be located in the physical world.

The third doctrine contributes to this perception in two ways.

First, as we saw in Chapter 2, there is a quick argument that leads directly from the third view to the conclusion that property dualism is correct (the appearance/reality argument). The main premises of this argument are the third view and the following very plausible principle about physical properties: Where *P* is any physical property, it is possible to distinguish between the appearance of *P* and the reality of *P*. It follows easily from these two premises that qualitative characteristics are not identical with physical characteristics.

Second, in the absence of an appearance/reality distinction, it is necessary to take all experientially grounded intuitions about qualia at face value, including those that pose a threat to physicalism. If an appearance/reality distinction was available, we might be able to explain dualism-promoting intuitions away, maintaining that they derive from appearances, and invoking the well known fact that appearances are often misleading. But this course is not open to us if qualia do not admit of an appearance/reality distinction.

An illustration: Consider the appearance that yellow objects characteristically present to us when they are viewed under standard conditions. This appearance is a qualitative characteristic. Call it *Y*. As many writers have observed, *Y* seems to us to be perfectly simple. Now according to the third doctrine, there is no difference between the way *Y* seems to us and the way it is in itself. So *Y* really is simple. But all of the physical properties that are associated with *Y* are extremely complex. This is true of the external properties that are associated with *Y*, such as properties of the surfaces that reflect yellow light, and also of the internal properties, such as the properties of the relevant information processing agencies. It follows that *Y* is not identical with any physical properties.

It is clear, then, that the third of our five views about awareness of qualia contributes to the plausibility of property dualism. What about the fourth view – the view that experiential awareness provides our *only* access to the essential natures of qualia? Does it contribute to the plausibility of dualism, too? Yes. Among other things, it plays a substantial and indeed essential role in the knowledge argument for property dualism. As we saw in Chapter 2, this argument appeals to a scientist, Mary, who knows everything there is to know about the physics and neuroscience of color, but who has never seen any colored objects, and who therefore has never been experientially acquainted with color qualia. Thus, Mary is someone who knows everything there is to know about the physical properties that are relevant to colors, but who has no real understanding of color qualia. This shows that color qualia are not reducible to physical properties. Or so it is claimed. Now it is clear that the argument presupposes that it is impossible to know the distinctive natures of color qualia unless one has been experientially acquainted with them. And this is precisely the claim that is made by the fourth view. Without the fourth view, the knowledge argument would collapse.

The fifth view claims that experiential acquaintance affords us access to all of the essential properties of qualia. This view also has a substantial metaphysical import, as can be seen by reflecting on Descartes's defense of his modal argument against an objection of Arnauld's. As we saw in Chapter 2, Arnauld objected that Descartes's idea of the mind might easily fail to capture its essential nature, the implication being that the mind might have an essential physical dimension that Descartes's idea of it failed to register. Responding to this concern, Descartes claimed that his idea of the mind was complete – that it did full justice to its essential properties. Reflection shows that a claim of this sort must either be a premise or a presupposition of any argument which purports to show that a category of mental items is metaphysically independent of the corresponding category of physical items. Now the fifth view is a claim of the sort in question. To be sure, it differs from Descartes's claim in that it is concerned with experiential access to mental items rather than ideas of them. Given, however, that our experiential access to qualia is the source of our ideas about them, it is precisely the fifth view that is needed as a premise or a presupposition for modal arguments about qualia.

4.4   EVALUATION OF THE FIRST TWO VIEWS

As I have stressed, all of the foregoing views about awareness of qualia are plausible. Indeed, they can seem incontrovertible. I wish to claim, however, that the first two of them are the only ones that can be accepted. The others must be rejected because they are incompatible with representational theories of awareness.

The first view claims that awareness of qualia is immediate (or in other words, that it is independent of inference and theoretical knowledge), and the second asserts that awareness of qualia is experiential. Reflection shows that there is nothing inherently problematic about either of these views, and also that they are compatible with the doctrine that awareness is representational. Further, it seems that we must presuppose these views in order for our talk about qualia to be recognizable as such. It would be absurd to maintain that awareness of pain involves a deductive or inductive inference *from* experience. Equally, it would be absurd to maintain that awareness of pains requires theoretical knowledge of some sort. Pains are just given to us. It is experience itself that puts us in touch with them.

4.5   EVALUATION OF THE THIRD VIEW

I turn now to the third of the foregoing views about awareness of qualia, the view that this form of awareness does not admit of an appearance/reality distinction. Unlike the first two views, this one is false.

Reflection shows that there are four rather different ways of drawing a distinction between appearance and reality.

First, there is the distinction between a system of justified or warranted beliefs that is concerned with an item and the facts involving that item that confer truth or falsity on the beliefs. Suppose, for example, that you are in a political discussion with someone, and he gives expression to some beliefs that strike you as quite wrong. Here you may say, "Well, that may be how the situation appears to you, but I can assure you that it presents a quite different appearance to me." When we say such things, we are viewing systems of beliefs as appearances.

I will refer to this first appearance/reality distinction as the *doxastic* distinction. I hasten to add, however, that doxastic appearances seem to involve evidence as well as beliefs. Thus, when we allude to doxastic appearances we seem to presuppose that the relevant beliefs are supported by evidence of some sort. I may *believe* that a comet will hit the Earth next week without having any evidence that this will happen, but it seems that it cannot *appear to me* that a comet will hit the Earth unless I have grounds for so believing.

Second, there is the distinction between the mode of presentation of an item and the item itself. The expression "mode of presentation" has been used in a number of rather different ways, but what I have in mind is a use according to which a property counts as a mode of presentation of an item if it is the property that we normally rely on in identifying the item, and in keeping track of it across contexts. Thus, for example, the property of being a person who looks like *this* (imagine here that I am pointing to Bill Clinton) is a mode of presentation of Bill Clinton, and the property of being a liquid that is transparent, colorless, odorless, and nourishing is a mode of presentation of water. It does not seem to be the case that *every* mode of presentation counts as an appearance. Rather, it seems that we apply the term "appearance" only to those modes of presentation that we rely on in identifying objects experientially, and in keeping track of them by methods that are experientially grounded. Within this limited range, however, the practice of speaking of modes of presentation as appearances seems quite robust. It is, of course, entirely natural to speak of the way Clinton looks as an appearance of Clinton, and to speak of the property of being a liquid that is transparent, colorless, odorless, and nourishing as an appearance that water presents to human observers.

Since Frege was responsible for bringing the expression "mode of presentation" into prominence, it is appropriate to refer to the second appearance/reality distinction as the *Fregean* distinction.[2]

Third, there is a distinction between the way an object looks, sounds, feels, tastes, or smells to an observer on a particular occasion, and the way the object is in itself. That is to say, there is a distinction between perceptual appearances and the corresponding realities. This is perhaps the appearance/reality distinction that figures most prominently in our everyday discourse. I will refer to it as the *perceptual* distinction.

Fourth, we are in effect drawing an appearance/reality distinction when we distinguish between the way an item is represented by the mind and the way the item is in itself. This *representational* appearance/reality distinction is closely related to the doxastic distinction, for systems of beliefs count as representations of the items with which they are concerned. But beliefs are not the only species of mental representations. Indeed, as we know from Chapter 3, representations figure constitutively in all forms of cognitive access. Accordingly, the representational appearance/reality distinction is much more inclusive than the doxastic distinction, though the doxastic distinction is an aspect or dimension of it. The representational distinction extends to all forms of awareness.

We can now appreciate that it is possible, after all, to draw an appearance/reality distinction with respect to experiential acquaintance with qualia. Experiential acquaintance is a form of awareness, and it therefore has a representational structure. This structure is not revealed by introspection, nor is it recognized by folk psychology, but nevertheless it is there. It follows immediately that the representational appearance/reality distinction extends to experiential acquaintance. That is to say, *for every quale Q, there is a distinction between the way Q appears to us and the way Q is in itself.* The third view about awareness of qualia is false.

This conclusion has several consequences that we should pause to appreciate. I begin by noting three general principles governing representational appearances. First of all, as is generally true of appearances, the relationship between the representational appearance of an item and the corresponding reality is contingent. Where P is any property, and R is

[2] See Gottlob Frege, "On Sense and Nominatum," translated by Herbert Fiegl in Herbert Fiegl and Wilfrid Sellars (eds.), *Readings in Philosophical Analysis* (New York, NY: Appleton-Century-Crofts, 1949), pp. 85–102.

the corresponding mental representation of P, (i) it is possible for R to be tokened even though there is no corresponding instance of P, and (ii) it is possible for P to be instantiated even though there is no accompanying token of R. Second, it holds as a general rule that the appearance of an item may be a very poor guide to the truth about the essential properties of that item. Representational appearances conform to this general principle, as do doxastic, Fregean, and perceptual appearances. A representation R may stand for P without explicitly encoding any information about P's essential properties. Moreover, any information about P's essential properties that R does encode is likely to be incomplete. Third, like doxastic, Fregean, and perceptual appearances, representational appearances may be systematically misleading. R may misrepresent P. Moreover, even if R represents P accurately, it may be positioned within the cognitive system as a whole in such a way as to foster false beliefs about P. This might happen, for example, if R is a representational atom – that is, if R is neither factorizable into more basic representations nor treated by the relevant cognitive agencies as equivalent to another representation that can be decomposed in this way. Suppose that R is a representation that is characterized by this sort of internal and systematic atomicity. Suppose also that R is the representation that a perceptual system, say vision, uses to keep track of P. Given these assumptions, we can see that an agent's perceptual experience of P might encourage the belief that P is itself atomic – that it is a simple, unanalyzable property. This could happen even if P is in fact quite complex.

Given that it is possible to draw a representational appearance/reality distinction with respect to experiential acquaintance with qualia, it follows from the first of these general principles that it can seem to an agent that he is experientially acquainted with a quale when in fact he is not. That is to say, it is in principle possible for there to be illusions and hallucinations concerning qualia. It also follows that there can be instances of qualia that are not objects of experiential acquaintance. It is in principle possible, for example, for an agent to be in pain without being aware of that fact. Further, it follows from the second principle that acquaintance with qualia may fail altogether to provide information concerning their essential properties, and also that, if it does provide such information, the information may be incomplete. Finally, it follows from the third principle that acquaintance with qualia may systematically mislead us concerning the properties of qualia. The representation that figures in a fact of acquaintance may misrepresent its object, or it may foster a false belief about the object as a result of facts involving its role in the cognitive economy of the relevant agent.

I conclude this discussion of the third view about qualitative awareness by noting that misrepresentation is actually quite common in perception, which suggests that it may be quite common in experiential awareness generally. There are many familiar perceptual illusions. A number of these occur only in highly restricted contexts, but others pervade a whole domain of perceptual experience. For example, Dennis Proffitt and his colleagues have found that we tend to perceive hills as having steeper slants than they actually possess, and that this effect is magnified when we are tired.[3] They have also determined that hills tend to look steeper when they are seen from the top than when they are seen from the bottom. We should not view these tendencies as visual deficiencies. On the contrary, as Proffitt points out, it seems likely that we evolved with them because they are beneficial: the first one gives us a preference for avoiding hills, which prevents unnecessary expenditures of energy, and the second one gives us a preference for choosing slopes with lesser slants when we are descending hills, which reduces the risk of accident. These observations remind us that perceptual systems are not necessarily in the business of avoiding error. Systematic error can be to our advantage. Accordingly, we should not think that perceptual error is exceptional, or that its significance is marginal.

4.6   EVALUATION OF THE FOURTH AND FIFTH VIEWS

The fourth doctrine about awareness of qualia claims that the distinctive nature of qualia can only be grasped via experiential acquaintance, and the fifth asserts that experiential acquaintance provides us with full access to the essential natures of qualia. Despite the intuitive appeal of these doctrines, we can now see that there is no obligation to accept either of them.

The motivation for the fourth view is undercut by the considerations which establish that there is an appearance/reality distinction for qualia. Consider, for example, the quale Y that is associated with perceptual experience of the color yellow. We are experientially acquainted with Y. According to the fourth view, this is our only access to the essential nature of Y. This was initially plausible, but now we know that there may be a significant difference between the way in which Y appears to us and the way it is in itself. Among other things, this creates logical room for the thesis that Y may be a complex physical property. The fact that Y seems to

[3] See, e.g., Dennis R. Proffitt, "Embodied Perception and the Economy of Action," *Perspectives on Psychological Science* 1 (2006), 110–122.

us to be simple does not preclude this thesis. Suppose now that the thesis is correct. Under this assumption, it is possible to answer questions about the essential nature of *Y* without being acquainted with it. As is the case with any physical property, we can explore its essential nature by using the methods of natural science – experiment, statistical analysis, and the construction of explanatory theories. We are not required to rely exclusively on acquaintance. Indeed, there will be no great loss if we forego the information about *Y* that is provided by acquaintance. That information is not privileged – it is simply information involving an appearance of *Y*, an appearance that it has in virtue of being represented in a certain way.

In sum, we now have an option of embracing a hypothesis about our epistemic access to *Y* that is flatly incompatible with the fourth view. Moreover, this alternative hypothesis is actually more appealing than the fourth doctrine. As we saw in Section 4.3, the fourth view can be used to support property dualism, which is in many ways an unappealing position. The ontological commitments of the alternative hypothesis are more conservative and therefore preferable.

We also have grounds for rejecting the fifth view. At the end of the last section we observed that representations can fail to do justice to, and can even fail altogether to register, the essential natures of the items they represent. Thus, a perceptual representation of water provides no information about the molecular structure of water, a line drawing of a house contains no information about the materials from which the house was constructed, and a photograph of a mouse contains no information about the mouse's DNA. There is logical room, therefore, for the idea that experiential representations fail to encode information about the essential nature of qualia. In particular, even though experiential representations fail to reveal that qualia are essentially physical, it is permissible for us to hold this. But of course, if we have the option of holding it, then we should hold it; for it is obviously superior to dualistic alternatives in a variety of respects, including simplicity and explanatory coherence.

4.7   THREE DUALISM-PROMOTING INTUITIONS
ABOUT QUALIA

We have been considering a family of views about awareness of qualia that play an important role in arguments for property dualism. I would like to turn now to examine three intuitions concerning qualia themselves, as opposed to awareness of qualia, that contribute to the plausibility of property dualism. One of these is the intuition that experience reveals each quale to have a distinctive individual nature that precludes any sort of reduction to other properties. When we try to think of any individual quale as being identical with another property, we have a sense that we are confronting the absurd or impossible, much as we do when we try to think of a round square or an integer between one and two. An individual quale is just too different from other properties for a reduction even to be entertainable. The second intuition affirms that qualia share a property that cannot be described in non-metaphorical language, but that is experienced whenever a quale is encountered. Qualia seem to have a kind of phosphorescence or iridescence that all other properties lack. They burst upon us like rockets exploding in the night sky. They are *alive*. By comparison, all other properties are dead. The third intuition counsels that qualia are intrinsic properties. To recognize an instance of a quale as such, it suffices to focus one's attention on the instance itself. One need not take account of its relations to other things. This third intuition weighs against reduction because the physical properties with which qualia might most naturally be identified are often highly relational. Thus, for example, pains share many properties, such as locations, with bodily disturbances that involve or portend bodily damage. But damage is a complex property that involves relations between events at the site of the damage and the future welfare of the organism. Again, the visual qualia that are presented by gray objects do not depend only on the surfaces of the objects themselves, but on their surrounds as well.

It seems likely that everyone has these three intuitions. This is one of the reasons why dualism has such a powerful appeal, even for those who are convinced that it must somehow be wrong.

4.8 ASSESSMENT OF THE INTUITIONS

I will begin by arguing that if we embrace a representational account of experiential awareness, it is possible to explain the first intuition away. To fix ideas, I will focus on the quality we are aware of when something looks yellow to us. We feel that there is an unbridgeable gulf between this quality and all of the physical and functional properties that are involved in color vision. Indeed, the idea that it might turn out to be identical with any of these properties strikes us as absurd. While acknowledging the force of this intuition, I will maintain that there is no obligation to take it at face value. Representational theories of awareness *predict* the intuition. We need not take it at face value because theories that are compatible with physicalism predict that it will occur.

When things look yellow to us, we are deploying a representation that is different than all of the representations that we deploy when things look other ways to us, different than all of the representations that are involved in non-visual experiential awareness, and different than all of the conceptually structured representations that science makes available. Let us say that this representation represents the characteristic Y. Now of course, the mere fact that we use a special representation to keep track of Y could not by itself give rise to an abiding impression that when we are aware of Y we are aware of a characteristic that is distinct from all other characteristics. This merely creates the possibility of such an impression. The impression itself arises from our sense that it would be inappropriate to *identify* Y with another characteristic.

We are all familiar with the fact that there can be multiple representations of a single characteristic, and we all avail ourselves, from time to time, of the option of identifying a characteristic that we initially grasp via one representation with a characteristic that we initially grasp via a different representation. But when we identify one characteristic with another, we are obliged to appeal to the fact that the characteristics are represented by distinct representations in explaining and justifying the identification. Only in this way is it possible to account for the fact that it is necessary to go beyond what experience itself reveals about the characteristics in order to appreciate the real nature of their relationship.

Now we must ask: Is it appropriate to invoke the difference between a property-qua-represented and a property-as-it-is-itself in determining whether Y is identical with some other property? From the perspective of common sense, the answer is "no." We are aware of Y in virtue of participating in facts of the form x *looks yellow to z*; and when we view such facts from the perspective of common sense, we find no reason to suppose that they constitutively involve representations. That is to say, folk psychology affords no glimpse of the representations that are constitutively involved in our experience of Y. We can only appreciate the existence of those representations from a highly theoretical perspective. (As we have noticed on several occasions, representationalism receives little support from introspection and folk psychology. It is a *highly* theoretical position.) Accordingly, we do not see how it could be true that Y might have a nature that is not revealed by experiential awareness. If there is no apparent distinction between Y-as-represented-by-experience and Y-as-it-is-in-itself, it cannot possibly be appropriate to go beyond what experience reveals about Y in assessing Y's relationship to other characteristics.

It may be useful to recast this line of thought in a somewhat different form. Suppose that *P1* is a characteristic that is revealed by perception, and suppose also that for some reason it is deemed desirable to identify *P1* with a prima facie different characteristic *P2*. In order to explain and justify the identification, which involves going beyond the impression of *P1* that perception itself provides, it is necessary to explain how it is possible to grasp *P1* perceptually without appreciating its identity with *P2*. It is normally possible to provide such an explanation by invoking some sort of appearance/reality distinction. Thus, we might distinguish between *P1* itself and a property that serves as the mode of presentation for *P1*. Or, if there is no other property that serves as the mode of presentation for *P1*, as will be the case if our awareness of *P1* is direct, then we might distinguish between *P1*-as-it-is-in-itself and *P1*-as-it-is-represented by a perceptual representation. But, to repeat, we must invoke some such contrast in order to explain why the identity of *P1* with *P2* is not revealed by experience itself.

Now let us turn to consider the special case of the characteristic *Y*. Is it possible to identify *Y* with some other characteristic, say *Y**? If we are to do so, there must be a way of explaining how it is possible to grasp *Y* experientially without appreciating its identity with *Y**. This means that we must invoke an appearance/reality distinction of some sort. But since *Y* is a quale, folk psychology does not recognize a distinction between appearance and reality in this case. It fails to register the representational character of our awareness of *Y*, and by the same token, it fails to support any ambitions that we might have to identify *Y* with another characteristic.

This completes my account of how representationalism explains our impression that *Y* is distinct from all other characteristics. Of course, in addition to explaining that impression, representationalism offers a perspective from which it is appropriate to reject the impression as illusory. Unlike folk psychology, it gives us the option of identifying *Y* with a physical characteristic.

In addition to receiving support from the intuition that there is an unbridgeable gulf separating individual qualia from all other properties, dualism also receives support from the intuition that all qualia differ from other properties in that they have a special phosphorescence or *vivacity*. Vivacity can only be explained, I think, in terms of metaphors. Consider the contrast between a glowing red coal and the pile of ash that surrounds it, the contrast between the lights shining below you as you fly over a town at night and the inky blackness that contains them, and the contrast between a single blare of a trumpet and the silence that it interrupts. We all feel that there is a contrast between qualitative characteristics and their non-qualitative colleagues that is in some sense similar to these contrasts. It is the former contrast that I mean to invoke in speaking of vivacity. That is to say, a vivacious property is one that contrasts with *all* other properties in the way that redness contrasts with grayness, in the way that illumination contrasts with blackness, and in the way that blaring contrasts with silence. Qualia are vivacious because they are vivid, luminous, and iridescent. By contrast, all other properties are flat, dull, and lifeless.

Although the temptation to suppose that vivacity is characteristic of qualia can seem irresistible, I would like to suggest that qualia seem vivacious to us only because of the *way* in which we are aware of them. Suppose, as is plausible, that it is possible to see all of the modes of awareness that put us in touch with qualia as modes of a single form of awareness that is experiential in character. Suppose, in other words, that the following principle is correct:

(Q) For any characteristic P, P is qualitative just in case P is available to us via experiential awareness.

Now consider the following two hypotheses:

(H1) Qualia share a special intrinsic feature, vivacity, that distinguishes them from all other properties.

(H2) Qualia do not have a special intrinsic feature that distinguishes them from all other properties, but only seem to do so because of the special character of experiential awareness.

Given (Q), it is not possible to make a case for the superiority of (H1) over (H2) by citing a characteristic that seems to us to be vivacious but that is not an object of experiential awareness. Nor is it possible to make a case for the superiority of (H1) by citing a characteristic that is an object of experiential awareness but does not seem to be vivacious. The characteristics that seem to us to be vivacious are exactly the ones that seem to be qualitative, and (Q) tells us that qualitative characteristics are exactly the ones that are objects of experiential awareness. Hence, given (Q), we are in principle free to reject (H1) and to embrace (H2) in its stead. In other words, we are free to reject the idea that vivacity is revealed to us by experiential awareness, and to say instead that it is constituted by this form of awareness.

So far, however, the latter option is just an abstract possibility. Nothing has been said about how we might exploit the special character of experiential awareness in giving a concrete explanation of vivacity. But it is not hard to proceed to a more concrete level. Thus, it seems quite reasonable to say that qualia seem vivacious because they are *given* to us. They are immediately before the mind, impressing themselves upon us in a way that no mere object of thought nor belief ever could. They are just *there*. They seem to us to contrast with all of the properties that we grasp in other ways because of this thereness. That is to say, qualia seem to us to be vivacious because we are aware of them all in the same way, and that mode of awareness is characterized by *presentational immediacy*.

To complete this deflationary explanation of vivacity, I need a theory of experiential awareness which shows that it is possible to appeal to experiential awareness without incurring any dualistic commitments, and which provides a metaphysically thin account of presentational immediacy. But just such a theory is provided by Chapter 3. As the reader may recall, that chapter explains experiential awareness as a form of cognitive access that satisfies the following eight conditions: it is conscious; it is direct or immediate; it has Moorean transparency (that is, introspection does not reveal a representational structure); it can put us in touch with objects, properties, and events that are too complex to be easily characterized in conceptual terms; it can put us in touch with properties that are highly determinate; it is highly particularized, in the sense that it always connects us with facts involving specific individuals (rather than facts that could be expressed using quantifiers or purely attributive descriptions); it is governed by a form of attention that can enhance resolution and figure/ground contrast; and it is a form of receptivity, in the sense that (apart from the influence of attention), it is not subject to endogenous, voluntary control. It is not immediately obvious, perhaps, that awareness of qualia has all of these features, though I think that this claim will be sustained by our future deliberations. (The case for the claim includes elements of the discussion of awareness of visual qualia in Chapter 5 and also elements of the discussion of awareness of pain in Chapter 6.) All that I need to assert at present is that awareness of qualia is characterized by directness, Moorean transparency, and receptivity; for as we noticed in Chapter 3, it is plausible that presentational immediacy can be explained in terms of these three characteristics.

Suppose you are currently experiencing a pain. It is evident, I think, that your awareness of the pain is direct in the sense that it does not depend on inference *from* experience or theoretical knowledge. Further, when you introspectively consider this experience, you do not encounter anything that would count as a mental representation of pain.

Introspection discloses just one particular in this case – the pain itself. Nor does introspection disclose an internal organization of any other kind. All that it reveals about your experience is that it is experience of a pain. Accordingly, your experience of pain is characterized by Moorean transparency. Finally, it is clear that awareness of qualia is in the domain of receptivity rather than that of spontaneity. It is up to you to decide whether you will attend to a pain, but once you have decided to bestow your attention upon it, what you will experience is not cancelable by rational assessment, and is not subject to voluntary control. Whether you will attend is up to you. What attention reveals is *given*.

As noted, it is plausible that when one is aware of an item via a mode of access that has these three characteristics, it will seem that the item is simply presented to you. It will seem to you that the item is simply *there*.

If you find my explanation of vivacity in terms of presentational immediacy inadequate, my guess is that you do so because you are thinking that perceptual awareness of various physical properties possesses all of the characteristics that I have used to define presentational immediacy. To amplify, my guess is that you are moved to at least some degree by the following line of thought: "When we are perceptually aware of such objective physical properties as objective shape, objective size, and objective velocity, our awareness is characterized by directness, Moorean transparency, and receptivity. Hence, on the foregoing account of presentational immediacy, perceptual awareness of certain physical properties is presentationally immediate. But it is clearly not true that the properties in question are qualitative, and it is also clearly not true that they seem to us to be vivacious. So it cannot be true that the vivacity of qualia can be explained in terms of presentational immediacy. At least, this cannot be true if the foregoing account of presentational immediacy is correct."

If this conjecture about your mental state is correct, then it is reasonable for me to hope that you will eventually be persuaded to accept my account of presentational immediacy, and with it my account of vivacity. Thus, in Chapter 5 I will maintain that our perceptual awareness of objective physical properties is not *unqualifiedly* direct, but only *comparatively* direct, being mediated by perceptual awareness of certain relational, viewpoint-dependent properties that I call *appearances*. Since I will also argue that perceptual qualia are to be identified with appearances, it will follow from my theory of perception that qualia are the *only* perceptible characteristics whose apprehension is characterized by Moorean transparency, receptivity, and *unqualified* directness. By the same token, it will follow that my account of vivacity in terms of these three characteristics does *not* predict that certain objective physical properties will seem to us to be vivacious. Accordingly, if I have characterized your concerns correctly, they should be dispelled by developments in later chapters.

This brings us to the third of the three dualism-promoting intuitions that we noted in the previous section. According to this intuition, qualia are intrinsic properties of the items that possess them. They do not involve relations between the instantiating items and other things, for it is possible to be aware that an item has a quale without taking its relations to other things into account. Thus, for example, one need not attend to the behavioral consequences of a sensation in order to determine that it is a pain, nor need one take note of the beliefs and desires that the sensation occasions. This intuition is dualism-promoting because, in many cases, science has revealed that the physical properties with which qualia are most intimately associated are highly relational in character.

Fortunately, representational theories of experiential awareness have the resources to explain impressions of intrinsicness away. It is always possible to explain why a property seems to us to be intrinsic by saying (i) that the relevant system of representation does not explicitly encode the information that the property is relational, and (ii) that it is the system that we rely on most heavily and most fundamentally for information about the property. Of course, the fact that it is possible to explain an impression of intrinsicness in this way has no tendency to show that the property is *not* intrinsic. The point is just that the explanation allows us to dismiss intuitions about the intrinsicness of qualia as mistaken if we have independent reasons for identifying them with relational properties.

4.9   WHY THE ARGUMENTS FOR PROPERTY DUALISM FAIL

We have already seen that representational theories of experiential awareness provide a foundation for objections to several of the arguments for property dualism that we considered in Chapter 2. In this section I will expand those earlier remarks into a systematic critique of the arguments.

1. The second premise of the Cartesian modal argument is the following claim:

Second premise: When we conceive of pain, we conceive of it completely, in the sense that in conceiving of it we do justice to all of its essential properties.

This premise is crucial to the argument. Without it, the argument would be vulnerable to an Arnauldian objection to the effect that in conceiving of pain, we might be conceiving of something that has a "hidden" physical nature, something that does in fact involve cortical activity of some sort. As Arnauld's original objection to Descartes makes quite clear, this objection has considerable force, for we know from examples (such as Arnauld's example of someone who conceives of a right-triangle without conceiving of it as having the Pythagorean property) that it is possible to conceive of items in ways that fail to do full justice to their essential natures. It is crucial that the objection be blocked.

The question now arises: How can we be sure that the second premise is true? What gives us the right to believe that in conceiving of pain we thereby have in view its full essential nature? When we consider these questions in relation to the discussions in Sections 4.2–4.6, we can see that it is impossible for advocates of the Cartesian argument to answer them in a satisfactory way. Thus, the concept of pain that is in play in discussions of property dualism is clearly an experiential concept, in the sense that its content derives from the fact that we use it to keep track of a property that is revealed to us by experience. Given that this concept of pain must fully capture the essential nature of pain if the Cartesian argument is to succeed, it follows that the essential nature of pain must be fully accessible to us when we experience pain. But it is precisely this thesis about the essential nature of pain that is called into question by the observation that experiential awareness of pain is representational. There is no guarantee that experiential representations of pain will do full justice to its essential properties. But this means that we have no good reason to think that in conceiving of situations involving pain we are always conceiving of genuine possibilities. In particular, for all we know, it may be that when it seems to us that we are coherently conceiving of a situation in which pain exists but is not accompanied by cortical activity of type φ, we are actually conceiving of a situation that is objectively impossible – that is, a situation in which there is φ-activity that is not accompanied by φ-activity. It follows that the Cartesian argument gives us no reason to accept property dualism.

We will find reason to strengthen this objection as we proceed. Thus far I have claimed only that we are not epistemically entitled to accept the second premise, but in Chapter 6 we will find reason to think that the premise should be rejected. Among other things, Chapter 6 sketches a theory of the form and content of the representations that are involved in experiential awareness of pain. That theory implies that there is much about the nature of pain that these representations fail to capture. I will also propose theories that have similar implications concerning the representations that subserve experiential awareness of perceptual qualia and the representations that subserve experiential awareness of emotional qualia.

2. I turn now to the knowledge argument. The main component of this argument is the intuition that the superscientist Mary learns something new when she encounters a red object for the first time. More specifically, it is the intuition that when Mary sees the red object, she becomes acquainted for the first time with how red things look, or in other words, with the appearance they present to normal observers like herself. This appearance will strike Mary as being quite different than all of the properties that she has encountered in her work as a vision scientist. The intuition affirms that this impression of Mary's is correct. The appearance *is* quite different than the properties she has encountered in the past.

Now it must be granted that it will *seem* to Mary that she is aware of something new in being aware of the appearance. We are not obliged to accept her impression at face value, however, for we can explain it by appealing to the fact that the representation that supports Mary's awareness of the appearance is one that her visual system has never before deployed. Because she is using a novel representation, the appearance would seem different to Mary even if it was a familiar physical property – say, the property of reflecting light that causes long wavelength receptors to fire more vigorously than middle wavelength receptors. Even though this property is an old friend, she has never before apprehended it via a system of experiential representation that is sensitive to wavelength combinations, and that positions represented items in a similarity space based on arithmetical relationships among wavelengths. In view of the differences between this system and the systems she has used in her scientific work (that is, the conceptual system involved in theory construction and the achromatic perceptual systems that she relies on in her black and white laboratory), it is no surprise that she has an impression of novelty when she first sees red.

It turns out, then, that representational theories of experiential awareness present us with alternatives to the idea that Mary's impression of novelty must be substantially correct. It follows from this that the knowledge argument is invalid. The argument requires additional premises ruling out the alternative hypotheses. But more: given what we know today about the representational systems that the visual system deploys, it seems very unlikely that an effort to rule out the alternatives would meet with success. For we know enough today to know that the representational systems that support experiential awareness of color differ substantially from other systems of representation, and that they are therefore likely to give rise to impressions of difference, at least in situations like the one in which Mary finds herself.

There is an analogy between Mary's situation and the situation of someone who has often seen rough surfaces but never touched one, and who is finally given an opportunity to explore a rough surface tactually. (Suppose that she is blindfolded when she does this.) It would not be hard, perhaps, for this person to infer that she is now touching a surface that would look rough if she could see it; but for the first moment or two she might well have an impression of novelty. It would clearly be appropriate to explain this impression by appealing to the fact that she is now aware of roughness in a very different *way* – that is, via a very different system of perceptual representation. Explanations of this sort are very plausible. The factors to which they appeal are obviously relevant, and obviously have sufficient power to do the requisite explanatory work.

3. As we saw in Chapter 2, Nagel's first premise has considerable intuitive appeal:

Facts about the qualitative character of an experience are fully accessible only from the point of view of the being who is the subject of the experience.

Even staunch opponents of dualism are attracted by this doctrine. I will maintain, however, that there is no good reason to accept it.

In justifying the doctrine, Nagel maintains that we can grasp the qualia of another creature only insofar as those qualia are similar to qualia that we have experienced ourselves. This view postulates two ways of grasping qualia:

(a) by directly experiencing them, and
(b) by extrapolating along lines of similarity from qualia we have grasped via direct experience.

In addition to asserting that we can grasp qualia in these two ways, Nagel in effect denies that there is any other way of gaining access to them. (By "grasping qualia" and "gaining access to qualia," I here mean "grasping the intrinsic natures of qualia" and "gaining access to the intrinsic natures of qualia." Nagel would not deny that we can gain access to the causal powers of qualia by means other than (a) and (b).)

No doubt it can *seem* to be true that we must apprehend the intrinsic natures of qualia either in way (a) or in way (b) if we are to grasp them at all. But *why* does this seem to be the case? More particularly, what is the motivation for holding that (a) is the only *basic* way of apprehending qualia, that it must provide the foundation for all other apprehensions?

(I will hereafter call this *Nagel's claim about basic awareness*.) Reflection shows that the motivation is complex. I wish to suggest that it has three main components.

One component is the perception that gives rise to the knowledge argument – the perception that when one has a new qualitative experience, one is aware of a property that is altogether new, a property that one has not previously encountered. If immediate experience could provide us with access to properties that were altogether new to us, no matter what properties we had previously come to know via other sources, then it would have to be true that immediate experience provides our *only* form of access to those properties. Thus, intuitions about novelty lead directly to Nagel's claim about basic awareness.

The second component is the perception that, as a matter of brute fact, the intrinsic qualitative natures we encounter via immediate first personal acquaintance are not available to us via any other form of cognitive access. Consider pain, for example. It seems to us that pains have bodily locations, but we do not encounter items that strike us as painful when we see or touch areas of the body where pains are occurring, or when we explore those areas with sophisticated technical devices. One could observe the neural activity in a damaged foot forever without having a clue that it was a locus of pain. The same is true of the areas of the brain that are responsible for processing signals from damaged areas. In order for it to be possible for us to see or touch a pain, it would have to be true that pain has a physical dimension, having to do with neural activity, that is not revealed to us by direct acquaintance. Equally, if we were to apprehend color qualia by visually or tactually exploring the visual system, or by examining it with laboratory equipment, it would have to be true that color qualia have a physical nature that direct acquaintance does not reveal. But neither pain nor color qualia could have a hidden physical dimension. This follows immediately from the perception that they do not admit of an appearance/reality distinction.

The third component of the motivation for Nagel's claim about basic awareness is the intuition that the qualia we encounter via immediate firstpersonal acquaintance are *not even similar to* the properties we encounter in other ways. That is, it seems to us that it would be impossible to anticipate the distinctive nature of any quale by extrapolating along lines of similarity from non-qualitative properties. Experience gives us no reason to think that qualia stand in relations of qualitative similarity to physical properties, and no reason to think that they are linked to physical properties by relations of physical similarity. Moreover, given that there is no appearance/reality distinction for qualia, we cannot say that qualia might stand in relations of similarity that our experience fails to reveal. In the case of qualia, relationships of similarity and dissimilarity are determined entirely by what is revealed in immediate experience. Or so it can seem.

None of these components of the motivation for Nagel's claim about basic awareness is compelling. We have already seen that it is possible to explain the sense that one is aware of something new when one has a new qualitative experience in a way that is entirely compatible with physicalism. Moreover, it is clear from the foregoing exposition that the second and third components stand or fall with the doctrine that qualia do not admit of an appearance/reality distinction, and by now we are well aware that this doctrine is wrong.

4. In reviewing Levine's formulation of the explanatory gap argument, we found that he posits an intimate tie between explanation and conceivability. According to Levine, if a set of facts Σ_I is reductively explainable in terms of another set of facts Σ_2, then, once one has the members of Σ_I and Σ_2 fully in view, it should be literally inconceivable that the members of Σ_2 might exist without being accompanied by the members of Σ_I. Having asserted this premise, he goes on to claim that it is always possible to conceive of physical facts existing without being accompanied by qualitative facts. It follows immediately that qualitative facts cannot be reductively explained in terms of physical facts; and it follows from this in turn, Levine maintains, that a fairly robust version of property dualism must be true.

Is Levine's premise about the relationship between explainability and conceivability correct? It depends on what is meant by "conceivability." To conceive of something is to represent it conceptually. It may well be true that the possibility of a reductive explanation depends on what can be conceived using concepts that reflect the essential natures of the phenomena being represented, but it seems unlikely that it should depend on what we can conceive using whatever concepts lie ready to hand. This can be seen by reflecting on the cases that are most relevant to our present concerns – that is, cases in which we conceive of situations by deploying the commonsense concepts that we use to represent qualia. Our use of these concepts is governed largely by the information about qualia that is provided by experiential awareness. As we have observed, experience may well distort the nature of qualia, and may well fail to do justice to, or even to give some indication of, their essential natures. Accordingly, it may well be the case that our ability to conceive of physical facts that are not accompanied by qualitative facts is entirely without ontological significance. But if it is without ontological significance, then how can it have any bearing on whether it is in principle possible to give an explanation of qualitative facts in terms of physical facts? The question of whether it is possible to give a reductive explanation of this sort is a question about the world. (Levine will of course have to agree with this, given that he wishes to draw a conclusion with ontological significance.) The answer should not be thought to depend upon what can be represented using concepts that may very well not reflect the real nature of the world.

5. The appearance/reality argument opens by claiming that it is impossible to draw an appearance/reality distinction with respect to qualia, and then goes on to observe that it clearly is possible to draw an appearance/reality distinction with respect to physical properties. These doctrines lead quickly to the conclusion that property dualism must be true.

The first thing we should notice about this argument is that there are several different ways of interpreting it. This is because, as we noticed in Section 4.5, there are several different appearance/reality distinctions. There is a *doxastic* distinction between a subject's warranted beliefs about an item and the facts involving the item to which the beliefs correspond, a *Fregean* distinction between the properties we rely on in identifying an item and the less accessible properties of the item, a *perceptual* distinction between the properties of an item that are presented to us perceptually and the properties of the item that we are not perceiving, and a *representational* distinction between the way an object is represented and the way it is in itself. Which of these distinctions, if any, provides us with an interpretation of the argument that confers truth on both of its premises?

The doxastic distinction has no tendency to support the argument, for the first premise comes out false when we think of it as a claim concerning the relationship between beliefs about qualia and the corresponding facts. Beliefs about qualitative states can easily be false. My favorite example of this is Roger Albritton's fraternity case (to which I have already alluded).[4] Consider a ceremony in which several students who are being initiated into a fraternity are bound and blindfolded, and are warned that they will be penalized heavily for failing to conform to orders. In fact, they are told, they will be slashed with a knife. Suppose that a particular student fails to perform as required, and is told to expect the worst. Suppose finally that instead of slashing him with a knife, his tormentor quickly draws an icicle across his body. It

---

[4] Albritton gave this example in a seminar at Harvard in 1971.

seems likely that, for a moment at least, the already terrified student will believe, falsely, that he is actually in pain. This is of course a case of conceptual priming. We can all find less dramatic instances of it in our own experience.

What about the Fregean distinction? It is clear that the first premise comes out true when we interpret it in terms of this distinction, for it is clear that there is no difference between the property we rely on in identifying pains as such and the property of being a pain. It is pain itself that we rely on in identifying pains. Reflection shows, however, that when the first premise is interpreted in terms of the Fregean distinction, its truth has little metaphysical significance. On this interpretation, it says no more than that our access to pain is direct. But whether access to a property is direct or indirect is a relative matter – it depends on the *mode* of access, the *way* in which one is aware of the property. Often it is possible to be aware of a property via two modes of access, and when this happens, it may be true that one mode is direct while the other is indirect. Accordingly, when the first premise is interpreted in terms of the Fregean distinction, we must understand it as claiming that our access to pain is direct *insofar as we are aware of pain via inner sense.* This claim cannot by itself support a conclusion about the metaphysical nature of pain; for it is compatible with the claims (i) that pain is identical with a certain physical property P, (ii) that we fail to appreciate this identity because awareness of pain via inner sense involves representations that fail to register the physical nature of pain, (iii) that we can be aware of P (and therefore of pain) perceptually (for example, by viewing fMRI images), and (iv) that our *perceptual* awareness of P (and therefore of pain) via vision is indirect, being mediated by awareness of various appearance properties (e.g., by the ways the relevant fMRI images look to us). Clearly, if these claims are true, any dualistic account of pain is mistaken. Hence, it is necessary to rule them out before one can proceed from the first premise of the argument to a dualistic conclusion. But this means that the appearance/reality argument begs the question. When the first premise of the argument is interpreted in accordance with the Fregean distinction, several additional premises are needed. Moreover, as reflection shows, the task of establishing these additional premises as correct is tantamount to the task of establishing dualism.

I turn now to perceptual appearance/reality distinction. When it is interpreted in terms of this distinction, the first premise claims that there is no difference between the ways qualia seem to us when we grasp them perceptually and the ways they are in themselves. To see that this claim is intuitively plausible, at least with respect to perceptual qualia, observe that it is common to identify perceptual qualia with the ways external objects seem or appear to us. If we accept this identification, then the claim says, in effect, that there is no difference between the ways perceptual appearances *appear* to us on the basis of perception and the ways perceptual appearances are in themselves. This has the ring of truth. Indeed, it is not immediately clear that its denial is a coherent thesis. We will not be able to arrive at a final evaluation of the claim, however, until we have taken a closer look at the nature of perceptual appearances in the next chapter. To anticipate the outcome of that discussion, we will find that it is after all possible to distinguish between the ways perceptual appearances appear to us and the ways they are in themselves, and that there is indeed good reason to draw such a distinction. Thus, we will in the end have grounds for rejecting the claim, and with it the third version of the appearance/reality argument.

This brings us to the representational distinction. Is it possible to confer truth on the first premise of the appearance/reality argument by interpreting it as the claim that it is impossible to distinguish between qualia as represented and qualia as they are in themselves? No. It can seem that the claim is true when one considers it from the perspective of folk psychology, but this is one of the areas in which folk psychology gets things badly wrong.

6. The introspection argument begins plausibly with the claim that as far as we can tell, qualitative states resist characterization in terms of the concepts and principles of physical theories. There is, for example, no basis in our experience of pain for applying the concepts that we use in describing neurons and neural activity. When we are experientially aware of pain, we do not thereby have any ground for supposing that we are aware of axons and dendrites, nor any ground for supposing that we are thereby aware of action potentials and the flow of neurotransmitters. Moreover, unlike physical states, pains are resolvable into minimal units, *minima discriminabilia* that have no constituent structure. Or so it seems. But can we trust appearances in this case? The argument faces this question directly, and answers it by saying that the reality of pain is the very same thing as the appearance of pain. Like all qualia, pain wears its intrinsic nature on its sleeve. Accordingly, if pain consisted of neural activity, and individual pains were decomposable into microevents corresponding to

microconstituents of neural events, our experience of pain would make these things apparent to us.[5]

For reasons that are now familiar, this argument must be set aside.

4.10   CONCLUSION

In this chapter we have considered a number of claims and arguments that appear, at first sight, anyway, to provide strong support for property dualism. In all cases, the claims and arguments have proved on examination to be badly flawed. They may *seem* to promote property dualism, but this is an illusion.

We cannot of course move directly from the foregoing lines of thought to the conclusion that property dualism is false, but I think we are entitled to draw this conclusion when we combine the lines of thought with the observation that the burden of proof is entirely on the shoulders of those who advocate dualism. We have an epistemic right to prefer theories that represent reality as simple and unified to theories that represent it as

---

[5] Questions concerning *qualitative simplicity* have arisen at several different points in this chapter. It may be useful to collect the scattered observations about this topic into an organized whole.

Qualitative entities fall into two metaphysical categories – on the one hand, there are qualitative *properties*, and on the other, there are *concrete qualitative states*. Corresponding to these categories are two forms of qualitative simplicity. Certain qualitative properties, such as the way yellow things look, seem to us to be simple, where this means that it seems to us that it cannot be analyzed into more basic properties. Also, it seems to us that concrete qualitative states can be decomposed into parts that are minimal – parts that have no parts of their own. These are both ways in which qualitative entities *seem* to us to be simple. When they are combined with the thesis that there is no difference between appearance and reality in the case of qualitative entities, they yield ontological conclusions – conclusions abut metaphysical simplicity. In this way, we arrive at the conclusion that yellow is a metaphysically basic property, and also at the conclusion that the parts of a pain are *minima discriminabilia* are metaphysically atomic, ultimate building blocks of reality. Both of these conclusions can be used to support dualistic doctrines.

As we have observed at several points in this chapter, a representationalist can respond to arguments for dualism that proceed from claims concerning the *apparent* simplicity of qualitative entities by showing that, initial impressions to the contrary notwithstanding, it is possible to distinguish between the appearance of a quale and the corresponding reality. What I would like to emphasize here is that it may well be possible for a representationalist to go further. In addition to blocking arguments from apparent simplicity to dualism, it may well be possible for a representationalist to offer deflationary explanations for both of the two forms of apparent simplicity. Indeed, we can see that this *will* be possible in any case in which a qualitative entity x is represented by an experiential representation R that is a representational atom – that is, a representation that is neither factorizable into more basic representations nor treated by the relevant cognitive agencies as equivalent to another experiential representation that can be decomposed in this way. If R provides a subject with his primary access to the qualitative entity x, and R is characterized by this sort of internal and systematic atomicity, then we can see that the subject's experience of x would encourage the belief that x is itself atomic – that it is a simple, unanalyzable entity. This would happen even if x is in fact quite complex.

complex and disjointed. Accordingly, if dualism cannot be *shown* to be true, we can and should set it aside as false.

I have now completed my assessment of current theories of qualia and qualitative awareness. In the next three chapters I will present a new theory – a theory that has certain affinities with the view I earlier called "Harmanian representationalism," and that has a broadly physicalist motivation, but that diverges from all current theories at a number of points. At present the theory makes no claim to completeness. It provides explanatory accounts of visual qualia, pain and other sensory qualia, and emotional qualia. I hope, however, that it will be plausible to the reader, as it is to me, that its central doctrines can be extended so as to apply to qualia of other sorts as well.

CHAPTER 5

*Visual awareness and visual qualia**

In this chapter I will be concerned with perceptual consciousness, and with what is going on when objects appear to us perceptually in various ways. I will begin by urging that perception always involves awareness of appearances. Then I will explain awareness of perceptual qualia in terms of awareness of appearances. Since all awareness is essentially representational in character, this will give us a representational theory of perceptual qualia. Having stated the theory, I will go on to spell out some of its metaphysical consequences, and to defend it against two powerful objections, one that is based on Swampman and another that is based on inverted spectra.

I will focus almost entirely on vision, and more particularly, on visual awareness of size and shape. Much that I will say will not generalize to other perceptual domains, but I believe that the more abstract and general claims apply to hearing and the other standard perceptual modalities as well as to vision.

5.1 APPEARANCE AND REALITY

When I wish to refer to the view that perception involves awareness of special properties that are distinct from the objective physical properties of external objects, I will speak of the *appearance view*. The principal motivation for this view comes from perceptual relativity – that is, from the fact that the way objects appear to us depends systematically on such factors as distance, angle of view, and lighting. To appreciate this motivation, consider the following line of thought: "It seems to be true that when we participate in facts of the form *x looks F to y*, we are aware of properties of *some* kind. After all, facts of the given form have

---

* Most of Sections 5.1–5.4 and part of Appendix II are excerpted from my contributions to Christopher S. Hill and David J. Bennett, "The Perception of Size and Shape," *Philosophical Issues* 18 (2008), 294–315.

a proprietary phenomenology, and phenomenology implies awareness of properties. So we must ask: What is the nature of the properties that we are aware of when we participate in such facts? In particular, could it be true that we are aware of the objective physical properties of external objects? Reflection on perceptual relativity leads immediately to a negative answer. What we are aware of is how objects look to us, and how objects look to us depends on distance, lighting, and so on. It is clear that the objective physical properties of external objects do not depend on factors of this sort. Hence, it cannot be true that we are aware of objective properties when objects look various ways to us. The properties we are aware of must belong to a special category. So the appearance view is correct."

I will eventually try to make this line of thought more precise, but before I do so, it will be useful to review the traditional philosophical discussions that invoke perceptual relativity. In assessing the motivation for the appearance view, it is important to keep it in mind that perceptual relativity has always seemed to philosophers to be something that can be taken for granted. It has always been recognized, it seems, that an object of perceptual awareness must appear a certain way to the observer, and that the way it appears depends on distance and other contextual factors.

Perceptual relativity has figured prominently both in epistemological discussions of perception and in metaphysical discussions. To begin with the epistemological literature, various authors have cited relativity in arguing for the unreliability of the senses. Sextus Empiricus was an early and passionate advocate of arguments of this sort. In discussing perception, Sextus' primary objectives were, first, to show that appearances tend to oppose one another, and second, to show that there is no criterion that can be used to distinguish between the appearances that provide access to objective properties and the appearances that have no objective validity. He relied heavily on considerations of relativity in pursuing these goals. Here, for example, is what he says about appearances of shape: "[T]he same stoa viewed from either end appears tapering but from the middle completely symmetrical, and from afar the same boat seems small and stationary but from close up large and in motion, and the same tower appears round from afar but square from close up."[1] Descartes, who was also principally concerned with epistemological issues, echoes these observations in the following passage: "Sometimes towers which had looked round from a distance appeared square from close up; and enormous

---

[1] Benson Mates, *The Skeptic Way* (Oxford: Oxford University Press, 1996), p. 104.

statues standing on their pediments did not seem large when observed from the ground."[2] In effect, Descartes is here endorsing Sextus' view that the relativity of appearances makes it inappropriate to view the senses as reliable sources of information about reality.

The metaphysical use of perceptual relativity can be traced back at least to Plato's *Theaetetus*. In modern philosophy it first achieved prominence in the writings of Berkeley and Hume, both of whom relied heavily on relativity in arguing for the doctrine that the immediate objects of perceptual awareness are mental in character. Relativity also figured prominently in discussions of the sense datum theory in the first half of the twentieth century. Thus, for example, in the initial chapter of *The Problems of Philosophy*, Russell famously argued from the relativity of appearances to the conclusion that awareness of appearances cannot be explained as awareness of objective physical properties, but must instead be identified with awareness of properties of sense data.[3] Here is a typical passage:

The *shape* of the table is no better. We are all in the habit of judging as to the "real" shape of things, and we do this so unreflectingly that we come to think that we actually see the real shapes. But, in fact, as we all have to learn if we try to draw, a given thing looks different in shape from every different point of view. If our table is "really" rectangular, it will look, from almost all points of view, as if it had two acute angles and two obtuse angles. If opposite sides are parallel, they will look as if they converged to a point away from the spectator; if they are of equal length, they will look as if the nearer side were longer. All these things are not commonly noticed in looking at a table, because experience has taught us to construct the "real" shape from the apparent shape, and the "real" shape is what interests us as practical men. But the "real" shape is not what we see. And what we see is constantly changing in shape as we move around the room; so that here again the senses seem not to give us the truth about the table itself, but only about the appearance of the table. ... Thus, it becomes evident that the real table, if there is one, is not the same as what we immediately experience by sight or touch or hearing. The real table, if there is one, is not immediately known to us at all, but must be an inference from what is immediately known.... Let us give the name of "sense data" to the things that are immediately known in sensation... .[4]

As I understand it, Russell's line of thought in this passage begins with the relativity of appearances and winds up with the conclusion that awareness

---

[2] Rene Descartes, *Meditations on First Philosophy*, in John Cottingham, Robert Stoothoff, and Dugald Murdoch (eds.), *The Philosophical Writings of Descartes*, Volume II (Cambridge: Cambridge University Press, 1984), p. 53.

[3] Bertrand Russell, *The Problems of Philosophy* (Oxford: Oxford University Press, 1959).

[4] *Ibid.*, pp. 10–12.

of appearances cannot be explained as awareness of objective physical properties, but must instead be identified with awareness of properties of sense data. It is an explicit premise of the argument that how things look to us is always in flux, as a result of changes in such factors as position and lighting, and also that this fluctuation precludes identifying the appearances of things with objective physical properties of external objects. In addition, it is clear that there is a background assumption to the effect that we must be aware of properties of *some* kind in virtue of participating in facts of the form *x looks F to y*. Thus, Russell's line of thought incorporates the main elements of the argument we considered at the beginning of this section.

The sense datum theory eventually encountered some important objections, and as a result, there was little discussion of perceptual relativity in the closing decades of the twentieth century. But perceptual relativity has returned to prominence in recent years. Moreover, as of yore, it is used in contemporary philosophy to motivate the appearance view. Thus, we find versions of the classical argument for the appearance view in the work of Sydney Shoemaker, Michael Huemer, and Alva Noë.[5]

I will soon provide a more detailed exposition of the classical argument, but before I do this, I should remind the reader of a distinction between two different senses of expressions like "looks" and "appears."

There is a sense of "looks small" in which it can be correctly applied both to a toy car that one holds in one's hand and to a real car that one sees on the road far ahead. In this sense, the expression can also be applied to a tall building that one sees from a plane, and even to an immense star that one sees from the Earth. When one says that an object looks small to an observer, using "looks small" in this *phenomenological* sense, one is not claiming that the observer's perceptual experience supports the judgment that the object really is small. One is not saying that the observer's experience represents the object as small. Rather one is drawing an analogy between the observer's current visual experience and the visual experiences he has when he is viewing objects that are reasonably close at hand and really are small.

The phenomenological sense of "looks" is also to be found in claims about apparent shape and apparent color. It is permissible to apply "looks elliptical" both to an object that really is elliptical and is perpendicular to

---

[5] Sydney Shoemaker, *The First Person Perspective and Other Essays* (Cambridge: Cambridge University Press, 1994); Michael Huemer, *Skepticism and the Veil of Perception* (Lanham, MD: Rowman and Littlefield, 2001); and Alva Noë, *Action in Perception* (Cambridge, MA: MIT Press, 2004).

the observer's line of sight, and to a round coin that is tilted away from the observer. Equally, it is permissible to apply "looks dark brown" both to a piece of chocolate and to a portion of a tan wall that is cloaked in shadow.

In addition to the phenomenological sense of "looks," there is also what is often called its *epistemic* sense. When we say that an item looks small to an observer, using "looks small" in this second sense, we mean that the observer's current visual experience provides adequate evidential support for the belief that the object is small. When we have this second sense in mind, we would not be willing to say that a car looks small to an observer if the car is at an appreciable distance from the observer, for when a car is at an appreciable distance from an observer, the observer's visual experience presents him with "pictorial cues" that are indicative of distance. Thus, for example, when an object stands at some distance from an observer, the features of the object seem indistinct. In a case of this sort, the observer's experience supports the belief that he is seeing a car of normal size, but a car that is rather far away. Accordingly, using "looks" in its epistemic sense, it is correct to say that the car looks to be of normal size, despite the fact that it is also correct to say, using "looks" in its phenomenological sense, that the car looks small.

We can also use "looks" in its epistemic sense to talk about appearances of other kinds. Thus, it is quite appropriate to apply "looks round" to a coin that is tilted away from an observer, and to apply "looks tan" to a portion of a wall that is poorly illuminated, provided that the observer's visual experience attests to this fact about the lighting.

Both of these senses are interesting, but I will be focusing here on the phenomenological sense, for that is the one that figures in classical discussions of perceptual relativity and the appearance view. I will use the expressions "looks-p" and "appears-p" to signify that the terms "looks" and "appears" are being used in their phenomenological senses.

5.2 AN ARGUMENT FOR THE TRADITIONAL VIEW

I turn now to the task of giving a more precise version of the classical argument running from perceptual relativity to the appearance view. It seems to me that when all of the premises are made fully explicit, the argument looks something like this:

First premise: When an observer is consciously perceiving an object, and the observer's awareness of the object is visual, there is a way that the object looks-p to the observer. That is to say, for some F, the object looks-p F to the observer.

Second premise: When an object looks-p a certain way to an observer, the observer experiences a phenomenology that is characteristic of that way of appearing. That is to say, for every *F* there is an associated visual phenomenology *P* such that an object looks-p *F* to an observer just in case the observer is experiencing *P*.

Third premise: When an agent has an experience with a certain associated phenomenology, *P*, as a result of participating in a fact of the form *x looks-p F to y*, the observer is visually aware of certain properties – properties that are constitutive of *P*. It is natural to call these properties *appearance properties*.

Lemma: When an observer is consciously perceiving an object, and the observer's awareness of the object is visual, there is a way that the object looks-p to the observer, and its looking-p that way consists in part in the observer's being aware of certain appearance properties.

Fourth premise (Perceptual Relativity): The ways that objects look-p to an observer are constantly changing. They change with such contextual factors as distance, lighting, etc.

Fifth premise: If the ways that objects look-p to observers vary with such factors as distance, lighting, etc., then the phenomenologies that are associated with those ways of looking-p vary with those factors as well, as do the appearance properties that are constitutive of those phenomenologies.

Sixth premise: If the appearance properties that observers are aware of in virtue of participating in facts of the form *x looks-p F to y* vary with such factors as distance, lighting, etc., then those properties cannot be identical with objective physical properties of external objects.

Conclusion: When an observer is consciously perceiving an object, and the observer's awareness of the object is visual, there is a way that the object looks-p to the observer, and its looking-p that way consists in part of the observer's being aware of certain appearance properties. These properties are distinct from the objective physical properties of external objects.

Several of the premises of this argument require qualification and/or defense, but none of them seems beyond repair. They are on the whole quite plausible, and together they seem to make a strong case for the appearance view.

The first premise is one of the ones that require qualification. It claims, in effect, that conscious visual perception always has an experiential dimension. Reflection shows that this claim is called into question by cases of "amodal" visual awareness. Suppose, for example, that an observer is looking at a dog that is partially obscured by the slats of a picket fence. There is a sense in which it is true to say that the observer is visually aware of the occluded parts of the dog, but there is no experience of the parts in question. It could not be said that the occluded parts look-p a certain way to the observer. This is a reasonable objection, but there is also a reasonable response. In the case described, awareness of the occluded parts of the dog *depends on* visual awareness of the other parts. In general, it seems to hold that when one is amodally aware of an object (or an object part), one's awareness depends on awareness of one or more other objects (or object parts). It also seems to hold that these other objects satisfy the first premise. That is to say, amodal awareness seems to be grounded in experiential awareness. By the same token, it seems possible to meet the present objection by restricting the first premise to forms of visual awareness that are not grounded in this way in other forms of awareness.

I turn now to the third premise, which claims, in brief, that when one has a perceptual experience with a certain associated phenomenology, *P*, one is ipso facto aware of certain properties as instantiated – properties that are constitutive of *P*. Claims of this sort are challenged by adverbial theories of phenomenology. According to adverbial theories, having an experience with an associated phenomenology consists in being in a mental state that has certain adjectival determinations (or in undergoing a mental process that has certain adverbial determinations), not in being aware of instantiated properties. My response to this objection is that adverbialism fails to acknowledge the intimate relationship between phenomenology and awareness. Indeed, as we saw in Chapter 3, it is in the end forced to deny that there is first order, experiential awareness of phenomenology. This is just wrong. It is non-negotiable that we are aware of phenomenology – this is how we know of its existence. Moreover, our awareness of the phenomenological dimension of an experience is experiential awareness. That is to say, awareness of phenomenology is located at the level of experience itself; it is not an adventitious, meta-cognitive awareness, and it does not involve conceptualization. Adverbialism fails to do justice to these fundamental facts. Indeed, it is forced to deny them.

There is also a second concern about the third premise. Someone with a representational theory of awareness might object as follows: "It may be true in many or even most cases that one is aware of certain properties in having an experience with an associated phenomenology, but it is also true that there are occasions on which having an experience with an associated phenomenology consists in *representing* certain properties as instantiated rather than being aware of them as instantiated. This is shown, for example, by dreams and hallucinations. In such cases one's experience has a rich phenomenological dimension, but it would be wrong to characterize them by saying that they involve awareness of properties. What one should say is that in dreams and hallucinations we *represent* properties as instantiated."

As an ardent fan of representational theories of awareness, I fully appreciate the force of this objection. I think, however, that it can be met by making relatively modest adjustments in the argument. Thus, the argument will retain its force and philosophical significance if the third premise is changed to read as follows:

When one has an experience with a certain associated phenomenology, *P*, one represents certain properties as instantiated. Moreover, in *most* cases one is *aware* of those properties as instantiated. This is true whenever the properties are in fact instantiated, and one stands in an appropriate causal relation to the instantiating event or object. The properties in question are constitutive of *P*.

Once this claim is substituted for the third premise, it becomes necessary to make compensatory adjustments elsewhere in the argument. But the new version of the argument retains the basic structure of the old version, and its conclusion has roughly the same content.

This brings me to the fourth premise, which is an endorsement of perceptual relativity. Perceptual relativity is a very plausible doctrine, and as we have seen, it has often been taken as obviously true in the history of philosophy. Its plausibility has several sources. I will mention two. (As usual, I will focus on relativity of size and shape.)

First, we become aware of the fact of relativity when we attend to objects whose relationship to us is changing. Consider a case in which an SUV moves slowly away from you. If you are attending to the SUV's apparent size, you will be aware of it as constantly shrinking. Equally, provided that you are attending to appearances, you will be aware of a continuous change of shape when you see a disk rotate on its horizontal axis.

Second, relativity is brought home to us when we attend simultaneously to the appearances of objects that are the same in point of objective properties, but that stand in different relations to us. This happens, for example, when one compares the apparent size of a hand held to close to one's face with the apparent size of a hand held at arm's length, and also when one compares the apparent shape of a book that is standing on end with the apparent shape of a book that is lying flat on the table. Provided that one's relations to two objectively similar objects are sufficiently different, attention easily reveals that they present different appearances.

The remaining premises seem to hold up to scrutiny pretty well on their own.

5.3 APPEARANCE PROPERTIES AND VISION SCIENCE

Interestingly, vision scientists have on the whole been more guarded in their attitude toward perceptual relativity than philosophers. They have tended to acknowledge that objects can present appearances that are quite different than their objective properties, but they have often expressed reservations about the idea that conscious visual perception generally or normally involves awareness of appearances. I will try to characterize these reservations in the present section, and will formulate replies to them.

In a well known discussion, Stephen Palmer distinguishes between two forms or modes of perception that he calls the "proximal mode" and the "distal mode." Here is the passage in which he first draws this distinction:

> An interesting approach … that has been taken by a number of theorists is to posit the existence of two different modes of visual perception. What we will call the *proximal mode* reflects mainly the properties of the retinal image, or proximal stimulus. What we will call the *distal mode* reflects mainly the properties of the environmental object, or distal stimulus.[6]

Palmer holds that the proximal mode and the distal mode are often combined, but he seems to think that we can switch back and forth between the two modes, adopting one to the exclusion of the other. He writes:

> Which perceptual mode you are in can be strongly influenced by explicit instructions. … If you were shown two identical disks at different distances in an experiment, for example, and were asked to compare the "apparent sizes of the two objects," you would probably settle into the distal mode and report them as being about the same in size. If you were then shown the same display and were asked to compare the "sizes of the objects' images as they appear from where you are standing," you would probably switch to proximal mode and report that the larger one appeared bigger. … If there are indeed two aspects of conscious perception that correspond to the proximal and distal modes, perceptual judgments can easily go one way or the other, depending on the instructions and the task.[7]

As Palmer notes, a number of other vision scientists have drawn closely related distinctions. (Palmer explicitly cites Carlson, Gibson, Mack, and Rock.[8]) Some of these scientists have shared Palmer's view that perceptual

---

[6] Stephen Palmer, *Vision Science* (Cambridge, MA: MIT Press, 1999), p. 313.

[7] *Ibid.*, p. 314.

[8] See V. R. Carlson, "Orientation in Size Constancy Judgments," *American Journal of Psychology* 73 (1960), 199–213; V. R. Carlson, "Instructions and Perceptual Constancy Judgments," in W. Epstein (ed.), *Stability and Constancy in Visual Perception* (New York, NY: Wiley, 1977), pp. 217–254; James J. Gibson, *The Perception of the Visual World* (Boston, MA: Houghton Mifflin, 1950); Arien Mack, "Three Modes of Visual Perception," in M. H. Pick (ed.), *Modes of Perceiving*

experience can exhibit one of the two modes to the exclusion of the other, and have maintained, in addition, that observers normally make use only of the distal mode. Use of the proximal mode, they have maintained, occurs only when one is animated by special interests, such as an interest in drawing objects according to the principles of linear perspective, or when one is in unusual perceptual circumstances, such as those that obtain when one is viewing houses on the ground from an airplane window. Because they hold this view, and because they also hold that we are aware of appearances only when we adopt the proximal mode, these scientists are skeptical concerning the pervasiveness or generality of awareness of appearances.

It seems to me that there are two main reasons for skepticism of this sort. (i) If one holds that attending to appearances occurs only when one has special interests, or is in unusual perceptual circumstances, and one also holds that awareness requires attention, then one will inevitably be drawn to a skeptical position. Now it is in fact plausible, on introspective grounds, that we do not normally explicitly attend to appearances. Moreover, the view that awareness requires attention is suggested by a number of recent scientific findings. (What I have in mind here is work on change blindness, inattentional blindness, the attentional blink, and related matters.[9]) Thus, there is a package of defensible views about

---

and Information Processing (Hillsdale, NJ: Earlbaum, 1978), pp. 171–186; and Irvin Rock, *The Logic of Perception* (Cambridge, MA: MIT Press, 1983).

[9] See, e.g., the discussions of these topics in Palmer, *Vision Science.*

I will briefly describe a famous series of change-blindness experiments and note their bearing on questions of awareness and attention.

In the experiments I have in mind (see Ronald A. Rensink, J. Kevin O'Regan, and James J. Clark, "To See or Not to See: The Need for Attention to Perceive Changes in Scenes," *Psychological Science* 8 (1997), 368–373), a subject was shown a computer screen containing an image of a certain scene (e.g., one involving a fairly large airplane) for 240 milliseconds. This image was followed by a mask – a uniformly gray image – that lasted for 80 milliseconds. The third and final image was largely the same as the first one, but differed from it in one fairly substantial respect (e.g., one of the engines of the airplane was missing). Like the first one, this third image lasted for 240 milliseconds. The series of these three images was repeated over and over until the subject detected the difference between the first and third images. In most cases, it took a surprisingly long time for the subject to note the change – sometimes several minutes.

In interpreting these experiments, Rensink and his colleagues pointed out that in order to detect a change, it is necessary for a subject to store a representation of the item that underwent a change in working memory. This is because detecting a change involves comparing a memory of how an object was prior to the change with a current perception of the object. Now the capacity of working memory is quite limited, so it can represent only a few components of the depicted scene at any one time. This means that the subject is forced to scan components of the scene serially, recording them three or four at a time in working memory. It takes a while to cycle through all of the components, with the result that it takes a surprisingly long time to detect a change. Attention is relevant to this explanation of the data because attention is in effect the gatekeeper of working memory – more specifically, it is the agency that creates copies of perceptual

attention that provides motivation for skepticism. (ii) Another reason for being drawn to skepticism has to do with the fact that visual awareness is normally shaped by constancy transformations – that is, by operations that work to reduce differences in input that can be attributed to such contextual factors as distance, angle of view, and lighting. It appears that experiential awareness occurs after these transformations have been applied, and that, as a result, differences in appearances are often marginal, to the extent that they exist at all. Now vision scientists tend to be much more keenly aware than philosophers of the work done by constancy transformations. Hence, they are much less likely to attribute importance to perceptual relativity.

I will reply first to (i) and then to (ii).

(i) stands or falls with the claim that attention is required for awareness of appearances. There are four considerations which suggest that this claim is mistaken. First, when one starts to attend to the appearance that an object is presenting, one's experience of the object remains substantially the same. There is no abrupt discontinuity in the phenomenology. Consider, for example, a case in which one starts to attend to the apparent size of a car in the remote distance. It is not as if the portion of one's experience that is devoted to the car undergoes a fundamental change. There is a change of some sort, but it is not a major structural change. (It would, for example, be quite wrong to say that the car looked-p large or normal-sized to you pre-attentively, and that it started to look-p small when you began to attend to its apparent size. It would also be quite wrong to say that the car looked-p no way at all to you pre-attentively. It is not even clear what it would mean to say something of this sort. What would it mean? That pre-attentively one had no experience of the car at all?) Moreover, reflection shows that the portion that remains the same is the portion that helps to make true the claim that the car looks-p small to one. The phenomenology that is relevant to its looking-p small is part of the phenomenology that is preserved.

Second, consider a situation in which you are visually aware of an object O, but are not attending to the apparent size of O. Suppose now that you turn away from O and that you ask yourself how large O looked-p to you. Suppose also that your strategy for answering this question involves summoning up an experiential memory, or memory image, of your perception of O. If you are like me, this image will not support a precise answer to

---

representations in working memory. It follows that when a subject eventually achieves awareness of a change, he does so as a result of attention.

the question of how large *O* looked, but it will enable you to give a rough answer. Since the image makes it possible for you to answer the question, it must be true that the image attributes a certain apparent size to *O*. That is to say, it must be the case that this apparent size is part of the representational content of the image. You are able to answer the question because it is possible for you to attend to this attributed or represented size, and to derive a perceptual judgment from what attention reveals. Assuming that the image is a fairly accurate replica of the original experience, it follows that the content of the original visual experience was also concerned with an appearance: it too represented the apparent size of *O*. But this means that you were aware of the apparent size of *O* when the original experience was occurring. Since by hypothesis you were not *attentively* aware of the apparent size at that time, we have a case in which there is nonattentive awareness of an appearance property. Moreover, since there is nothing special about the case, we can infer that awareness of appearance properties is the norm.

Third, there is a consideration that arises from vision science itself. In normal circumstances, we are consciously aware of the relative distances and relative orientations of the objects that we see. Thus, for example, I am currently aware that the bookshelf on my left is farther away than my desk, and also that the former stands at a different angle relative to my line of sight than the latter. These are just physical facts about these objects that I register more or less automatically. Now when vision scientists are concerned to explain awareness of facts of this sort, they normally appeal to what they call "forms of pictorial information." An example of pictorial information is the fact that parallel lines appear to converge as they recede into the distance. Another example is the fact that items that are farther away appear to be closer to the horizon than items that are closer to hand. A third example is the fact that the apparent sizes of objects tend to decrease as the objects move farther away. And a fourth example is that the apparent shape of an object tends to change in definite ways as the orientation of the object changes. Like the various other forms of pictorial information, apparent convergence, apparent closeness to the horizon, apparent size, and apparent shape are all registered by photographs – whence the name "pictorial information." Moreover, it is clear that they can also be registered by conscious visual experiences. Now let us ask: Are pictorial factors *generally* registered at the level of conscious visual experience, or does this happen only when we explicitly attend to them? The fact that we are generally consciously aware of relative distance and relative orientation provides strong evidence that the answer should be "generally." Thus, if it is true, as it seems to be, that we are generally aware of relative distance and relative orientation, and it is also true, as vision scientists are wont to maintain, that we are aware of relative distance and relative orientation in virtue of being aware of pictorial factors, then it must be the case that we are generally aware of pictorial factors, including apparent size and apparent shape.

The fourth reason for thinking that we are generally aware of appearances is that such awareness appears to play a role in categorization. Thus, a series of studies by Michael Tarr and his associates on object recognition seem to have established that success in recognition tasks is heavily influenced by the viewpoint-dependent properties of the objects that subjects are required to recognize.[10] (Recognition of an object is facilitated if the subject is occupying a perspective on the object that is similar to the perspectives the subject has occupied during past encounters with the object.) Tarr's results do not address questions concerning the specific nature of the viewpoint-dependent properties to which subjects are sensitive, but they do provide support for the general thesis that the viewpoint-dependent properties are normally registered at the higher levels of visual processing.

We may conclude, then, that there are good reasons for thinking that awareness of appearance properties does not require attention – or at least, that it does not require the sort of highly focused attention that occurs when one explicitly notes an appearance and classifies it as such. It must be acknowledged, however, that this is a complex topic which requires further consideration. I will return to it in Appendix I.

I turn now to (ii), which urges that the scope of perceptual relativity is considerably reduced by the role of constancy transformations in shaping perceptual experience. I of course wish to acknowledge the importance of constancy transformations in visual processing, but it seems possible to me to appreciate the significance of that role while also acknowledging that our perceptual experience of objects shows the influence of distance, lighting, and so on. Indeed, there are three reasons for thinking that the transformations leave considerable latitude to relativity. One derives from the experimental literature. As I will emphasize in Appendix II, there is considerable experimental evidence that the transformations do not altogether eliminate the influence of contextual factors. They compensate for

---

[10] See, e.g., Michael J. Tarr, and H. H. Bulthoff, "Is Human Object Recognition Better Described by Geon Structural Descriptions or by Multiple Views?" *Journal of Experimental Psychology: Human Perception and Performance* 21 (1995), 1494–1505.

differences in inputs that are due to such factors, but the compensation is generally partial, even in circumstances in which excellent information about the factors is available to the visual system. There is generally a certain amount of "underconstancy."[11] Second, there is also introspective evidence for the claim that the transformations do not fully normalize representations of objects. As we noted in Section 5.2, when one attends to how objects look-p to one, one finds that their appearances are constantly changing, and that objects with similar objective properties generally present different appearances. Often the discrepancies are small, but even when this is true, there are circumstances in which they can be detected. Third, there is a continuity argument. We find it hard to detect differences in appearance when the contextual differences are small. On the other hand, when the differences in the relevant contextual factors are sufficiently large, there are always manifest differences in the ways objects look-p. We notice them immediately when we are attending to appearances. It is plausible that appearances that are manifestly different are connected by series of appearances whose differences are so small as to be virtually undetectable – at least without highly focused attention and careful comparisons.

5.4   THE NATURE OF APPEARANCES

What has been said thus far about the nature of appearances is quite sketchy. The picture I have provided consists entirely of the following five claims: (i) appearances are properties that are encountered in perceptual experience; (ii) access to appearances is unmediated and non-inferential – it is not the case that there are other properties such that we are aware of appearances in virtue of being aware of those other properties; (iii) appearances vary with such contextual factors as distance, angle of view, and lighting; (iv) appearances are not identical with the objective physical properties of external objects; and (v) awareness of appearances is a general, pervasive feature of perceptual experience. These claims leave many questions open – for example, the question of whether appearances are exemplified by internal mental objects or by external objects. These remaining questions are quite numerous and tend to be very difficult. I

---

[11] See, e.g., Irvin Rock, *An Introduction to Perception* (New York, NY: Macmillan Publishing Company, 1975), pp. 30–32; H. A. Sedgwick, "Space Perception," in K. R. Boff, L. Kaufman, and J. P. Thomas (eds.), *Handbook of Perception and Human Performance: Vol. 1: Sensory Processes* (New York: Wiley, 1986), pp. 21.1–21.57 (especially 21.1–21.23); and Palmer, *Vision Science*, pp. 314–317.

will not be able to address them fully here. But I would like to amplify what has been said thus far in two ways. First, I would like to under-score doctrine (iv) by discrediting a certain last-ditch effort to deny it. And second, I would like to argue for the view that appearances are not properties of internal mental objects, but are rather relational viewpoint-dependent properties of external objects.

Anyone who wishes to deny (iv), and who accordingly holds that the objective physical properties of external objects are the *only* properties that are represented by perceptual experiences, must face the following question: If the view is correct, then why do perceptual experiences show the effects of perceptual relativity? If the properties that visual expe-riences represent are enduring traits of external objects, then why are the ways that external objects look-p in constant flux? We now observe that there is an answer to this question that enjoys a certain prima facie plausibility. It is possible to maintain that visual experiences represent objective properties while also maintaining that they systematically *mis-represent* them, and that the degree of misrepresentation varies with con-textual factors like distance and lighting. Suppose you are watching an SUV as it moves away from you. As its distance increases, the SUV looks smaller and smaller. According to the view we are now considering, your experience continues to represent the objective size of the vehicle, but as the distance of the vehicle increases your representation of its object-ive size becomes more and more inaccurate. Thus, the idea is to explain perceptual relativity as failure to achieve accuracy in representing object-ive properties. To appreciate that this view is initially plausible, consider the fact that the constancy transformations play a role in shaping visual experience. This fact provides powerful motivation for any view which incorporates the claim that visual experiences represent objective prop-erties. After all, a constancy transformation is by definition a proced-ure that normalizes representational content by reducing the influence of contextual factors like distance and lighting on perceptual represen-tations. It is natural to regard transformations answering to this defin-ition as procedures for producing representations that do a better job than sensory inputs of keeping track of objective physical properties. But when we regard the transformations in this way, it is but a short step to the claim that the experiences they produce are representations of objective properties.

Despite its initial plausibility, reflection shows that this *misrepresenta-tion theory* of visual experience has a fatal flaw. If it was true that visual experiences represent objective properties, and also that they misrepresent such properties in ways that vary with contextual factors, then our views about the objective properties of external objects would be in constant flux. Whenever an object moved a few feet away from an observer, or even a few inches, it would be necessary for the observer to adopt a new view about the objective size of the object. Equally, a small change in the slant of an object would call for a new view about its objective shape. It is clear, however, that our views about the objective properties of external objects are much more stable than this. Generally speaking, when the contextual relationship between an object and an observer undergoes a change, the observer retains his grasp of the object's objective properties. He is not required to adopt a new view of them, or even to consider a change in his view. The misrepresentation theory must be rejected because it denies this truism. But then there must be a mistake in the reasoning that leads to the theory. What is it? The answer is that it is a mistake to infer the claim that experiences represent objective properties from the fact that the constancy transformations play a role in shaping them. This would be a legitimate inference if the transformations achieved full constancy. But since they do not, it is entirely appropriate to entertain alternative views about the representational content of visual experiences.

I turn now to the question of whether the objects that exemplify appearances are internal and mental or external and physical. My answer is that considerations having to do with the *transparency* of visual experience favor the second view. More particularly, they favor the view that the objects that exemplify appearances are "ordinary" physical objects such as tables, chairs, trees, and human bodies.

Visual experience is said to be transparent because introspection reveals no objects of visual awareness other than ordinary physical objects.[12] That is to say, when we consider our visual experience introspectively, we find no grounds for saying that awareness of ordinary objects is mediated by awareness of objects of some other kind. It is not mediated by

---

[12] The form of transparency that I mean to be discussing here is different than both of the two forms of transparency that I distinguished in Chapter 3 – Harmanian transparency, which claims that introspection provides us with no information about the intrinsic natures of perceptual experiences, but only with information about their representational characteristics, and Moorean transparency, which maintains that introspection provides us with no information either about the intrinsic natures of perceptual experiences or about their representational characteristics. The view that experience has the third form of transparency, the form that is under discussion here, can be factored into the following two claims: (i) it does not normally seem to us that we are aware of internal mental objects (such as images or sense data) when we consider perceptual experiences introspectively, and (ii) it does seem to us that we are directly aware of external physical objects in three-dimensional space.

awareness of internal mental objects, and it is not mediated by awareness of "extra-ordinary" physical objects, such as retinal images or packets of structured light in the area immediately before one's eyes. Rather, it seems that we open our eyes and ordinary objects are simply *there*. Now if appearances are properties that we are aware of in visual experience, and the only objects of visual awareness are ordinary physical objects, then it must be true that appearances are properties of ordinary objects. Surely it could not be true that we are visually aware of properties without being aware of the objects that instantiate them. In general, awareness of properties entails awareness of objects. Hence, introspection makes it reasonable to suppose that commonsense physical objects are the bearers of appearances.

It turns out, then, that while appearances are not identical with the intrinsic physical properties of ordinary physical objects, they are properties of those objects of *some* sort. Given this conclusion, it is natural to adopt the view that appearances are *relational* properties of ordinary objects. Of course, there are many kinds of property that answer to this description. To mention only two, there are relational properties that objects have in virtue of their relations to points in physical space, such as the property of subtending a visual angle of n degrees with respect to a point, and there are relational properties that objects have in virtue of causing activity of certain sorts in the visual systems of observers, such as the property of projecting an image of a certain shape onto the retina of an observer. So the view that we are now endorsing is actually quite vague. Even so, however, it substantially improves the picture of appearances that is afforded by doctrines (i)–(v) above.

I will not attempt here to say anything more definite about the nature of appearances (or *A-properties*, as I will henceforth call them). What has been said thus far provides a grasp of them that suffices for present purposes. That is, for present purposes it suffices to think of A-properties as relational, viewpoint-dependent properties of external objects that satisfy the following conditions:

(i) A-properties are properties that are encountered in perceptual experience.
(ii) Access to A-properties is unmediated and non-inferential – it is not the case that there are other properties such that we are aware of A-properties in virtue of being aware of those other properties.
(iii) A-properties vary with such contextual factors as distance, angle of view, and lighting.

(iv) A-properties are not identical with the objective physical properties of external objects.

(v) Awareness of A-properties is a general, pervasive feature of perceptual experience.

There is of course a certain redundancy in this characterization – claim (iv) follows from the thesis that A-properties are viewpoint dependent.

As will, I hope, become clear in the next section, where I put A-properties to use in explaining visual qualia, the present account of A-properties provides all that we need to know in order to understand the phenomenology of visual experience. I hasten to acknowledge, however, that it is highly desirable to know more about the nature of A-properties. After all, if the lines of thought in the foregoing sections are correct, A-properties play a very large role in visual and other forms of perception. Unfortunately, we are not in a position today to settle on any reasonably comprehensive picture of their nature. But more can be said than has been said thus far, provided that the additional claims are put forward tentatively. I will take a cautious few steps toward bringing A-properties into sharper focus in Appendix II.

5.5 VISUAL QUALIA

I will be guided in this section by Jaegwon Kim's observation that perceptual qualia "are, by definition, the ways that things look, seem, and appear to conscious observers."[13] It seems to me that this remark nicely captures the consensus about that nature of perceptual qualia that we find in the literature.

I will interpret Kim's remark as the claim that perceptual qualia are A-properties, and as implying that awareness of perceptual qualia is experiential awareness of A-properties. These views seem correct to me – that is, I hold that if we are to think of perceptual qualia and awareness of perceptual qualia at all, this is how we must think of them.

To amplify a bit, I wish to recommend a theory of visual qualia that makes the following claims:

(a) Visual qualia are A-properties – that is, relational, viewpoint-dependent properties of external objects.

(b) Our most basic form of access to visual qualia is a form of experiential awareness.

[13] Jaegwon Kim, *Philosophy of Mind*, 2nd edition (Cambridge, MA: Westview Press, 2006), p. 225.

(c) Like all other forms of awareness, this one is representational in character.

(d) Accordingly, visual qualia are governed by an appearance/reality distinction – it is necessary to distinguish between visual qualia as represented and visual qualia as they are in themselves.

Of course, these claims spell trouble for the traditional epistemological views about awareness of visual qualia – that it is a form of non-interpretive acquaintance, that is flawless and therefore utterly trustworthy, and that it provides us with a comprehensive grasp of their essential natures. And by the same token, they add detail to the objections to property dualism that we originally considered back in Chapter 4. As we saw there, the main arguments for property dualism presuppose that there is no appearance/reality distinction for awareness of qualia. Assuming that (a)–(d) are defensible, there is a rationale for denying that this is true of awareness of visual qualia. What we know of perceptual qualia is limited to what is explicitly registered by the perceptual representations that support our awareness of them. Moreover, these representations may foster beliefs about visual qualia that distort or even badly misconstrue their nature.

I will now say a few things in explanation and defense of these four doctrines.

It must be acknowledged that doctrine (a) runs counter to much, and perhaps most, of the traditional and contemporary writing about visual qualia. Qualia are supposed to be mental – that is, to be properties of psychological states. But (a) represents them as properties of external objects, albeit properties that such objects have in virtue of their relations to perceivers and/or points of view.

But this is only part of the story. While (a) seems quite odd when one first considers it, reflection shows that it is forced upon us by a variety of considerations. First, it is truistic that visual qualia are properties that are accessible to us via immediate experiential awareness. A-properties also satisfy this condition. Second, visual qualia vary with such contextual factors as distance and lighting. As we have had numerous occasions to observe in the present chapter, the same is true of A-properties. Third, since visual qualia are revealed by specifically visual experiences, it must be true that the things that exemplify them are objects of immediate visual awareness. Transparency considerations show that the objects of immediate visual awareness are external physical objects. There are other considerations that might be added to these three, but the present ones should suffice to remove any initial doubts about doctrine (a). Visual qualia are A-properties.

Doctrine (b) is, I think, embraced by everyone who is willing to talk about qualia at all, so it requires no defense, given the qualia-realism that I am presupposing here. Moreover, while doctrines (c) and (d) certainly require defense, they follow from a more general thesis that is defended at length in Chapter 3 – the thesis that all forms of awareness, including experiential awareness, have a representational structure.

As the reader will have observed, thesis (d) has an arresting consequence: it implies that there is an appearance/reality distinction that *is defined over appearances*. A-properties are appearances of external objects, and (d) tells us that it is possible to distinguish between the appearance of an A-property and the corresponding reality. Thus, according to (d), there is such a thing as the way an appearance appears to one, and also such a thing as a failure of an appearance to appear the way it actually is. These doctrines are of course radically at variance with the theory of visual appearances that is implicit in commonsense psychology, but they flow ineluctably from representational accounts of visual awareness, and it is therefore necessary to accept them.[14]

It seems, then, that while the package consisting of (a)–(d) has some surprising and counter-intuitive consequences, we should in the end feel comfortable about accepting it. One of its components (doctrine (b)) is not in need of defense, and the others are eminently defensible.

I conclude this section by observing that it is possible to draw a useful distinction between the *qualia that one is aware of* in virtue of having a perceptual experience and the *phenomenal character* of the experience. If one is aware of qualia in virtue of having a perceptual experience, it must be true that the object of awareness is actually instantiating the A-properties that one's experience attributes to it. These A-properties are the qualia. Thus, the qualia that one is aware of in virtue of having an experience

---

[14] I am presupposing here that although there is no pre-theoretical motivation for speaking of appearances of perceptual appearances, there is no conceptual incoherence in speaking this way. This presupposition seems appropriate because we distinguish in commonsense discourse between, say, a table's presenting a trapezoidal appearance and a subject's being aware of that appearance. Given this distinction, and given also that, as we know from Chapter 3 and Chapter 4, all forms of awareness are representational, it is to my mind appropriate and even natural to say that it is possible to draw an appearance/reality distinction with respect to perceptual appearances. My sense that it is appropriate is reinforced by the fact that we recognize that an object can present an appearance without a subject's being aware of the appearance, and by the fact that we recognize that a subject can have an experience *as of* an object that is presenting a certain appearance without there actually being an object that is presenting the appearance. (The latter occurs, for example, in dreams.) Incidentally, the fact that appearances are "separable" in these ways from awareness and experience distinguishes appearances from pain. It seems that pain cannot occur without the relevant subject's being aware of the pain, and that it is impossible for a subject to have an experience *as of* pain without really being in pain.

are A-properties that the relevant object actually has. On the other hand, the phenomenal character of an experience is the set of qualia that one's experience *attributes to* the object of awareness. Reflection shows that it is possible for an experience to attribute qualia to an object of awareness even though the object fails to instantiate those qualia. This would happen, for example, if an ocular disorder caused an observer to represent an object of awareness as having an A-property that is characteristic of green objects on an occasion when in fact the object was blue and was reflecting light in the way that is characteristic of blue objects. (Thus, it would happen if, as a result of some sort of a yellowing of the macula, an object looked-p green to an observer, even though it would have looked-p blue to him if he had not been suffering from the yellowing.) In a case of this sort, the experience has a certain phenomenal character but one is not aware of actual instances of the qualia that are included in the phenomenal character. There is representation of qualia but no awareness of qualia.

More generally, the phenomenal character of a perceptual experience is the set of qualia that the experience represents as instantiated by objects of awareness. In most cases, there is an actual object of awareness and one's experience attributes the qualia to that object. It can also happen, however, that there is no real object that counts as the object of awareness. In a case of this second sort, one's experience represents a set of qualia as instantiated, but it cannot be said to attribute these qualia to a real object. This is, of course, what happens in dreams and hallucinations.

5.6 SWAMPMAN

To complete my exposition and defense of this broadly representational system of ideas, I will respond to what are perhaps the best known and most fundamental objections to representational theories of perceptual qualia – the Swampman objection and the inverted spectrum objection. I will urge that both of these objections are fundamentally flawed.

As described in the standard accounts, Swampman is a human-like creature who comes into existence accidentally, as a result of quantum fluctuations of some kind, and who therefore cannot be said to have the teleological endowment that real human beings enjoy in virtue of natural selection.[15] As a special case of this general teleological deficiency,

---

[15] Donald Davidson was the first to appreciate the philosophical importance of creatures like Swampman. See his "Knowing One's Own Mind," *Proceedings and Addresses of the American Philosophical Association* 60 (1987), 441–458.

Swampman has no capacity to represent things perceptually.[16] But still, he is amazingly similar to real human beings. Indeed, we can suppose that he is a cell-for-cell duplicate of a particular human agent – an agent whom I will call "Hector." As a real human agent, Hector of course enjoys perceptual qualia, and there is a fairly stable intuition to the effect that Swampman enjoys them, too. How could he not, given that he is intrinsically just like Hector? But if it is true that Swampman is aware of perceptual qualia, then all representationalist accounts of perceptual qualia must be wrong, including the one I have formulated above. Swampman cannot be said to represent A-properties – or anything else for that matter. So awareness of perceptual qualia cannot be explained in terms of representation of A-properties.

Why exactly does it seem to us that Swampman is aware of perceptual qualia? The answer is surely that it is part of our practice as folk psychologists to be guided by behavioral and physical similarities in attributing mental states. We attribute awareness of qualia to Swampman because he is similar to someone whom we know independently to be aware of qualia. Now it is not entirely clear how to visualize the logical underpinnings of attributions of this sort. On one account, our attributional inferences are best seen as analogical in character: we are guided implicitly by the perception that creatures who are similar in many fundamental respects are likely to be similar in other fundamental respects as well. On another account, our attributional inferences should be seen as inferences to the best explanation: we are guided by a desire to make the attributions that best explain the behaviors of a creature, and also by the perception that the best explanations will be the ones that most resemble our explanations of similar behaviors by other creatures. It is not clear which of these accounts is correct, and anyway, both of the accounts suffer from vagueness. That vagueness would have to be removed before either account could be accepted as correct. But even though it is not clear how exactly to reconstruct our attributional practice, it is pretty clear that attributions are guided by similarities. This is a large part of

---

[16] Although my arguments rarely depend on it, I am presupposing in this work that at the most fundamental level, the content of perceptual representations is determined by our biological endowments, and therefore ultimately by natural selection. Accordingly, Swampman has a particular relevance to the version of representationalism I prefer. But there are other versions of representationalism that do not see perceptual content as biologically determined. This makes it possible for them to deal with the Swampman problem by simpler arguments than the ones I deploy. For an attractive version of a view of this kind, together with an explanation of how it applies to Swampman, see Michael Tye, *Consciousness, Color, and Content* (Cambridge, MA: MIT Press, 2000), Section 6.4.

the reason why we feel that Swampman must have perceptual experiences like Hector's.

Now of course, even though Swampman is exactly like Hector in point of neural organization and therefore in point of behavior, he is very different than Hector in point of history. Hector enjoyed a normal development from an embryo, but Swampman was in effect created *ex nihilo*. Accordingly, our practice of being guided by similarities in attributing mental states would provide no help with respect to the question of whether Swampman is aware of qualia if we had any reason to think that awareness of qualia depends on historical factors, such as the selectional history of an individual's species. But we are strongly inclined to think that historical factors are irrelevant to questions about qualia. Thus, we incline to the view that in the case of qualia, at any rate, the relevant similarities have to do with intrinsic properties. If agents are intrinsically the same in other respects, they will be aware of the same qualia. Or so we are inclined to think.

We now have an explanation of why we feel confident that Swampman is aware of perceptual qualia, but we are not yet in a position to assess the validity of the perception. Before we can take its measure, we must also have some grasp of why it seems to us that the qualitative nature of a perceptual experience is intrinsic, in the sense that it is independent of the historical record. But we can, I think, derive an answer to this question from our earlier reflections concerning our introspective understanding of experiential awareness. As we have seen on a number of earlier occasions, the representational nature of awareness of qualia is not revealed by introspection. On the contrary, awareness of qualia is transparent to introspection: when we consider it reflectively, we are aware only of the qualia that serve as the objects of awareness, not of the internal structure of the relation that we bear to these qualia. By the same token, introspection discloses nothing that would suggest that awareness of qualia depends on selectional history. Experiential awareness seems to us to owe nothing to history because it seems to be perfectly simple, and therefore complete in itself.

Assuming that this explanation of why awareness of qualia seems to us to be independent of selectional history is correct, we are in a position to see what is wrong with the perception that Swampman resembles Hector in being aware of perceptual qualia. This perception depends ultimately on the fact that introspection does not attribute a representational structure to perceptual consciousness. As we have already observed, it is much better to view this fact as evidence of the limitations of introspection than as a reason for doubting that perceptual consciousness is representational. We know that representations are constitutively involved in all awareness, and therefore in perceptual consciousness. It follows directly from this fact that if introspection fails to reveal representations when it is directed on perceptual consciousness, then introspection has a blind spot. It does not reveal the whole truth about the phenomena in its domain.

It turns out, then, that we do not have a good reason to believe that Swampman is aware of perceptual qualia. To be sure, Swampman has states that *encode information about qualia*. To see this, observe first that since Hector has states that represent A-properties, he can be said to have states that encode information about such properties. (Generally speaking, if a state represents a property, then under normal conditions it covaries with that property, and therefore encodes information about it.) Accordingly, Hector can be said to have states that encode information about qualia. Second, observe that since Swampman stands in the same causal relations to the world as Hector, he stands in the same informational relations to A-properties, and therefore to qualia. So we should ask: Does the fact that Swampman registers information about qualia give us a reason to say that he is aware of them?

No. Encoding information about a set of properties does not by itself amount to awareness. Many things can be said to encode information about qualia, or at least to bear such information. For example, the behaviors that are shaped by states of awareness of qualia can be said to bear information about them. Reflection shows that these purely informational relationships have no relevance to the main question that is at issue in metaphysical discussions of qualia, which is whether qualia pose a significant threat to views of the Universe that represent it as comparatively simple and unified. The arguments that promote dualism depend crucially on intuitions about *awareness* of qualia. Thus, for example, they tend to presuppose that if qualia had a physical nature, our immediate experiential awareness of them would reveal that fact. There are no intuitions about states that encode information about qualia that can be substituted for these intuitions about awareness. Informational relations are just a species of causal relations. One cannot infer anything about the ultimate nature of a state from the fact that it stands in a causal relation to another state.

It can seem that the line of thought we have been following misses the point. Thus, it is natural to think that there is such a thing as how things are *for* Swampman, or from the perspective of Swampman, and that how things are *for* Swampman must be exactly the same as how things are *for* Hector. In other words, it is natural to suppose that if God could successively adopt the perspective of Swampman and the perspective of Hector, he would not be able to discriminate between them. It can seem that it misses the point of this intuition to say simply that there is no such thing as how things are *for* Swampman, or from Swampman's perspective, because Swampman cannot appropriately be said to be aware of anything. But reflection shows that it does not miss the point. It is a crucial component of the intuition that Swampman has a perspective – otherwise, how could God occupy his perspective? Moreover, it is a crucial presupposition of the intuition that having a perspective comes to something more than processing information about certain complex properties. If having a perspective came to no more than processing information about certain properties, then awareness of qualia would never have been thought to pose substantial metaphysical problems.

To be sure, the intuition dies hard, for it is encouraged by introspection and folk psychology, which tends on the whole to support the view that awareness of qualia is independent of representation, and is therefore the kind of thing that can supervene, whether causally or metaphysically, on intrinsic properties of neural states. As we have seen, however, this view about awareness of qualia is deeply misguided. Moreover, when the failings of the view are appreciated, and it is replaced by a more adequate picture, the intuition tends to dissipate, and the sense that Swampman *must* have experience of qualia tends to dissipate with it.

To summarize: Opponents of representationalist accounts of awareness of qualia often present Swampman as a kind of counterexample, claiming that he is aware of qualia but lacks the capacity to form and deploy representations. In responding to this view, I have allowed, in effect, that it would be reasonable to say that Swampman *possesses* qualia (for his senses can register A-properties and his perceptual systems can process information about them), but I have maintained there is no good reason to say that he is *aware of* qualia. The intuition that he is aware of qualia can be fully and plausibly explained away. Further, I have urged that the fact that Swampman possesses qualia is of little philosophical significance. Opponents of representationalism have various reasons for objecting to it, but the most important of these is that, as we have seen, it can be used to undercut the case for property dualism. More specifically, it can be used to show that awareness of qualia could fail to reveal their true nature, just as perceptual awareness of water fails to reveal its molecular structure. Hence, any philosophical significance that Swampman might be thought to have is due to the intuition that he has non-representational awareness of qualia. Once this intuition is discredited, the importance of Swampman dissipates. Since he is not aware of qualia, the fact that he possesses them has no tendency to reinstate the case for property dualism.[17]

5.7   EXPOSITION OF THE INVERTED SPECTRUM ARGUMENT

I turn now to the inverted spectrum objection. I will begin by stating the objection, and will then argue that it suffers from much the same flaw as the Swampman objection. Like the Swapman objection, I will suggest, it presupposes that awareness of qualia depends only on intrinsic proper- ties of the agent's current perceptual processing. This presupposition is initially appealing, but the motivation for it does not withstand careful scrutiny. It must be rejected.

The argument purports to show that it is possible to hold the represen- tational content of experience fixed while allowing the qualitative nature of experience to vary.

Let Normal be a normal human subject. Suppose that B is the brain state Normal is in when he sees something red under normal conditions, and that B^* is the brain state he is in when he sees something green under nor- mal conditions. Suppose further that Invert is an observer who belongs to a different species than Normal. The pathways leading from Invert's retinas to Invert's color processing centers are inverted relative to Normal's path- ways, but in all other respects, Invert's visual system is exactly the same as Normal's. It follows from these initial assumptions that the visual processing that red objects occasion in Normal is exactly the same, at all points after the point of inversion, as the visual processing that green objects occasion in Invert. Also, the visual processing that green objects occasion in Normal is exactly the same, at all points after the point of inversion, as the visual processing that red objects occasion in Invert. Thus, B is the brain state that Invert is in when he sees a green object under normal conditions, and B^* is the brain state he is in when he sees a red object under normal conditions.

---

[17] In addition to allowing that Swampman *possesses* qualia, I have in effect allowed that there is infor- mation about his qualia in the upper reaches of his visual system, and also in other higher level parts of his brain, including the parts that are associated in normal human beings with awareness and cognition. Perhaps, then, there is a sense in which it is true to say that Swampman is a *subject* who possesses information about his qualia. If so, can this claim be used to motivate any philosophical doctrines? In particular, can it be used to provide motivation for property dualism? No. The fact that a subject stands in informational relations to an item has in itself no tendency to show that the subject has a full cognitive grasp of the item's essential nature, or even that the subject is apprised of part of its essence. To see this, observe that we possess a great deal of perceptually acquired infor- mation about water. This information provides no insight into water's essential nature.

Since Normal is a normal human subject, it must be true that red objects look-p red to him when he sees them under normal conditions, for it holds as a general rule that red objects look-p red to normal human observers when they are seen in normal conditions. In combination with this fact, our assumptions entail that when Normal is in brain state B, the object he is seeing looks-p red to him. For similar reasons, we also know that green objects look-p green to Normal when he sees them under normal conditions, and that when Normal is in brain state B^*, the object he is seeing looks-p green to him.

Suppose now that both Normal and Invert are looking at a red object, x, under normal conditions, with the result that Normal is in B and Invert is in B^*. It must be true that x looks-p red to Normal. Moreover, since the phenomenal character of a visual experience is determined by how things look-p when one is having the experience, it must also be true that Normal is aware of reddish visual qualia. How does x look-p to Invert? We have the following facts:

Invert is in brain state B^*.
When Normal is in B^*, things look-p green to him.

It appears to follow from these facts that x looks-p green to Invert. The reason, I suggest, is that we find the following supervenience principle extremely plausible:

(SP) How an object looks-p to an observer is determined by the brain state that the observer is in when he/she is seeing the object.

It follows from (SP) that if an object causes two observers to be in the same high level visual state, then the object looks-p the same way to the observers. My suggestion, then, is that we accept (SP), and that since we do, it seems to us that x looks-p green to Invert, and also that Invert is aware of greenish visual qualia in virtue of seeing x.

Let us turn now to consider the representational contents of B and B^*. We have assumed that red things cause Normal to be in B and that they cause Invert to be in B^*, provided that they are seen under normal conditions. But we have also made a more far reaching assumption about the relationship between Normal's visual system and Invert's visual system. We have supposed that the two visual systems are just alike except that in Invert's system the wires leading from cones to later processing centers are inverted. This assumption entails that *all* of the external conditions that cause Normal to be in B cause Invert to be in B^*, and that *all* of the external conditions that cause Invert to be in B^* cause Normal to be in B. Moreover, we can easily assume that it has always been thus – that all through the evolutionary histories of the species to which Normal and Invert belong, the conditions that caused Normal's ancestors to be in B were the same as the conditions that caused Invert's ancestors to be in B^*. Another way of putting this is to say that the information that B encoded throughout the history of Normal's species is the same as the information that B^* encoded throughout the history of Invert's species. Now it is very plausible that the representational content of a visual state is determined by the information that the state encoded during the portion of evolutionary history when the relevant visual system was being shaped by selective pressures. Thus, our current assumptions appear to entail that B has the same representational content in Normal as B^* has in Invert. Moreover, similar assumptions and similar reasoning lead to the conclusion that B^* has the same representational content in Normal as B has in Invert.

We have now arrived at the following results: (i) x looks-p red to Normal and Normal is therefore aware of reddish qualia when he sees x; (ii) x looks-p green to Invert and Invert is therefore aware of greenish qualia when he sees x; and (iii) the representational content of Normal's current visual state is the same as the content of Invert's current state. It follows that qualia are independent of representational content: it is possible to fix the relevant representational facts without thereby fixing the relevant qualitative facts.

5.8 AN OBJECTION TO THE ARGUMENT

What should a representationalist do when he encounters this argument? Roll over and die? No. Suppose it is true that when an object looks-p a certain way to an observer, the observer is aware of the object as having a certain A-appearance. Now awareness involves representations: to be aware of a property P, one must token a representation of P. It follows that principle (L) is true:

(L) If an object looks-p a certain way to an observer, the observer is representing the object as having a certain property.

This result calls the supervenience principle (SP) into question. In effect, the supervenience principle says that how an object looks-p to one depends exclusively on the brain state one is in – questions about the representational content of the brain state are irrelevant. This clearly conflicts with principle (L).

It appears, then, that if it is true that one is representing an appearance property when an object looks-p a certain way to one, then (SP) is false. Since we know on independent grounds that one is representing an appearance property when an object looks-p a certain way to one, we are entitled to reject (SP), and with it the inverted spectrum argument. If (SP) is false, why does it seem so plausible? Part of the answer is of course that we know that it is possible to manipulate facts of the form *x looks-p F to y* by manipulating a subject's brain state; but this can't be the full explanation, because we know that it is possible, for example, to manipulate what someone believes by manipulating the brain, and we have no tendency to think that beliefs are determined exclusively by brain states. Evidently, the answer also has something to do with the fact that it is not immediately clear to us that facts of the form *x looks-p F to y* constitutively involve states that have representational content. A full answer must invoke the fact that the representational nature of visual perception is not manifest to us from the vantage point provided by introspection and commonsense psychology.

5.9   SUMMARY

We began by observing that considerations having to do with perceptual relativity appear to mandate the doctrine that we are generally aware of appearances in visual experience. We then agreed that appearance properties are best construed as relational, viewpoint-dependent properties of external objects. Our next step was to observe that, despite some initial intuitions to the contrary, it is all things considered best to identify visual qualia with appearance properties, and to adopt a representational account of awareness of visual qualia. Finally, we considered the objections to representational accounts of visual qualia that are most prominent in the literature. We were in the end able to see that both objections are undermined by flaws in the picture of awareness that is encouraged by introspection and folk psychology.

APPENDIX I

In Section 5.3 I described two reasons for doubting that we are aware of A-properties in the normal course of things. One of these reasons was an argument that can be formulated as follows:

> *First premise*: We rarely attend to A-properties.
> *Second premise*: Awareness of A-properties requires attention.
> *Conclusion*: We are rarely aware of A-properties.

This argument, which I will call *Argument A*, has a certain intuitive appeal. Moreover, as we observed, it seems that vision scientists often embrace the argument, or something like it, maintaining that the first premise has been confirmed by recent experimental work.

I objected to the conclusion of Argument A in Section 5.3, sketching four lines of thought which indicate that awareness of A-properties is the norm. As I see it, these lines of thought make a very strong case for my opposing view. More needs to be said, however, for while the four lines of thought provide grounds for rejecting the conclusion, they do nothing to undercut the motivation for the conclusion that is supplied by the premises. That is, they contradict the conclusion without explaining what is wrong with the rationale that leads people to embrace it. I will try to fill this lacuna in the present appendix.

What exactly are the considerations that lead people to accept the first premise? I think that the motivation for it is largely introspective. Thus, it seems that there is an introspectively discriminable type of mental state that it is natural to call *attending to an A-property*. When one is in a state of this type, one explicitly notes or recognizes that an object has a particular A-property – that is, one explicitly subsumes the object under a categorical representation of the property. In doing so, one confers a certain cognitive salience on the property, thereby enabling thoughts and various other attitudes that are focused on it (including, for example, judgments that compare the property to the A-properties of other objects). We have all been in states of this sort, and we all know that such states are comparatively rare, occurring only in special circumstances. These circumstances principally include ones in which one has undertaken a special task, such as drawing an object, that is specifically focused on A-properties, and ones in which the A-properties of an object diverge so radically from the norm that one's attention is grabbed by them. For examples of this sort of radical divergence, see Figures 5.1 and 5.2 on the next page.

It is, of course, highly unusual for feet to appear as large in relation to a person's body as the feet do in Figure 5.1, and for a surface that is uniform in lightness to appear as variegated as the chairs do in Figure 5.2.

I wish to claim, then, that introspection reveals that there is a form of awareness of A-properties that is clearly attentive in nature, and also that introspection also reveals that this form of awareness occurs only when there are unusual task demands or the object of awareness is presented in an unusual way. In short, as I see it, introspection shows that the first premise of the foregoing argument is correct.

What about the second premise of Argument A? What are the grounds for thinking that awareness of A-properties requires attention? It seems that there are grounds of two kinds – introspective and experimental. The introspective motivation has to do with the impression of novelty

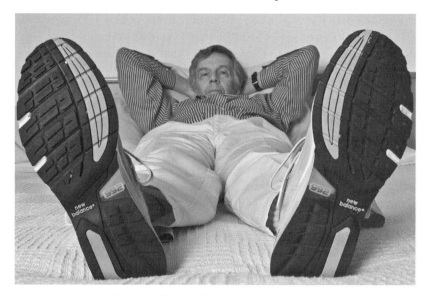

Figure 5.1 Radical Divergence: Example A.

Figure 5.2 Radical Divergence: Example B.

that tends to accompany attending to A-properties. When one attends to an A-property, one feels that one is getting *new* information about the object. Thus, one is often surprised when one comes to appreciate how large one's foot looks-p in relation to a desk that is located across the room, or when one comes to appreciate how trapezoidal a table looks-p when one sees it from one end. But if one is surprised when one attends to an A-property, then, it seems, it must be true that attention is providing one with new information about the object. And if attention provides one with new information about the object, then it must be true that attention is a necessary condition of acquiring information of that sort. This implies that the second premise of the foregoing argument is true. As for the experimental evidence for the premise, it derives from work on such phenomena as blindsight, inattentional blindness, and the attentional blink.[18] Subjects in the relevant experiments appear to be unaware of objects to which they are not attending. Taking this apparent lack of awareness at face value, many vision scientists have concluded that attention is required for awareness. The second premise is of course a special case of this more general claim.

To begin with the introspective motivation for the second premise, I wish to claim that it involves a hasty and inaccurate interpretation of what is going on when one attends to an A-property. Suppose that a certain subject S is trying to draw a distant building. Suppose that S has often seen the building from the same distance, but that she has never before explicitly noted its A-size. She may be quite surprised by how small the building looks-p to her, and this reaction may lead her to judge that she is getting new information about the building – that she is aware of its A-size for the first time. But now suppose that S starts to switch back and forth between attending to the A-size of the building and looking at the building in a different way – for the sake of definiteness, let us suppose, more particularly, that she alternates between attending to the building's A-size and attending to its objective physical size. Our subject S will eventually come to feel, I suggest, that that there is a very substantial continuity between what she is experientially aware of when she attends to the A-size and what she is experientially aware of when she attends to the objective size. That is, she will come to appreciate that the experiential phenomenology associated with the first mode of awareness is essentially the same as the phenomenology associated with the second mode. (This is another way of stating the main point of the first of the four arguments I presented in Section 5.3.) Further, when she recognizes the continuity, she will be inclined to withdraw her earlier judgment that she was aware of new information, and to replace it with the judgment that she was aware of old information in a new way. She had often before been aware of the A-size of the building, she will think, but had never explicitly noted its A-size. Further, she will think that it was this new take on old information that gave rise to her initial sense of novelty.

Why do impressions of novelty tend to accompany attentive awareness of A-properties? The answer has three parts. First, we do not normally attend explicitly to A-properties. When we attend to the properties of an object, we are much more likely to attend to its objective physical properties. Second, the information that becomes salient when we attend to the former properties is often quite different in character than the information that becomes salient when we attend to the latter properties. Objects that are in fact very large can look-p quite small, and objects that are in fact very small can look-p quite large. And third, it is the information that we acquire by attending to properties that provides the basis for the perceptual stereotypes or profiles that we use in thinking about objects. That is to say, when we are concerned to predict the behavior of an object, or to compare it to other objects, or to perform any one of a number of other cognitive tasks with respect to it, we tend to rely heavily on a perceptual profile of the object that derives from past episodes of attentive awareness. Now when we combine these three observations, we find that they provide an explanation of why attending to an A-property can occasion an impression of novelty; for they imply that when we attend to A-properties, we are often aware of properties that are quite different than the ones that figure in our normal ways of thinking about objects.

This brings us to the question of whether recent experimental work on phenomena like change-blindness, inattentional blindness, and the attentional blink makes it plausible that attention is required for awareness. Vision scientists are often inclined to think that this question should be answered in the affirmative. It should be noted, however, that this is by no means the only possible interpretation,[19] and also that there are other experimental data which appear to point in a quite different direction.[20] Moreover, what is most important for our purposes here, even if it is granted for the sake of argument that attention is required for perceptual awareness of objects (and parts of objects), it can still be quite reasonable to maintain that it is

[19] See, e.g., Jeremy M. Wolfe, "Inattentional Amnesia," in Veronika Coltheart (ed.), *Fleeting Memories* (Cambridge, MA: MIT Press, 1997), pp. 71–94.
[20] Michael Tye, "Content, Richness, and Fineness of Grain," in Tamar Szabó Gendler and John Hawthorne, *Perceptual Experience* (Oxford: Oxford University Press, 2006), pp. 504–530.

possible to be aware of A-properties without attending to them. At least, it can be quite reasonable to maintain this if one distinguishes between *implicitly* attending to A-properties and *explicitly* attending to them. To appreciate this point, consider a case in which a subject is attending to a distant SUV. In this case, I wish to claim, the SUV is presented to the subject *by* certain of its A-properties. That is to say, the subject's awareness of the SUV is partially constituted by awareness of its A-properties. Now it might be said to follow from this characterization of the subject that he is attending to certain of the SUV's A-properties. After all, it has been stipulated that the subject is attending to the SUV, and also that awareness of A-properties is partially constitutive of this attentive awareness. Perhaps surprisingly, I do not disagree with this observation – I think it is possible to understand it in such a way that it counts as true. But in the case I am asking you to imagine (which, by the way, I take to represent the norm), the subject does not *explicitly* attend to any of the SUV's A-properties. That is to say, his visual system does not form a separate categorical representation of an A-property and predicate it of the independently identified object. Hence, the A-properties of the object have no particular cognitive salience – their role is simply to present the SUV to the subject. In other words, the subject's awareness of them has none of the usual effects of explicit, focal attention. He attends to them only in the sense that he attends to an object that is presented by them. If he can be said to attend explicitly to any of the SUV's properties, the properties in question will most likely be objective physical properties, such as intrinsic shape and intrinsic size.

To summarize: The first premise of Argument A appears to receive strong support from introspection, but the motivation for the second premise evaporates under scrutiny. There are no compelling reasons for thinking that awareness of A-properties requires a form of attention that is in any sense special or rare. Hence, it is possible to reject the conclusion of the argument with impunity. To put the point in positive terms, we can embrace the view that awareness of A-properties is a general condition of perception without coming into conflict either with introspection or with vision science.

APPENDIX II

In Section 5.4 we adopted the view that A-properties are relational, viewpoint-dependent properties of external objects that satisfy the following conditions:

(i) A-properties are properties that are encountered in perceptual experience.

(ii) Access to A-properties is unmediated and non-inferential – it is not the case that there are other properties such that we are aware of A-properties in virtue of being aware of those other properties.

(iii) A-properties vary with such contextual factors as distance, angle of view, and lighting.

(iv) A-properties are not identical with the objective physical properties of external objects.

(v) Awareness of A-properties is a general, pervasive feature of perceptual experience.

This account of A-properties is certainly better than no account at all, but as we noticed at the time, it leaves many important questions about the nature of A-properties open. I will propose tentative answers to some of these questions in the present appendix.

When one considers the relational properties that seem initially to be good candidates for the role of A-properties, one will very likely be drawn – initially, at least – to the view that visual angles (defined with reference to the nodal point of the lens of the observer's eye) are especially strong candidates for the role of size appearances, and to the view that angular shapes are especially strong candidates for the role of shape appearances. (The angular shape of an object can for present purposes be identified with the set of all visual angles that are subtended by pairs of points on the boundary of the object's facing surface.) Angular properties are properties of ordinary physical objects, and it is clear that they vary with contextual factors. Moreover, they are known to figure in mathematical laws linking contextual factors such as distance to the objective sizes and objective shapes of external objects.[21] Because of these laws, an agent who has a firm cognitive grasp of angular properties might be able to use them to arrive at valuable conclusions about the objective world. Accordingly, it is plausible that the visual system represents angular properties at some level or other.[22] The present proposal simply makes this

---

[21] A good source is Palmer, *Vision Science*, pp. 232–3 and p. 321. There is a more extensive discussion of some of the laws governing angles in Robert Schwartz, *Vision* (Oxford: Blackwell, 1994), Chapter 2.

[22] A qualification. Angular properties provide a prima facie adequate foundation for explaining A-sizes, and also for explaining *certain aspects* of A-shapes. More particularly, they provide a prima facie adequate basis for explaining the aspects of A-shapes that might be called *silhouette appearances* (that is, the aspects that have to do with the way that *external boundaries* of facing surfaces look to an observer). But even when the matter is considered prima facie, there is little temptation to suppose that they provide an adequate basis for explaining three-dimensional shape-appearances. Three-dimensional shape-appearances are much more complex than silhouette appearances in that they involve the concavities and convexities of

plausible doctrine more definite by claiming that the level of experience is the level at which angular properties are represented.[23]

Unfortunately, while this proposal is characterized by simplicity, elegance, and explanatory power, it seems that we have no choice but to reject it. Size appearances share important properties with angular sizes. Most notably, perhaps, they decrease with increases in distance, just as angular sizes do. But apparent sizes are not proportional to angular sizes. Generally speaking, the size appearances that an object presents at different distances are more similar to one another than the corresponding angular sizes. Thus, when the distance of an object from an observer is doubled, the angular size of the object is decreased by half. But the change in apparent size is much less than that. Especially at close ranges, the rate of change in the size of an object as it moves away from you is significantly less than the rate of change in its angular size.

The reader can appreciate the truth of this remark by performing a few experiments. Hold your right hand a foot away from your face and your left hand at a distance of two feet. Does your left hand appear to be half as big as your right hand? No. Careful observation will reveal that your right hand looks bigger than your left, but the difference in apparent size is quite small. Now arrange three pens of the same size on a table before you, placing the first one at a distance of one foot, the second at a distance of two feet, and the third at a distance of four feet. Does the second pen appear to you to be half as big as the first? No. Does the third appear to you to be one fourth as big? No. Here the difference

---

the facing surface. As David Bennett has emphasized in recent work (see his "Phenomenal Shape Experiences, Shape Appearance Properties, and Shape Constancy," typescript, Brown University, 2008), it seems likely that a more elaborate explanatory framework is needed to account for them.

[23] There is a closely related proposal that should be mentioned. According to this second proposal, the A-size of an object is identical, not with the property of subtending a certain visual angle, but rather with a property of the form *projecting a retinal image of such and such a size*, and the A-shape of an object is identical, not with an angular property, but rather with a property of the form *projecting a retinal image of such and such a shape*. This proposal is equivalent to the angular properties proposal in the sense that it is possible to recover the size of a retinal projection uniquely from the corresponding angular size (and conversely), and it is possible to recover the shape of a retinal projection uniquely from the corresponding angular shape (and conversely). But the properties that figure in the angular properties proposal are all simpler (because more mathematical) than properties of the forms *projecting a retinal image of such and such a size* and *projecting a retinal image of such and such a shape*. (Note that the latter properties involve causal relations between external objects and retinal images.) Accordingly, it is easier to think about them, and it is also easier to see how the visual system might acquire the ability to represent them. This is why I give preference to the angular properties proposal in the text.

between the apparent size of the first pen and the apparent size of the second will be readily apparent, but the third pen will not appear tiny in relation to the first.

What is being claimed here about apparent sizes applies to apparent shapes as well. Differences in apparent shapes are not proportional to differences in angular shapes. Thus, for example, as a circular disk is rotated in depth, its apparent shape changes more slowly than its angular shape.

The fact that A-properties change at a very slow rate, at least as compared with angular properties, is due to constancy transformations that are applied prior to the formation of experiential representations.[24] One plausible suggestion about those transformations is that they take representations of angular properties as inputs, together with information of other kinds, and produce experiential representations as outputs. Inevitably, the outputs do not register proportions among the angular properties that serve as inputs.

Could it be true that experiential representations represent angular properties but systematically distort their nature? Could this be a case of systematic *misrepresentation*? Not if it is true, as seems quite plausible, that accurate representations of angular properties are among the inputs to the transformations that produce experiential representations. It is a fundamental tenet of vision science that visual processing *improves* the cognitive prospects of the organism. It does not worsen those prospects. But visual processing that took accurate representations of angular properties as inputs and delivered systematically distorted representations of angular properties as outputs *would* worsen the cognitive prospects of the organism. The visual system would be closer to the truth in the earlier stages of processing than at the later stages.

I regard this argument as assigning a burden of proof, not as a conclusive objection. There is reason to believe that systematic misrepresentation does occur at certain points in visual processing.[25] My point is that systematic misrepresentation of the sort that involves a *worsening* of cognitive prospects cannot be the norm. The burden of proof is on someone who claims that it occurs at a particular point.

The failure of the angular properties hypothesis is disappointing, but there is a valuable lesson that can be learned from its downfall. It is plausible, we have found, that we become aware of appearances of size and shape as a result of processes that take representations of angular properties as

---

[24] See Palmer, *Vision Science*, pp. 315–322, pp. 327–332.
[25] See e.g., Dennis R. Proffitt, Mukul Bhalla, Rich Gossweiler, and Jonathan Midgett, "Perceiving Geographical Slant," *Psychonomic Bulletin and Review* 2 (1995), 409–428.

inputs and subject them to constancy transformations. If this plausible view is correct, then it is natural to suppose that appearances are the values that are obtained when certain computable functions are applied to angular properties (together with various other quantities). It seems that the best available view of appearances is that they are properties that answer to this description. Unfortunately, since vision science has yet to describe the relevant transformations in detail, we cannot at present say more about appearances. For the present the best that can be said is just that *there exist* computable functions of angular sizes and angular shapes such that (i) the functions are in effect constancy transformations, (ii) they each take a number of arguments in addition to angular sizes and angular shapes, all of which are relevant to computing constancies, (iii) their values fall short of being genuine constancies, and (iv) their values are A-sizes and A-shapes.

The view that I am recommending here is a version of the more general view that *all* appearances are properties that show the influence of constancy transformations, but that they fall short of the degree of constancy that would make it appropriate to view them as objective properties. This more general view has been present in the literature for some time. Perhaps the earliest detailed formulation of it occurs in two papers by R. H. Thouless that appeared in 1931.[26] These papers are still enlightening to read. Here is what Thouless says about apparent sizes:

Here also it is to be noted that we are dealing not with an absolute constancy of phenomenal size but with a tendency to constancy. At no distance from the observer is it true to say that changing distance of the object makes no difference to phenomenal size. As the distance of an object changes, its phenomenal size changes, whether the object be far or near. It changes, however, less rapidly than does the size of the retinal image. The tendency to constancy is shown by the amount of change being a compromise between the changing size of the peripheral stimulus and the unchanging "real" size of the object.[27]

And here is what he says about apparent shapes:

If a subject is shown an inclined circle and is asked to select from a number of figures the one which represents the shape seen by him, he chooses without hesitation an ellipse. This ellipse, however, is widely different from the one which represents the shape of the inclined circle indicated by the laws of perspective, being much nearer to the circular form. The subject sees an inclined figure

[26] See Robert Thouless, "Phenomenal Regression to the Real Object I," *Journal of Psychology* 21 (1931), 339–359; and Robert Thouless, "Phenomenal Regression to the Real Object II," *Journal of Psychology* 22 (1931), 20–30.
[27] Thouless, "Phenomenal Regression to the Real Object I," 353.

neither in its "real" shape nor in the shape which is its perspective projection but as a compromise between them.[28]

These conclusions have been amply confirmed by later work.[29]

Because of Thouless's early and vigorous advocacy of a view that is closely related to the one I recommend, it is natural to express the latter view by saying that appearances are *Thouless properties* of ordinary physical objects.

In combination with views defended earlier in the present chapter, the claim that A-properties are Thouless properties entails that perceptual experience is generally and systematically concerned with Thouless properties. Now if this is so, there must be a reason *why* it is so. That is, it must be somehow cognitively beneficial for us to represent Thouless properties. What might the relevant benefits be? This is, I believe, a difficult question. It will be some time till cognitive science is able to answer it in a definite and final way. But it seems relevant that experiential representations play a large role in guiding present actions and planning future ones. If we are to act and plan in ways that serve our goals, and we are to do so on the basis of what experience tells us, then experience must make it possible for us to form more or less accurate beliefs about questions of two sorts – questions concerning the objective physical properties of external objects, and questions concerning the ways in which external objects are disposed in relation to us (that is, questions concerning how far away they are, questions concerning how they are slanted in relation to us, questions concerning how they are moving in relation to us, and so on). It seems that Thouless properties can simultaneously help us to answer questions of both kinds. Thus, since Thouless properties do a better job than angular properties of tracking objective physical properties, they provide a better platform than angular properties for inferences about the objective layout of the situation in which one's actions will take place. The inferences will be more rapid, and will also have more accurate results, than would otherwise be the case. But also, since they respect some of the features of angular properties, Thouless properties provide a platform for quick and reliable inferences to views about our egocentric relations to objects. Thus, for example, since they respect *orderings* of angular sizes (though not *proportions* of such sizes), they make it possible for us to arrive at roughly accurate views about distance relationships among objects that we know independently to be similar in objective size. In sum, by representing Thouless properties, we obtain benefits that would otherwise be achieved

[28] *Ibid.*, 339.   [29] For discussion see the works cited in note 11.

only by independently representing properties of two kinds – objective physical properties and angular properties. Mother Nature has killed two birds with one stone.

It appears, then, that there is much to recommend the idea that A-properties are Thouless properties.[30] But there is also a ground for concern. Thouless properties are properties that are obtained by applying certain constancy transformations to properties like angular size and angular shape. Accordingly, they are properties that are obtained by applying constancy transformations to properties that are in an important sense external to the agent. (From one perspective, it is natural to think that the external world extends to the retina but no farther.) But if Thouless properties are transformations of external properties, it is natural to suppose that they are themselves external. Accordingly, it seems that we ought to adopt this view.

Now if A-properties are Thouless properties, the externality of Thouless properties implies that A-properties are external. There are, however, considerations that have suggested to some investigators that A-properties should be seen as involving or depending constitutively on internal factors. Thus, how an object looks-p to an observer clearly depends systematically on attention, and also on the degree to which internal processing agencies have adapted to stimuli of a certain sort. Attention and adaptation are internal factors. Moreover, how something looks-p to an observer can be influenced by a range of more sporadic internal factors, such as disease and the effects of drugs. Given that how something looks-p to an observer depends on internal factors of these sorts, should we perhaps suppose that the truth-makers for propositions of the form "x looks-p F to y" include internal phenomena of some sort? To be a bit more specific, should we suppose that the A-properties that figure in the truth-makers are properties of the form *being an external object that is causing an internal state of the observer's visual system that has intrinsic property P*?

Although this move has seemed natural to some writers, it seems to me to be largely unmotivated. The truth-makers for propositions of the form "x looks-p F to y" are facts that consist of states of awareness and also of A-properties. Now on a representational theory of awareness, the

---

[30] A qualification is needed here – a qualification that is similar to the one that was needed in connection with the proposal that A-properties are identical with angular properties. (See note 21.) Thouless properties may well provide an adequate foundation for explaining A-sizes, and also for explaining those aspects of A-shapes that have to do with the external boundaries of facing surfaces. But they probably do not provide an adequate basis for explaining three-dimensional shape-appearances. Unlike those aspects of shape-appearances that have to do with external boundaries, 3-D shape-appearances involve the concavities and convexities. It seems likely that a more elaborate explanatory framework is needed to account for them.

states of awareness that figure in facts of the given sort are partially constituted by representations, and the A-properties that serve as objects
of awareness are represented by those representations. Accordingly, if
we are to say that certain "internal" properties figure in the facts, we
must show that they are represented by the representations in question.
That is, we must show that the properties are involved in the representations' contents. So the question arises: Does the fact that how things
look-p to an observer depends on such internal factors as attention and
adaptation provide us with a reason to think that internal properties are
represented by the relevant representations? Reflection shows, I suggest,
that the answer should be "no." Attention and adaptation are internal
factors, and they play a role in determining what representations the
visual system is producing at a given time. But the fact that a representation is produced by internal factors of a certain kind has no tendency
to show that properties of such factors figure in the *representational content* of the representation. In general, it is a mistake to draw inferences
concerning the content of a representation from information about its
etiology.[31]

---

[31] What about A-colors? Are they external? Provided that one views properties of retinal images as
external, it is arguable the answer is "yes." Thus, for example, we have reason to believe that when
an object looks-p red to an observer, the object is projecting a retinal image that involves appreci-
ably more activity in long wavelength cones than in middle wavelength cones, and about the same
amount of activity in short wavelength cones as in long wavelength cones and middle wavelength
cones combined. Let us say that if an object projects a retinal image of this sort, it has a *red projection
property*. Clearly, given that retinal properties count as external, red projection properties count as
external, too. Now red projection properties are not A-colors, for as Thouless pointed out, A-colors
reflect the influence of constancy transformations. But it seems that we can explain A-colors in terms
of color projection properties. It seems, for example, that we can say that an object counts as A-red
if (i) it has a red projection property, (ii) appropriate constancy transformations have been applied to
this property, and (iii) the output of the transformations falls within a certain range.

On this account, it seems natural to see red appearance properties as external, though of course a
great many internal agencies are involved in the processes by which subjects become aware of such
properties.

If we should accept an account of A-colors based on projection properties, considerations of
uniformity would provide motivation for embracing an account of A-sizes and A-shapes that was
based on certain related projection properties. Thus, for example, there would be motivation for
saying that an object counts as A-large if (i) it is projecting an image of size S on the retina, (ii)
appropriate constancy transformations have been applied to S, and (iii) the resulting quantity is
comparatively large. In general, on this new account, the sizes and shapes of retinal projections
would play the role of angular sizes and angular shapes in the Thouless-properties proposal –
that is, as inputs to the constancy transformations.

All things being equal, I prefer accounts that invoke angular properties to accounts that invoke
projection properties, for the former tend to be simpler and more elegant than the latter. But I can
appreciate the desirability of achieving uniformity, and it is clear that, depending on what theory
of A-colors we wind up with, uniformity might come into play here. (For additional discussion of
projection properties, see note 23.)

CHAPTER 6

Ouch!

The paradox of pain*

6.1 APPEARANCE AND REALITY

It is generally possible to distinguish between the appearance of an empirical phenomenon and the corresponding reality. Moreover, generally speaking, the appearance of an empirical phenomenon is ontologically and nomologically independent of the corresponding reality: it is possible for the phenomenon to exist without its appearing to anyone that it exists, and it is possible for it to appear to exist without its actually existing. It is remarkable, therefore, that our thought and talk about bodily sensations presupposes that the appearance of a bodily sensation is linked indissolubly to the sensation itself. This is true, in particular, of our thought and talk about pain. Thus, we presuppose that the following principles are valid:

(A) If x is in pain, then it seems to x that x is in pain, in the sense that x has an experiential ground for judging that x is in pain.

(B) If it seems to x that x is in pain, in the sense that x has an experiential ground for judging that x is in pain, then x really is in pain.

There are alternative ways of expressing these principles. For example, (A) can be expressed by saying that it is impossible for x to be in pain without x's being experientially aware that x is in pain, and (B) can be expressed by saying that it is impossible for x to have an experience of the sort that x has when x is aware of a pain without its being the case that x really is aware of a pain.

(A) appears to hold quite generally – even in cases that are somewhat outré. To appreciate this, recall that soldiers and athletes often sustain serious injuries but show no sign of being in pain, continuing to display normal

---

* Several portions of this chapter are excerpted from my paper "OW! The Paradox of Pain," in Murat Aydede (ed.), *Pain: New Essays on its Nature and the Methodology of its Study* (Cambridge, MA: MIT Press, 2005), pp. 75–98.

behavior until the end of the battle or the athletic contest, and perhaps even longer. They also deny that they are in pain. We may feel confused in try-ing to describe situations of this sort, but we realize that we have an obliga-tion to concur with the person who has the injury. If he or she denies that there is pain, and we have no reason to think that the denial is insincere, we will acquiesce in it, and indeed insist on its truth. We feel that it would be deeply absurd to override the testimony of the injured party.

We can appreciate the plausibility of (B) by reflecting on cases of phan-tom limb pain. When someone complains of pain in a limb that no longer exists, his or her testimony is taken as fact, provided only that there is no reason to suspect insincerity. To be sure, it will not seem correct, either to the person suffering from the pain or to external observers, to say that the pain is in the part of the body where it appears to be located, for by hypothesis there will be no such part. Because of this, it is true to say that there is a certain discrepancy between appearance and reality in such cases. But this is the only discrepancy. Thus, while we are prepared to say that the victim's perception that the pain is in the right leg is an illusion, we will allow, and in fact insist, that the pain is in all other respects as it appears to the victim. In particular, we will insist that it is a *pain*, thereby manifesting our commitment to principle (B).

It is important that we regard it as *absurd* to say that an agent is in pain in circumstances in which the agent is not aware of a pain, and that we regard it as *absurd* to say that an agent is not in pain in circumstances in which it seems to the agent that he or she is in pain. This suggests that we think of (A) and (B) as necessary truths – that is, as holding either because of deep metaphysical facts about our awareness of pain, or because of the a priori structure of our concept of pain.

There are several aspects of our thought and talk about pain that seem not to be fully in keeping with (A) and (B). I will mention one. We all know that pain has causal powers with respect to attention and aware-ness. When we are aware of a very intense pain, it seems to us that it has the power to keep attention focused on itself – indeed, a power to so engage attention as to make it difficult or impossible for us to honor other concerns and interests. Equally, as a pain increases in intensity, it seems to us to increase proportionally in its power to attract attention. Because of these phenomenological facts, we have a tendency to suppose that pain can exert an influence on attention even prior to our becoming aware of it. Thus, we say that pains can wake us up. On one very natural con-strual of this claim, it presupposes a picture according to which pain can exist prior to and therefore independently of awareness. According to this picture, there are pains that are so "small," so lacking in intensity, that they are incapable of attracting attention, and exist only at a subliminal level. But a pain of this sort can increase in intensity, thereby increasing also in its power to attract attention, and it may finally attain a level of intensity that enables it to open the gates of awareness. When this happens during sleep, we wake up.

Although this picture has a certain appeal, I doubt very much that it can be said to represent a dominant strand in our commonsense conception of pain. If we were fully committed to the picture, we would be prepared to consider it epistemically possible that an injured soldier actually has a severe pain, despite his professions to the contrary, but that there is something wrong with the mechanisms in his brain that support attention, and that this is preventing the pain from penetrating the threshold of consciousness. When I have asked informants to assess the likelihood of this scenario, however, they have all been inclined to dismiss it as absurd. The fact is that our discourse about pain is subject to divergent pressures. It serves a number of purposes and is responsive to a complex phenomenology. As a result, it is not entirely coherent. We resonate deeply to (A) and (B), but it should not surprise us that we are occasionally led to say things, and to feel the appeal of pictures, that cannot be fully squared with these principles.

At all events, I will go forward on the assumption that (A) and (B) strike us as fundamentally correct, and in fact seem to us to enjoy a kind of necessity. Whether the necessity in question has an ontological ground or is instead due to the a priori structure of our concept of pain is a question that I will defer to Section 6.5.

6.2   AWARENESS OF PAIN

The fact that pains do not admit of a substantive appearance/reality distinction is unfortunate, for it presents a serious challenge to an otherwise appealing account of what it is to be aware of a pain. Indeed, we should view the absence of an appearance/reality distinction here as *extremely* unfortunate, for the considerations that favor the account in question actually seem to mandate it. Thus, we have an antinomy. On the one hand, principles (A) and (B) appear not just to be true, but to be in some sense necessary. And on the other hand, there are considerations that seem to force us to embrace an account of awareness of pain that is flatly incompatible with (A) and (B). This is the "paradox of pain" that is cited in the subtitle of this chapter.

The account of awareness of pain that I have in mind here is one that likens awareness of pain to such familiar sorts of perceptual awareness as vision, hearing, and touch.

When we consider the familiar forms of perceptual awareness from an introspective perspective, we find that they share a number of features, and this impression is reinforced when we view them from the perspective of contemporary cognitive psychology. I will mention several of these common features.[1] It will be clear as we proceed, I believe, that awareness of pain possesses the features as well.

First, perceptual awareness involves subconceptual representations of objects of awareness. Reflection shows that we are able to perceive innumerable properties that we are unable to name or describe. It is often said that we can use demonstrative concepts, such as *that shade of color*, to specify these properties, but even if this observation was fully correct, which is highly questionable, given that animals seem to be capable of highly sophisticated perceptual representations while being very limited conceptually, it would not diminish the case for the view that the properties are represented subconceptually. This is because we must attend to a property perceptually in order to demonstrate it. The representations that are employed by perceptual attention when it provides grounding for demonstrative concepts cannot themselves be conceptual.

Awareness of pain also involves subconceptual representations. To be sure, awareness of pain often takes the form of a judgment to the effect that we are in pain, and judgments put concepts into play. But what we are aware of in being aware of pains can easily transcend the expressive powers of our conceptual repertoire. We have all been aware of pains that have a significant degree of internal complexity. Perhaps it would be possible to put together roughly adequate descriptions of such pains if they were to last long enough, without changing in any way, or if we could remember their particularities for a long enough time after they had disappeared. In actual fact, however, the task of describing them fully is way beyond our powers. What we are aware of is ineffable in practice if not in principle.

Second, all of the familiar forms of perception are associated with automatic attention mechanisms, and also with attention mechanisms that are under voluntary control. Among other things, such mechanisms can

---

[1] Inevitably, the present list of distinctive features of perceptual awareness overlaps with the list of features of experiential awareness in Section 3.6.

increase the resolution of our experience of an object of awareness, and heighten the contrast between an object of awareness and its background. The same is true of awareness of pain. We can attend to pains, and when we do, there is a higher level of resolution and also a more salient contrast between figure and ground.

Third, it is of the essence of perceptual representation to assign locations and other spatial characteristics to its objects. The same is true of awareness of pain.

Fourth, there are a priori norms of good grouping that determine the ways in which perceptual elements are organized into wholes. For example, we group visually presented dots together if they are alike in some respect – that is, if they share a neighborhood in space, or a shape, or a color, or a size, or a common fate. The same is true of groups of pains. Suppose that you have three pains, two in your palm and one in your wrist. The two in your palm will seem to form a unified whole of a certain kind. Equally, two pains that are alike in intensity, or that begin to exist at the same time, will seem to be members of a single "society," even if they lie at some distance from one another spatially.

Fifth, all forms of perceptual awareness have a proprietary phenomenology. The same is true, of course, of awareness of pain.

Sixth, perceptual awareness is particularized. I can form a belief that there are three books in a box without being en rapport with any of the particular books that make my belief true. Equally, I can believe that someone has been eating my porridge without having any relevant beliefs about a specific individual. But perceptual awareness is different. If I am perceptually aware of the presence of three books in a box, I must be in some sense perceptually aware of each of the individual books. Equally, if I am aware of the existence of a trio of pains in my arm, I must be aware of each individual member of the trio.

Seventh, perceptual awareness has a certain mereological determinacy. I can form a belief about an object without forming any belief about its parts. But unless an object of perception is atomic, a minimum sensibile of some sort, I am inevitably aware of a range of its parts in being perceptually aware of the object, and also of certain of the structural relationships among the parts. (I mean to be using "part" quite broadly here, so that it applies to temporal constituents of events and qualitative constituents of complex properties as well as to spatial parts of physical substances.) This is also true of awareness of pains. Pains are normally experienced as extended in space, and when they are so experienced, the parts are experienced as well, as are a number of the structural relationships among the parts.[2]

We have been reviewing certain of the common features of paradigmatic forms of perception that are visible from the perspective of introspection and/or the perspective of cognitive psychology. I have maintained that when we reflect, we can see that these features are shared by experiential awareness of pain. I now wish to point out that there are other commonalities that are visible from the perspective of cognitive neuroscience. More specifically, cognitive neuroscience provides many data which suggest that awareness of pain is fundamentally akin to haptic perception, thermal perception, and proprioception. It is widely held that the latter forms of perception owe their character and indeed their very being to the representational functions of certain structures in the somatosensory cortex. Insofar as we prescind from the emotional and behavioral phenomena that attend awareness of pain, and think of awareness of pain as awareness of a purely sensory state, we find that awareness of pain also owes its character and its being to representations in the somatosensory cortex.[3] Moreover, in addition to this global commonality, there are also many commonalities of detail – commonalities having to do with internal organization, relationship to sensory pickup systems, and connections to higher cognitive centers, such as those that are believed to be involved in attention. In view of these similarities, it would be very uncomfortable to withhold the label "perceptual system" from the structures that subserve awareness of pain while applying it to the structures that subserve, say, haptic perception.[4]

As I see it, then, we are obliged to accept the view that awareness of pain is constituted by representations that are fundamentally perceptual

[2] See Yaffa Yeshuran and Marissa Currasco, "Attention Improves Performance in Spatial Resolution Tasks," *Vision Research* 39 (1999), 293–305; and Marissa Currasco, Cigdem Penpecci-Talgar, and Miguel Eckstein, "Spatial Covert Attention Increases Contrast Sensitivity across the CSF: Support for Signal Enhancement," *Vision Research* 40 (2000), 1203–1215.

[3] The experiments that established this were done by Pierre Rainville. See Pierre Rainville, J. H. Duncan, D. D. Price, B. Carrier, and M. C. Bushnell, "Pain Affect Encoded in Human Anterior Cingulate but Not Somatosensory Cortex," *Science* 277 (1997), 968–971; and Pierre Rainville, B. Carrier, R. K. Hofbauer, *et al.*, "Dissociation of Sensory and Affective Dimensions of Pain Using Hypnotic Modulation," *Pain Forum* 82 (1999), 159–171.

[4] The picture I have just sketched is presented in much greater detail in Donald D. Price, *Psychological Mechanisms of Pain and Analgesia* (Seattle, WA: IASP Press, 1999), Chapter 5; and in Allan J. Basbaum and Thomas M. Jessell, "The Perception of Pain," in Eric Kandel, James H. Schwartz, and Thomas M. Jessell (eds.), *Principles of Neural Science*, 4th edition (New York: McGraw Hill, 2000), pp. 472–491. For discussion of the mechanisms that underlie other forms of bodily awareness, see Esther P. Gardner, John H. Martin, and Thomas M. Jessell, "The Bodily Senses," in Kandel, Schwartz, and Jessell, *Principles of Neural Science*, pp. 430–450; and Esther P. Gardner and Eric R. Kandel, "Touch," In Kandel, Schwartz, and Jessell, *Principles of Neural Science*, pp. 451–471.

in character, and by the same token, the view that awareness of pain is a form of perceptual awareness. Alas, in accepting these views, we come into conflict with principles (A) and (B), which deny that there is a substantive distinction between its seeming to one that one is in pain and its being the case that one is in pain. The reason for this conflict is that the relationship between perceptual representations and the items they represent is always contingent. Suppose that a perceptual representation R represents a property P. It is always possible for P to be instantiated without being represented by a corresponding token of R, and for R to be tokened without there being a corresponding instance of P. Because of this, if awareness of pain constitutively involves perceptual representations, it must be possible, at least in principle, for there to be pains that one is not aware of, and it must also be possible to be aware of pain, in the sense of having an experience just like the ones one has when one is aware of a pain, without one's actually being in pain. That is to say, there must be possible circumstances in which one is in pain without seeming to be in pain, and possible circumstances in which it seems to one that one is in pain without its actually being the case that one is in pain. But (A) and (B) deny that such possibilities exist.

It appears, then, that when we try to combine the folk psychological picture of pain and awareness of pain with various introspective and scientific facts, we arrive at an antinomy. I will eventually propose a way of dealing with this conflict, but before I do so, I would like to develop the foregoing remarks concerning awareness of pain into something resembling a theory, and to then work out the implications of this theory for questions about the nature of pain itself.

6.3 THE PERCEPTUAL MODEL

The foregoing arguments provide motivation for a view that I will call the *perceptual model* of awareness of pain. According to the perceptual model, awareness of pain is a form of perceptual awareness, fully on a par with such paradigmatic forms of perceptual awareness as vision and olfaction. It involves perceptual representations that are probably best seen as patterns of elevated activity in the somatosensory cortex. As is always the case with representations, these representations can occur independently of what they represent. Thus, it can seem to us that we are aware of pain when we actually are not. There can be hallucinations of pain.

Further, because awareness of pain involves representations, there is good reason to doubt that awareness of pain puts us in touch with the essential nature of pain. There is always a gap, and generally a very large gap, between the intrinsic nature of a phenomenon and the features of the phenomenon that are captured by perceptual representations of it. Thus, as we all know, while visual representations provide us with reasonably good access to some aspects of physical color, they reveal very little about the physical microstructure of color, or the ways in which perceived colors depend on relations between objects and their surrounds. There is no good reason to think that it should be otherwise in the case of awareness of pain. Thus, the perceptual model commits us to acknowledging that there is a gap, and quite possibly a very large gap, between pain as it is represented and pain itself, or in other words, between the appearance of pain and the underlying reality. By the same token, the perceptual model implies that we should be wary of philosophical theories of pain that are based on the assumption that it is possible to grasp the essential nature of pain via introspection. On the present account, introspective awareness of pain is a form of perceptual awareness, and is therefore probably a poor guide to the essential nature of its object.

I conclude this sketch of the perceptual model with a claim about the state of mind that we call the *experience of pain*. It seems natural to suppose that the experience of pain bears the same relation to awareness of pain as the experience of shape bears to awareness of shape. Now the experience of shape is what might be called the *subjective component* of awareness of shape: when one is visually aware of a shape, one must be having an experience of that shape, but it is possible to have an experience of a shape without being aware of that shape, as when a distorting lens causes a thin object to look thick. Visual experience of shape is what you get when you focus on that aspect of visual awareness of shape that involves only the perceptual experience of the subject. Conversely, visual awareness of shape occurs when one has a visual experience of shape that is veridical. We find much the same situation, I suggest, when we turn to consider the experience of pain in relation to awareness of pain. The experience of pain is the subjective component of awareness of pain, the component one arrives at when one focuses on that aspect of awareness of pain that involves only the experience of the subject. Conversely, awareness of pain occurs whenever an experience of pain is veridical.

6.4 THE BODILY DISTURBANCE THEORY

Up to now we have been concerned exclusively with questions about awareness of pain. I wish to turn now to consider the nature of pain itself.

Pains are presumably physical states of some kind, but *what* kind? There are a number of options here. We could say that pains are bodily disturbances that involve actual or potential damage.[5] We could also say that they are events in the tips of the nerves that detect damage – that is, in the tips of C fibers and Aδ fibers. A third possibility is to identify pains with processes in the spinal cord. Another is to identify them with certain events that occur in the early stages of processing of nociceptive signals in the brain – perhaps with events in the thalamus. Still another is to identify them with cortical events of some sort.

There is something to be said for each of these options. Thus, for example, there are modulatory processes in the spinal cord that have the effect of reducing the strengths of the nociceptive signals that arrive from the periphery. As a result, the level of nociceptive activity in the spinal cord is generally closer to the perceived intensity of pain than is the level of activity in peripheral damage detectors. This match between perceived intensity and level of activity is a reason, though not by itself a decisive reason, for identifying pains with processes in the spinal cord.

In the present section I will argue for a theory of the nature of pain that I will call the *bodily disturbance theory*. This view identifies pains with peripheral disturbances involving actual or potential damage. The reasons for accepting the view are individually quite strong, and taken together they seem – prima facie, at least – to be decisive. It is therefore surprising that it is also possible to make a strong case for an opposing view. According to this second view, pains are not bodily disturbances but somatosensory representations of bodily disturbances. I will state the case for the alternative proposal in Section 6.6.

The first reason for identifying pains with bodily disturbances is that our experiences of pain represent pains as having bodily locations. Thus, for example, I experience my current pain as being in my foot. The bodily disturbance theory is the only theory of pain that takes the apparent locations of pains at face value. Every other theory implies that our

---

[5] As David Bennett has pointed out to me, there is a problem with the idea that pains are bodily disturbances that involve actual or potential damage – it often happens that bodily disturbances are felt as pains even though they do not pose threats to the integrity of the parts of the body in which they occur. Migraine headaches are examples. This shows that if we are to identify pains with bodily disturbances, we will need to characterize the relevant disturbances in broader, more inclusive terms. It will be necessary, for example, to invoke abnormally high values of degrees of pressure and inflammation. I do not think, however, that it is widely off the mark to characterize the relevant disturbances as ones that involve actual or potential damage. This characterization does justice to the normal case. Because of this, and because of its simplicity, I will continue to rely on it in the sequel.

experiences of pain are systematically misleading, or illusory, insofar as they assign locations to pains. Now if the perceptual model is correct, the fact that the bodily disturbance theory takes our experience of pain at face value counts strongly in favor of the theory. This is because, as we all know, there is a general rule to the effect that we should prefer theories that take perceptual experience at face value to theories that treat it as systematically misleading. This does not mean that we are obliged to view perceptual experience as veridical in all circumstances. It is clear that perceptual evidence can be overridden in some cases. But it does mean that there is a prima facie obligation to view perceptual experience as veridical, and that its teachings cannot easily be set aside. Applying these points to the case at hand, we arrive at the conclusion that we should prefer the bodily disturbance theory to its competitors unless we encounter very serious internal problems as we attempt to develop it.

Before going on to consider additional reasons for embracing the bodily disturbance theory, we should pause to consider an objection to this first reason. According to the objection, we have already encountered a consideration which suggests that our experience of pain may be systematically misleading with respect to locations. Thus, we have seen that the perceived intensities of pains are not perfectly correlated with levels of peripheral activity. There is a much better correlation between perceived intensities and levels of activity in the spinal cord. This suggests that it is best to identify pains with events in the spinal cord, and by the same token, it provides a reason for thinking that our perceptual experience systematically misrepresents the locations of pains.

This objection has a certain initial plausibility, but I don't think that it is in any sense decisive. In effect, the objection points out that we must choose between saying that our perceptual representations of pains tell the truth about the locations of pains but lie about their intensities, and saying that our representations of pains tell the truth about the intensities of pains but lie about their locations. It seems right that we must make this choice, but it also seems that there are strong reasons for preferring the first option to the second. Thus, while it is true that the perceived intensities of pains are not perfectly correlated with levels of bodily activity, it is also true that there is a statistically salient correlation between these two variables. Accordingly, if we say that pains are identical with bodily disturbances, we thereby commit ourselves to saying that perceptual representations of intensities are systematically misleading, but we do not thereby commit ourselves to saying that they are altogether wrong. On the contrary, we will be giving them a qualified endorsement, maintaining that their testimony about intensities is to a large extent correct. On the other hand, if we say that pains are located in the spinal cord, we will be forced to conclude that perceptual representations of the locations of pains are altogether erroneous. We will not have the option of saying that they are largely correct. In view of this asymmetry, it is clear that we will show more respect for our perceptual representations of pain by embracing the theory that identifies pains with perceptual disturbances than by embracing the theory that they are nociceptive signals in the spinal cord. Both theories commit us to saying that our representations of pain tell lies, but the former theory accuses the representations of less dishonesty than the latter theory.

The second reason for accepting the bodily disturbance theory is that experiences of pain attribute spatial properties other than locations to their objects. Experiences of pain represent their objects as having sizes and also as having spatial parts – parts that stand in various relationships to one another. Thus, you may experience a pain as extending over a large region of your left forearm, and you may also experience it as having a grating structure, with regions of high intensity alternating with regions of low intensity. The bodily disturbance theory is the only one that fully endorses spatial attributions of this sort. It implies that they are entirely and literally correct. Other theories treat them quite differently.

The third reason for accepting the bodily disturbance theory begins with the truism that we are aware of pains. Now awareness involves representations, and when one is aware of *x*, the object of awareness, *x*, is identical with the object that is represented by the representation that is involved in one's state of awareness. Indeed, it is natural to say that the state of awareness *inherits* its object from the representation that is involved in the state – or in other words, that the representation *determines* the object of awareness. In particular, then, what one is aware of when one is aware of a pain is whatever it is that is represented by the somatosensory representation that is involved in the state of awareness. Now it is pretty clear that nociceptive somatosensory representations have the function of encoding information about bodily disturbances involving stress or damage. But if nociceptive somatosensory representations have the function of encoding information about bodily disturbances, then it is plausible that they *represent* those disturbances. Hence, it is reasonable to say that one is aware of a bodily disturbance when one is aware of pain. But it follows immediately from this that pains are identical with bodily disturbances.

To summarize: (i) What one is aware of when one is aware of a pain is determined by the somatosensory representation that is involved in one's state of awareness. It is whatever it is that is represented by the representation. (ii) The representation represents a bodily disturbance involving stress or damage. Hence, what one is aware of when one is aware of a pain is a bodily disturbance. But this means that pains are bodily disturbances.

I should perhaps say a bit more in explanation of premise (ii) – the claim that the somatosensory representations that are involved in awareness of pain represent bodily disturbances. When we look at the relevant neuroscientific facts, it becomes quite clear that these representations encode information about bodily disturbances of the relevant sort. But it can be true that a state or event encodes information about x without being true that the state or event represents x. To represent x, the state or event must have the *function* of encoding information about x. Why should we think that somatosensory representations have the function of encoding information about bodily disturbances? This view is made plausible, I suggest, by the fact that higher cognitive centers, such as the ones responsible for planning, initiating, and guiding action, have a vital *need* for information about bodily disturbances of the given sort. In particular, they are more in need of information about bodily disturbances than of information about activity in the spinal cord or brain. Thus, if higher cognitive agencies are to protect the organism from harm, and prevent harms from becoming worse, they need an accurate, continuously updated map of the peripheral loci where there is actual or potential damage. If equipped with such a map, these agencies can take steps to end threats and to protect areas that have already incurred harm. But without such a map, the agencies would be blind. So there is a pressing need for information about disturbances. Now it is very natural to think that the informational requirements of higher cognitive agencies play a large role in determining the representational contents of perceptual representations. As far as I know, this view is sustained by all current theories of perceptual representation.

This brings us to a fourth reason for thinking that pains should be identified with bodily disturbances. This one has to do with reference. The referent of a complex demonstrative such as "that man" or "this apple" is determined in part by attention. "That man" refers to Mervin P. Gerbil because I am focusing my attention on Mervin as I utter or think the words. Now it is plausible that we focus attention on bodily disturbances when we use complex demonstratives involving "pain." Thus, as we know, attention enhances the processing of information about whatever it is that is being attended to. Because of this, we can figure out what is being attended to in any particular case by determining which streams of information are being most deeply processed. It is pretty clear that it is information about bodily damage that is most deeply processed when we attend to pains. So we have: (i) the referent of "that pain," etc. is whatever we are attending to when we utter or think those words; (ii) what we attend to in such cases are bodily disturbances; (iii) the referent of "that pain" is always a pain; so (iv) pains must be bodily disturbances.

A fifth reason has to do with the fact that we consult bodily disturbances in assessing claims about pain for truth or falsity, and in answering questions about pains. Is the pain in my foot worse than it was yesterday? To answer this, I must attend to the pain. But the considerations we have just reviewed indicate that attending to a pain involves attending to a bodily disturbance.

It appears, then, that there are several fairly strong reasons for embracing the perceptual disturbance theory. I now observe that this theory fits together quite nicely with the perceptual model of awareness of pain that we considered earlier. They are fully compatible – indeed, to some extent, anyway, they are mutually reinforcing. Accordingly, it is reasonable to combine them under a single label, and to view this combination as a unified theory. I will henceforth refer to them as the *perceptual/somatic theory*.

The perceptual/somatic theory makes the following claims: First, awareness of pain is perceptual in character. Second, such awareness essentially involves representations. Third, the experience of pain is the subjective, experiential component of awareness of pain. It occurs when a perceptual representation of pain acquires whatever properties are needed for a perceptual representation to become conscious. Fourth, awareness of pain is governed by an appearance/reality distinction and is therefore an unreliable guide to the essential nature of pain. Fifth, pain itself should be kicked out of the mind and relocated in the regions of the body where our perceptual experience represents it as being located. Sixth, the experience of pain can occur without being accompanied by pain itself, as in cases of phantom limb. There are hallucinations of pain. And seventh, pain itself can occur without being accompanied by the experience of pain, as in cases of severe battlefield injuries.

As this summary makes clear, the perceptual/somatic theory is flatly incompatible with the two principles from folk psychology that we considered at the outset, principle (A) and principle (B):

(A) If x is in pain, then it seems to x that x is in pain, in the sense that x has an experiential ground for judging that x is in pain.

(B) If it seems to *x* that *x* is in pain, in the sense that *x* has an experiential
      ground for judging that *x* is in pain, then *x* really is in pain.

Accordingly, if we accept the perceptual/somatic theory, we must reject
these principles. Now it is not immediately clear what such a rejection
would amount to, for it is not immediately clear what we should say about
the semantic and epistemic status of the principles. That is to say, it is not
immediately clear whether they should be seen as constitutive of the concept of pain, and as a priori in epistemic status, or they should instead be
seen as very deeply entrenched empirical claims. In the first case, if we
were to reject them, we would in effect be eliminating the commonsense
concept of pain and replacing it with a new and less problematic one. In
the second case, in rejecting them we would be undertaking a revision of
theory but not a conceptual revision. I don't know how to settle the question about the status of (A) and (B) with any sort of finality, but in the
next section I will advance some considerations which suggest that the
first possibility is more likely. It is plausible that (A) and (B) are constitutive of the commonsense concept of pain, and are also a priori.

   In stating the perceptual/somatic theory, I have distinguished sharply
between the experience of pain, which I take to be a perceptual state,
and pain itself, which I have identified with a certain type of bodily disturbance. Before concluding this exposition of the theory, I should note
that it is actually necessary to draw a threefold distinction. In addition to
distinguishing between the experience of pain and pain itself, we should
distinguish both of these factors from what we might call *pain affect*, the
sense that pain is something bad or noxious. Further, we should recognize
that in addition to being distinguishable, these three factors are separable,
both clinically and experimentally: it is in principle possible for each to
occur independently of the others. In cases of phantom limb pain there is
an experience of pain and also pain affect, but these factors are not accompanied by a bodily disturbance of the right sort, with the result that there
is no pain. In cases of pain asymbolia, there is an experience of pain and
also pain itself, but the subjects say that their pains do not bother them,
and that they do not hurt. Accordingly, we have to view such cases as ones
in which the experience of pain and pain itself occur, but in which they are
not accompanied by pain affect.[6] In cases of battlefield wounds and serious sports injuries, there is damage to the body and also torrential activity
in Aδ fibers and C fibers. Accordingly if we accept the bodily disturbance

---

[6] See, e.g., Nikola Grahek, *Feeling Pain and Being in Pain* (Oldenburg: Bibliotheks- und
Informationssystem der Universität Oldenburg, 2001).

theory, we are obliged to view such cases as ones in which there is pain. But as we observed earlier, there is no experience of pain in such cases and no pain affect. Finally, I note that there are reports of cases in which subjects report pain affect but deny that they are experiencing pain. Cases of this sort are very rare but apparently they do occur.[7]

6.5   THE COGNITIVE ROLE OF THE CONCEPT OF PAIN

The perceptual/somatic theory is internally coherent and deeply motivated by a broad range of introspective, philosophical, and scientific considerations. As we recently observed, however, it conflicts with the intuition that awareness of pain does not admit of an appearance/reality distinction. What is the nature of this conflict? Is it merely empirical, or does the theory challenge folk doctrines that are partially constitutive of the concept of pain? I will try to answer this question in the present section. That is to say, I will attempt to explain the semantic and epistemic status of the folk principles I have called (A) and (B).

The explanation I wish to propose has three components. The first component is a pair of claims about the rules that govern the use of the folk concept of pain – or rather, to be more precise, that portion of the use that consists in forming simple first person beliefs involving the concept. The second component is a narrative that explains the plausibility of the folk picture of pain in terms of our conformity to these rules. And the third component is an account of why it is natural, given our practical and cognitive interests, to have a concept that is governed by the rules, and to embrace the folk picture that grows out of them.

To begin, then, I claim that the folk concept of pain is governed by rules that are more or less equivalent to (R1) and (R2):

(R1)   One is fully and unqualifiedly entitled to form a first person judgment of the form *I am in pain* if one is currently having an experience of pain.

(R2)   One is not entitled to form a first person judgment of the form *I am in pain* unless one is currently having an experience of pain.

There must of course be many other rules that govern the concept of pain – for example, rules concerning the use of the concept in more complex first person judgments. But I think we can afford to ignore all other rules in the present context.

---

[7] See *ibid.*, pp. 100–103.

I now observe that (R1) and (R2) have some remarkable consequences. Thus, (R1) implies that if one is currently having an experience of pain, then one is entitled to believe that one is in pain no matter what additional information one happens to possess. That is, immediate experience provides an entitlement that cannot be overridden by information of other sorts. In particular, (R1) implies that experience provides one with an entitlement that cannot be overridden by a physician's testimony that there is absolutely nothing wrong with one's body, nor even by testimony of one's own eyes to the effect that the relevant part of one's body is missing. According to (R1), the entitlements provided by immediate experience are absolute. The consequences of (R2) are no less remarkable. It implies that there is no information about one's body, or about any other part of the physical world, that can provide one with an entitlement to believe that one is in pain. When it comes to beliefs about pain, immediate experience is the only source of entitlements.

When we consider these consequences of (R1) and (R2), we can see, I believe, that if a subject is conforming to these rules, then he or she will have absolutely no motivation for distinguishing between the appearance of pain and the reality of pain. When we draw an appearance/reality distinction with respect to a phenomenon φ, it is because we know that immediate experience is a fallible guide to beliefs about the existence and nature of φ's. That is, it is because we know that the testimony of immediate experience can be overridden and/or made unnecessary by information about φ's that comes from other sources. But a subject who is conforming to (R1) can never have an experiential ground for a positive belief about pain that is overridden by information of some other kind. He or she will never encounter information that calls such beliefs into question. And a subject who is conforming to (R2) will never be in a situation in which he or she lacks an experiential ground for holding a positive belief about pain but has a ground of some other sort. By the same token, the subject will never acquire information which shows that experience failed to alert him or her to the existence of a pain.

In sum, a subject who is conforming to (R1) and (R2) will never have reason to think that there is a tribunal other than immediate experience to which judgments about pain must answer. But it is precisely the conception of such a tribunal that provides the motivation for distinguishing between appearance and reality in other areas of cognitive endeavor. Insofar as there is no tribunal, other than that provided by immediate experience itself, to which a class of judgments must answer, there can be no ground for thinking that experience itself provides a less than perfectly trustworthy guide to reality.

Is it true that the folk concept of pain is governed by (R1) and (R2)? I think we can see that it is true, and also understand why it is true, by noticing that we have a very powerful motive for having a concept that can be used to keep track of the experience of pain – that is, to encode and store information about the experience. The motivation comes from the causal powers that are possessed by experiences of pain, or, equivalently, by the somatosensory representations that constitute such experiences. It is these somatosensory representations that directly control the activity in the anterior cingulate cortex and in the limbic system that determines our affective response to pain. Pain affect occurs when and only when a somatosensory representation of the right sort is tokened. And of course, it is pain affect that makes pain itself so important to us. Without the response, pains would be of no more interest to us than tingles and mild sensations of pressure. We would hardly take notice of them at all. These considerations show that it is essential that we keep close tabs on somatosensory representations of the given sort. By keeping close tabs on them, we are simultaneously keeping close tabs on the impression that a pain is occurring and on that which confers significance on this impression.

Of course, somatosensory representations are not the only items that have the power to produce pain affect. Bodily disturbances have this power, too. But the causal efficacy of the representations is much more substantial than that of the disturbances. The causal linkage between the representations and pain affect is disrupted only in extremely rare clinical and experimental conditions. It is an extremely tight causal relationship. The casual relationship between bodily disturbances and pain affect is much easier to disrupt. Indeed, it is even disrupted by sleep. Moreover, it is dependent on the casual relationship between somatosensory representations and pain affect. Bodily disturbances have the power to cause pain affect only insofar as they have the power to cause somatosensory representations. Accordingly, it is much less important that we have a concept that can be used to keep close tabs on bodily disturbances than that we have a concept that can be used to keep close tabs on representations of the relevant sort.

We now have an explanation of why it is not apparent to us from the perspective of folk psychology that it is possible to draw an appearance/reality distinction with respect to pain.[8] In a nutshell, the explanation

---

[8] There is also another explanation – an explanation that derives from the fact, much discussed in earlier chapters, that the representational nature of experiential awareness is not in evidence

maintains that the possibility of drawing such a distinction is invisible to us because the rules governing the use of the commonsense concept of pain recognize no sources of warrant for judgments about pain other than experiences of pain. It also claims that we have adopted these rules because it is fundamentally important to us to have a concept that can be used to keep track of the somatosensory representations that govern the comings and goings of pain affect.

The present inquiry into the cognitive role of the concept of pain was prompted by questions about the semantic and epistemic status of principle (A) and principle (B), the two folk principles that preclude an appearance/reality distinction for pain. Are the principles constitutive of the concept of pain or merely well entrenched generalizations? Are they a priori or empirical in character? We have now found reason to think that the principles arise from deep and abiding interests, and that the interests in question are practical rather than predictive and explanatory in nature. Assuming that this view is correct, it is probably best to think of the two principles as tied to the concept of pain in a deeper and more fundamental way than any merely empirical generalizations could be. And by the same token, it is probably best to suppose that if we were to reject the principles, we would in effect be revising our conceptual scheme, and not merely making empirically motivated adjustments in a predictive/explanatory theory.

6.6 REVISIONARY METAPHYSICS

In Sections 6.2, 6.3, and 6.4 we found that there are very powerful reasons for embracing the accounts of pain and awareness of pain that are offered by the perceptual/somatic theory. But we also found that embracing them would bring us into conflict with principles (A) and (B) – that is, with the folk principles that preclude an appearance/reality distinction for pain. We now know that these principles are partially constitutive of the concept of pain. By the same token, we now know that if we were to embrace the perceptual/somatic theory, we would in effect be jettisoning or radically revising the folk concept of pain. So we must ask: Given that

when such awareness is viewed from the perspectives of introspection and folk psychology. We fail to see that experiential awareness of pain admits of an appearance/reality distinction because we do not ordinarily appreciate that such awareness involves representations. (If we did appreciate this, we would see that it is possible to distinguish between pain-as-it-is-represented and pain-as-it-is-in-itself.) In effect, then, it is overdetermined that we do not appreciate that awareness of pain admits of an appearance/reality distinction.

embracing the theory would in effect deprive us of the commonsensical concept of pain, does it make sense to embrace it? Is it the best available option, all things included?

We saw that the folk concept of pain serves an important purpose – that of encoding information about somatosensory representations of bodily disturbances involving actual or potential damage, the representations that control the comings and goings of pain affect. (I will hereafter refer to these items as *D-representations*.) Because of this, any course of action that commits us to eliminating or radically revising the commonsense concept of pain would have significant practical costs. Can we afford to incur these costs? It seems unlikely that we can. It is vitally important that we have a device for registering facts about D-representations, for storing information about such facts in memory, and for framing generalizations about them.

It turns out, then, that there is a problem with embracing the perceptual/ somatic theory. Moreover, this first problem is accompanied by a second one. We have found that principles (A) and (B) are partially constitutive of the concept of pain. As we will see in a moment, it is possible to use this fact as the basis for an argument that the concept of pain refers, not to bodily disturbances involving actual or potential damage, but rather to D-representations. But this means that (A) and (B) provide motivation for the view that pains *are* D-representations. We have been assuming that the perceptual/somatic theory is the best available account of pain and awareness of pain; but if there is a strong reason for viewing pains as D-representations, we have no right to proceed on this assumption. Instead of seeing the perceptual/somatic theory as the best available option, we should perhaps see it as a proposal that is called into question, or even refuted, by a competing proposal with equal or superior credentials.

Here is an argument for the view that the concept of pain refers to D-representations: "As we have seen, the non-existence of an appearance/ reality distinction for pain is best explained by supposing that the concept of pain is used to encode information about experiences of pain. Since experiences of pain are constituted by D-representations, it follows that the concept of pain is used to encode information about D-representations. Now if a concept serves the purpose of encoding information about X's, then it should be seen as referring to X's. What could reference be other than the relation that a concept bears to the items it is used to keep track of? But this means that the concept of pain refers to D-representations."

Interestingly, there are other ways of arguing from (A) and (B) to this conclusion about the reference of the concept of pain. Here, briefly, is a second way: "We regard a first person ascription of pain as indefeasibly justified if the person who makes the judgment in question is currently enjoying an experience of pain – that is, if a D-representation is currently occurring in his or her somatosensory cortex. But to regard a judgment as indefeasibly justified is tantamount to regarding it as true. Hence we are committed to seeing a first person ascription of pain as true just in case the relevant agent is tokening a D-representation. It follows that D-representations are the truth-makers for first person ascriptions of pain, and it follows from this in turn that the concept of pain refers to D-representations."

Let us pause to take stock. There is strong motivation for adopting the perceptual/somatic theory. If we take that course, however, we will be committed to rejecting (A) and (B), and by the same token, committed to eliminating or radically revising the commonsense concept of pain. The latter move would have significant practical costs. But also, (A) and (B) provide motivation for a theory of pain that is an alternative to the perceptual/somatic theory – viz., the theory that pains are D-representations. It is by no means clear that we should prefer the perceptual/somatic theory to this competing proposal, or even that it is rationally permissible to do so. Indeed, it might be thought that we have a kind of antinomy here: two well motivated accounts of the nature of pain that sharply conflict with one another.

Here is our old friend, the paradox of pain, emerging in a new guise.

Fortunately, as I see it, anyway, we are now in a position to understand the source of the paradox, and to see how to deal with it in a final and fully satisfactory way. The problems facing us arise from the fact that folk psychology tries to use a single concept, the concept of pain, to keep track of two very different things – bodily disturbances involving actual or potential damage, and somatosensory representations of such damage. Folk psychology permits and even requires us to think of pains as things that have bodily locations and other spatial properties. Moreover, it requires us to think of pains as objects of experiential awareness. Because of the latter requirement, it can also be said to require us to think of pains as things that can be understood by investigating this form of awareness. But when we investigate it, we are led ineluctably to the conclusion that it is a form of perceptual awareness, and that its objects are bodily disturbances. In effect, then, folk psychology mandates the view that the folk concept of pain refers to bodily occurrences. On the other hand, as we have just been noticing, the concept serves interests that connect it intimately with high level representations of bodily occurrences. Because of this, we are in effect required to see the concept as referring to such representations. Thus, we are forced to say that the concept refers to bodily disturbances, and also to say that it refers to D-representations. Now much of the time, the fact that the concept has this dual role is invisible to us, for in normal cases, an agent is undergoing a bodily disturbance of the relevant sort just in case he or she is tokening a D-representation. But these two things are in principle dissociable, and in fact become dissociated in certain cases of injury and in cases of phantom limb pain. Because of this, it is literally impossible to have a single, internally coherent theory of the nature of pain. A theory of pain can honor those aspects of the use of the folk concept that connect it with peripheral disturbances, or it can honor those aspects of its use that connect it with D-representations. But if it is to be consistent, a theory cannot honor all of those aspects simultaneously.

We have now arrived at a plausible diagnosis – a plausible account of the factors responsible for the paradox of pain. Assuming that this diagnosis is correct, we can easily agree on a form of therapy. If the paradox arises because we use the concept of pain to keep track of two different and dissociable items, then we can remove the paradox by replacing the concept with two new ones, each of which will be used to keep track of just one of the two items. More specifically, we should introduce a concept that can be used exclusively to keep track of bodily disturbances involving actual and potential damage, and also a second concept that can be used exclusively to keep track of D-representations. Once the concepts have been introduced, we can substitute the first one for all occurrences of the concept of pain in the perceptual/somatic theory, thereby protecting that theory from the objections we encountered earlier in the present section. This will of course clear the way for unqualified acceptance of that deeply and multiply motivated theory.

Actually, reflection shows that we need *three* new concepts to do the work that is done in everyday life by the concept of pain. In addition to registering the comings and goings of bodily disturbances and D-representations, the concept of pain is used to register the comings and goings of pain affect, which consists principally of the response of the limbic system to the occurrence of D-representations. Just as bodily disturbances and D-representations are dissociable from each other, so both are dissociable from pain affect. Accordingly, if we are to avoid conflicts and meltdowns, we must have the means of keeping track independently of all of these items.

It turns out, then, that the form of conceptual fission that we are contemplating here is more complex than the form that is found in the standard examples from the history of science. Indeed, as far as I know it is unique. Standard examples such as heat/temperature involve binary fission. The present case is an example of ternary fission.

In summary, it would be good to have a set of concepts that enabled us to distinguish sharply among the experience of pain, pain itself, and pain affect, and to talk coherently about these three quite different items. Since we cannot do these things using the commonsense concept of pain, there is a reason for setting that concept aside and replacing it with three new concepts that have separate conceptual roles. Such a replacement would clearly benefit both science and philosophy.

6.7   CONCLUSION

We have found that our use of the concept of pain is subject to a variety of countervailing pressures, and that it suffers from a form of semantic incoherence as a result. But also, in addition to this negative result about the concept of pain, we have uncovered a set of extra-conceptual facts that can be summarized as follows: First, experiences of the sort we call "experiences of pain" are quasi-perceptual states, where this means that they share a range of important functional and informational characteristics with paradigmatic perceptual states. Presumably there are also underlying representational similarities. Second, the objects on which these states are directed have peripheral locations, and are in fact to be found in the parts of the body to which we refer our pains. And third, the characteristic properties of these objects are properties having to do with damage and stress.

What have authors had primarily in mind when they have spoken of pain qualia? Have they meant to refer to properties of somatosensory perceptual states or to properties of the peripheral disturbances that such states represent? Given the incoherence of the commonsense concept of pain, there is no one answer to this question. I will assume here, however, that the literature on pain qualia is on the whole best understood as concerned with properties of bodily disturbances. This is the only assumption that allows us to make sense of the fact that contributors to the literature are fully committed to the idea that pain qualia are properties with which we are immediately acquainted in virtue of having experiences of pain. Pain qualia are taken to be properties that we know, and moreover, properties that we know by experiencing them. They are objects of experiential awareness. This view is one of the few that are shared by members of all camps.

On this picture pain qualia have a quite different metaphysical nature than the qualia that are revealed by such standard forms of perceptual awareness as vision and hearing. According to the picture, pain qualia are properties of highly circumscribed events in specific regions of the body. They are therefore quite different than the properties that have been identified with perceptual qualia in earlier chapters. Perceptual qualia have been said to be A-properties, where A-properties are viewpoint-dependent properties of external objects – properties that external objects have in virtue of their relations to the perspectives or viewpoints occupied by observers. The reason for this divergence is that awareness of bodily disturbances does not share the perspectival character of the standard perceptual modalities. Experiential awareness of pain does not involve changes like the changes in visual experience that occur when we move closer to an object, or the ones that occur when the intensity of the lighting is increased, or the ones that occur when the orientation of the object of awareness undergoes a change. In short, awareness of pain does not involve awareness of A-properties. It follows immediately, of course, that pain qualia *cannot* be identified with A-properties. They have to be identified with properties whose realization is confined to circumscribed, continuous regions.

CHAPTER 7

Internal weather

The metaphysics of emotional qualia

Although it is widely and perhaps universally recognized that the emotions have large and richly textured qualitative dimensions, there is no standard inventory of emotional qualia. Accordingly, for much of its compass, the present chapter will be concerned with the enterprise of identifying emotional qualia and classifying them. The more theoretical enterprise of explaining emotional qualia will be less prominent. In the end, though, we will find that emotional qualia conform to the theory of perceptual and bodily qualia that has been developed in earlier chapters. This will make it possible for us to explain them, and thereby to bring them into the domain of science and naturalistic metaphysics.

7.1 SOMATIC THEORIES OF THE EMOTIONS

Whatever else the category of emotional qualia may encompass, it is clear that it includes a large range of bodily sensations. When I am afraid my body is engaged in my fear: my heart throbs, I have butterflies in my stomach, the rate of my breathing increases, and my hands grow cold and clammy. All of these physical conditions have a sensory dimension. A throbbing heart feels quite differently than one that is beating at a normal rate, and an agitated stomach feels quite differently than one that is at rest. Disgust is also characterized by a set of bodily conditions. When a smell disgusts me I gag, my eyes water, my nose wrinkles, my lips curl, and I may wretch. Each of these conditions has a proprietary qualitative character. There are of course emotions that are less extensively and saliently somatic than full blown fear and disgust – for example, mild surprise. But even in the case of paradigmatically "mental" or psychological emotions, careful attention generally reveals qualitative bodily accompaniments. These accompaniments range from the qualia associated with small changes in facial expression to the qualia associated with such generalized and pervasive conditions as being energized and being in a state of relaxation or tension.

Insofar as emotional qualia can be identified with sensory characteristics of bodily states, it is possible to assimilate them to pain qualia, and thereby to bring them within the purview of the theory of qualia and qualitative awareness that I have been developing. Thus, for example, to the extent that the qualia associated with fear can be located within the body, it is natural to suppose that our awareness of them is perceptual (or quasi-perceptual), and to hold that it is possible to explain the way they appear to us by invoking syntactic, functional, and semantic properties of perceptual representations. In general, in view of our conclusions about pain in Chapter 6, it is appropriate to think that bodily qualia are in principle intelligible, even though it may be necessary to make adjustments in our conceptual scheme in order to describe and explain them in a fully satisfactory way. To the extent that emotional qualia are in and of the body, they participate in this intelligibility.

It is therefore a matter of some importance to map the space of emotional qualia and to determine what portion of that space is ultimately somatic in character. Does the space consist mainly of somatic qualia? Is it plausible that it consists entirely of somatic qualia? If not, where exactly do the boundaries between somatic and non-somatic qualia fall? These questions are of fundamental importance for our inquiry.

In seeking answers for them it is useful to consider the history of attempts to answer a set of closely related but more general questions. The question of whether emotional qualia are largely somatic is paralleled by the question of whether emotions are themselves largely somatic. And the question of how to draw the boundary between somatic and non-somatic emotional qualia, if indeed a boundary exists, is paralleled by the question of how to draw a boundary between the components of emotions that are bodily and the components that are psychological and mental. As is well known, these questions about the scope of the bodily dimension of emotions have figured prominently in the psychological and neuroscientific literature for decades. While inconclusive, these discussions have produced a number of valuable insights, and it therefore seems wise to review them before proceeding with our investigation of emotional qualia. The insights have implications concerning emotional qualia that we will find helpful.

William James initiated discussions concerning the somatic nature of the emotions in 1884.[1] James sketched and persuasively defended a version

---

[1] William James, "What is an Emotion?" *Mind* IX (1884), 188–205. Reprinted in Knight Dunlap (ed.), *The Emotions* (Baltimore, Williams and Wilkins, 1922), 11–30. All citations of James refer to pages in this volume.

of the extreme view that emotions consist entirely of states of awareness that register certain bodily changes – specifically, the changes that we undergo when we encounter stimuli of biological significance. I will summarize James's paper and will then describe the closely related views of the contemporary neuroscientist Antonio Damasio. We will be able to acquire a sense of the terrain in this area by considering the proposals of these figures and some of the objections that have been brought against them.

All theories recognize that the body responds adaptively to biologically significant stimuli, and these responses are felt or perceived by a monitoring system in the brain. James was impressed by the complex and multi-dimensional character of the responses. In effect, he observed, they involve the whole body – the cardiovascular system, the endocrine-hormonal system, the digestive system, the musculoskeletal system, and so on. He was also impressed by the extent to which these bodily changes are registered by the cerebral monitoring system. He found it natural to think that the richly embroidered texture of an emotion can be explained in terms of the complex structure of the cerebral representation that registers it.

These perceptions led to the following proposal: "My thesis ... is that *the bodily changes follow directly the* PERCEPTION *of the exciting fact, and that our feeling of the same changes as they occur is the emotion.*"[2] This prominently located passage explicitly identifies emotions with perceptions of bodily states, and I think this is the general tenor of James's discussion. At all events, I will interpret him here as being fully committed to this identification.

It should be noted, however, that there are a few passages in which he seems to incline to the view that emotions are not perceptions of bodily conditions, but rather bodily conditions themselves. This is true, for example, of a footnote in which he acknowledges that it can seem to one that one is experiencing fear even though one's body is not undergoing the relevant cardiac and visceral changes. The passage I have in mind runs as follows:

It must be confessed that there are cases of morbid fear in which objectively the heart is not much perturbed. These however fail to prove anything against our theory, for it is of course possible that the cortical centres normally percipient of dread as a complex of cardiac and other organic sensations due to real bodily change, should become *primarily* excited in brain-disease, and give

---

[2] *Ibid.*, p. 13.

rise to an hallucination of the changes being there, – an hallucination of dread, consequently, consistent with a comparatively calm pulse, etc.[3]

Of course, if dread is a perceptual representation of accelerated heartbeat, etc., then it would be wrong to describe a token of the representation that is not accompanied by these bodily phenomena as *hallucination of dread*. One should say instead that dread exists in cases of this sort but is hallucinatory: one experiences real dread, but that state of dread misrepresents the current state of the body.[4]

Apart from atypical passages of this sort, James steadfastly maintains that each emotion is constituted by a perceptual representation of a set of bodily changes. One of his main concerns is to convince us that the bodily dimensions of emotions are "much more far-reaching and complicated than we ordinarily suppose." Another is to get us to share his view that these bodily occurrences are consciously perceived: "every one of the bodily changes, whatsoever it be, is *felt*, acutely or obscurely, the moment it occurs."[5] (In evaluating this claim, by the way, it is important to remember the adverb "obscurely." James is not urging that we are explicitly and separately aware of each component of an array of bodily changes. Rather, his view seems to be that the microcomponents of bodily processes are registered by somatosensory perceptions in the way that microcomponents of external physical events are registered by visual perception. The microcomponents contribute causally to the signal that is processed, with the result that the ensuing representation can be said to encode information about them. But we cannot discriminate them.)

James gives several arguments for his theory. Two of these are especially relevant to our concerns. First, there is the famous *subtraction argument*. James invites the reader to imagine an emotion. The reader's image of it will, James is sure, include representations of accompanying bodily phenomena. He asks the reader to subtract these representations one-by-one from the original image, and then, at the end of the process, to see whether anything essential to the emotion remains. The reader is to ask, "Can the notion of anger (or whatever) get a foothold here?" He feels sure that the reader will answer "no." He writes: "If we fancy some strong emotion, and then try to abstract from our consciousness of it all the feelings of its characteristic bodily symptoms, we find that we have nothing left behind, no 'mind-stuff' out of which the emotion can be constituted, and that a cold and neutral state of intellectual perception

[3] *Ibid.*, p. 24.   [4] *Ibid.*, p. 14.   [5] *Ibid.*, p. 16.

is all that remains."[6] I will call James's second argument the *induction argument* because it has to do with inducing an emotion. The idea is that we can, for example, induce a state of happiness or quasi-happiness by voluntarily producing the bodily conditions that normally characterize that emotion. James would have us relax, smile broadly, straighten our posture, and then ask whether we do not feel something akin to happiness. He is confident that our answer will be in keeping with his theory. (Of course, we will not feel unqualified or full-strength happiness, for we will not have willed all of the relevant bodily conditions into existence. We could not have done this – many of these conditions are outside the realm of voluntary control.)

In addition to marshalling supporting arguments, James discusses several reasons for concern about his theory. I will mention two of these. First, there were in his time, as there are today, clinical data suggesting that patients suffering from bodily anaesthesia, such as victims of spinal cord injuries, are capable of experiencing emotion. Second, there are emotions that seem to be purely psychological in character – James's examples are the "moral, intellectual, and aesthetic feelings."[7] Referring to these emotions, he develops the objection as follows:

Concords of sounds, of colors, of lines, logical consistencies, teleological fitnesses, affect us with a pleasure that seems ingrained in the very form of the representation itself, and to borrow nothing from any reverberation surging up from the parts below the brain. ... We have, then, or some of us seem to have, genuinely *cerebral* forms of pleasure and displeasure, apparently not agreeing in their mode of production with the so-called standard emotions we have been considering.[8]

Since perceptions of music and logical ideas can "immediately arouse a form of emotional feeling,"[9] it cannot hold in general that feelings are perceptual representations of bodily phenomena.

James does not have much of interest to say about the problem posed by spinal cord injuries, so I will not review his discussion of it here. On the other hand, Damasio deals with the problem quite effectively; I will discuss his response to it a bit later on. James's discussion of the "higher pleasures" objection is more illuminating. Speaking of cases of "purely cerebral" emotions, he says the following:

Unless in them there actually be coupled with the intellectual feeling a bodily reverberation of some kind, unless we actually laugh at the neatness of the mechanical device, thrill at the justice of the act, or tingle at the perfection of

---

[6] *Ibid.*, p. 17.   [7] *Ibid.*, p. 25.   [8] *Ibid.*, p. 25–26.   [9] *Ibid.*, p. 26.

the musical form, our mental condition is more allied to a judgment of *right* than anything else. And such a judgment is rather to be classified among awarenesses of truth; it is a *cognitive* act.[10]

He goes on to speak of the comparative "dryness" of the cognitive act, "the paleness and absence of all glow." It is not characterized by feeling, in James's eyes, so it has no emotional character.

Although it is partially persuasive as it stands, this reply to the "intellectual pleasures" argument is incomplete. It is necessary to conjoin it with an account of the hedonic properties of experiences which denies that pleasure or pleasantness is ultimately qualitative in character. I offer such an account in Section 7.3 – an account which maintains that the pleasantness of an experience is a functional property. There is, I believe, nothing about James's theory that would prevent him from embracing this additional claim.

I turn now to Damasio. Unlike James, Damasio distinguishes sharply between emotions and feelings. (He acknowledges that this distinction does some violence to ordinary usage, but maintains that it is warranted by its theoretical utility.) An emotion begins either when a perceptual system detects a stimulus that has some bearing on the welfare of the organism (an "emotionally competent stimulus"), or when a stimulus of this sort is recalled from memory.[11] This leads to the activation of a set of cortical and subcortical agencies, including the ventromedial prefrontal cortex, the cingulate cortex, and the amygdala, that can trigger and regulate a bodily response.[12] The bodily response is an adaptive reaction to the emotionally competent stimulus,[13] and it is genuinely multi-dimensional, consisting of cardiovascular phenomena, endocrine-hormonal phenomena, musculoskeletal phenomena, and so on. Depending on its specific composition, the bodily response is designed either to support behavior that is appropriate to the eliciting stimulus, or to support a suitable internal accommodation to the stimulus. Damasio regards it as the culmination and principal component of the emotion. The entire emotion consists of this bodily response, the initial perception or memory of the eliciting stimulus, an evaluation of that stimulus,[14] and the ensuing activity of the cerebral regulatory agencies. A feeling, on the other hand, is entirely mental or psychological in character.[15] The principal component of a feeling

---

[10] *Ibid.*, p. 26.
[11] Antonio Damasio, *Looking for Spinoza: Joy, Sorrow, and the Feeling Brain* (Orlando, FL: Harcourt, Inc., 2003), p. 53 and p. 57.
[12] *Ibid.*, p. 59.   [13] *Ibid.*, p. 30 and p. 49.   [14] *Ibid.*, p. 54.   [15] *Ibid.*, p. 28.

is a perceptual representation of the somatic component of an emotion.[16] Often this representation is the only component.[17] In other cases, how- ever, a feeling includes states of awareness of two other sorts – specifically, an awareness of the thoughts that are occasioned by an emotion, and an awareness of the speed and other adverbial characteristics of the concur- rent mental processes. When I am sad, for example, in addition to being aware of such bodily conditions as a general lack of energy and a slack- ness of the facial muscles, I may note that my thoughts keep returning to the events that initially caused the downturn in my mood, and I may also note that my mental processes are slow and lacking in fluency. In a case of this sort, my feeling of sadness has three components – a state of bodily awareness and two states of introspective, psychological awareness. Summarizing this picture, Damasio says the following: "*a feeling is the perception of a certain state of the body along with the perception of a certain mode of thinking and of thoughts with certain themes.*"[18]

Damasio tells us a number of other things about feelings. One impor- tant claim is that a feeling is at least potentially conscious.[19] This is neces- sary if a feeling is to perform its job of informing the agent of the current condition of his body. Another important claim is that feelings are highly variegated and quite complex.[20] Damasio defends this claim by inviting us to attend to our own feelings, and also by providing elaborate descrip- tions of examples, such as feelings of lust and feelings of pride. Damasio also presents and lays out considerable experimental justification for a theory concerning the cortical sites that support feelings. It appears that the principal sites are the somatotopic maps in the insula and the second- ary somatosensory cortex. A pattern of activity in these sites is in effect a perceptual representation of the somatic component of an emotion.

As we saw, James allows for cases in which somatosensory represen- tations occur without being accompanied by the corresponding bodily phenomena. Like sight, hearing, and the other outer perceptual modal- ities, somatosensory perception can be hallucinatory. Damasio takes up this idea and develops it in considerable detail, under the label "'as if' feelings."[21] An "as if" feeling is a token of a perceptual representation of the body that is not brought about in the usual way, by a wave of somatic activity, but rather by cerebral activity of some sort. In many cases, the trigger is a process in a high level cognitive agency, such as episodic mem- ory or the visual imagination. "As if" feelings are generally less vivid and

---

[16] *Ibid.*, p. 86–87.   [17] *Ibid.*, p. 89.   [18] *Ibid.*, p. 86.   [19] *Ibid.*, p. 110.
[20] *Ibid.*, p. 87 and p. 94.   [21] *Ibid.*, pp. 115–121.

complex than the feelings that are caused by bodily phenomena, but they are nonetheless qualitatively similar to their more robust colleagues.

This brings us to Damasio's discussion of the problem posed by patients with spinal cord injuries. Although the data involving such patients are somewhat discordant, they on the whole indicate that it is possible to have recognizable emotions in the absence of the information about the state of one's body that is normally carried by the spinal cord. Some studies even indicate that spinal patients can have fairly intense emotions. On the face of it, therefore, the data pose a substantial threat to somatic theories of emotions and emotional experience. Damasio responds to this challenge in several ways. One of his arguments is that the spinal cord is not the only source of information about the body – the vagus nerve is another important source, as is the bloodstream, which carries information in chemical form.[22] Another argument appeals to the neural channels leading directly from the face to the brain. On all accounts facial expressions play a large role in emotions, even when emotions are experienced in solitude, and the feelings that register these expressions play a correspondingly large role in emotional experience.[23] In combination with several others that Damasio gives, these arguments are quite powerful. They would be circumvented, however, if future research were to show that emotional experience can continue in a fully robust form even when all of the sources of bodily information are blocked or substantially attenuated. This is one of the reasons why "as if" feelings are an essential component of Damasio's theory. "As if" feelings can be triggered by central processes, including the very perceptual states that normally initiate adaptive bodily responses. To be sure, these feelings are less vivid than the corresponding veridical perceptions; but this is actually a virtue from Damasio's perspective, for he interprets the data involving spinal patients as showing that their emotional experiences are impaired or restricted to some degree.[24]

I do not myself agree with somatic theories of emotion. They are certainly right to emphasize the behavioral and other bodily dimensions of emotion, and the role that perception of these dimensions plays in emotional phenomenology. But they have trouble explaining the psychological aspects of emotion other than qualitative awareness. Thus, as a group they have little to say about the process by which external stimuli are evaluated for ecological and social significance. What

---

[22] Antonio Damasio, *The Feeling of What Happens: Body and Emotion in the Making of Consciousness* (New York: Harcourt, Brace, and Company, 1999), p. 289.
[23] *Ibid.*, p. 290.   [24] *Ibid.*, p. 289.

dimensions are relevant to these evaluations, and what is the nature of the representational scheme in which they are couched? To what extent are they automatic and under stimulus control, and to what extent are they under the control of flexible high level programs? Questions of this sort should be fully and deeply engaged by a theory of the emotions, not marginalized or ignored altogether. Another shortcoming is that somatic theories have trouble explaining what it is for an emotion to have an intentional object or target. My anger is directed at Congress, my fear at the snake, and my envy at the neighbor who owns a Porsche. These intentional facts seem to be inextricably bound up with the other dimensions of their respective emotions. It seems, however, that somatic theories lack the resources to explain how emotions acquire intentional objects, or the role that a representation of an intentional object plays in the course of an emotion. From the perspective of a somatic theorist, the intentional object of an emotion would have to be either the eliciting stimulus or the current state of the body, for these are the represented items on which somatic theories place the greatest emphasis. But neither of these objects has the right properties. Thus, in many cases, the intentional object of an emotion is quite different than the eliciting stimulus. I may become incensed with Congress as a result of reading of a bombing in a country on the other side of the world. Here the intentional object of my emotion is Congress, or perhaps its Neanderthal behavior, not the eliciting stimulus, which is a certain newspaper article. Nor is it appropriate to identify the intentional object of my wrath with the condition of my body. My anger is directed at Congress, not at my breathing or pulse rate. There are also other problems with somatic theories. For example, it is beginning to be clear that the emotions have deep and systematic connections with perception, reasoning, learning, memory, and the imagination. Damasio has shown that somatic theories may be able to account for some of these liaisons, but it seems unlikely that such theories will be able to do full justice to all of them. Moreover, even if they can explain the liaisons, they will be forced to classify them as contingent side effects of emotions, not as fundamental and constitutive. But why should the flaring of one's nostrils be thought more essential to one's anger than one's thoughts and images of retribution?

On the other hand, while somatic theories of emotion run into insurmountable problems, due to their tendency to minimize psychological components, they help us to appreciate the resources of somatic theories of emotional qualia. Thus, as we will see in a moment, both of the Jamesian arguments for somatic theories of emotions that we considered earlier – the subtraction argument and the induction argument – can be reformulated so as to provide support for somatic theories of emotional qualia. The arguments appear to be quite effective. Further, Damasio's experimental work provides considerable support for the claim, essential to somatic theories of emotional qualia, that our grasp of emotional qualia is perceptual. Thus, as we observed, Damasio and his associates have shown that the bodily changes that are involved in emotions give rise to highly intricate representations in the insula and the secondary somatosensory cortex. It is independently plausible that representations of this sort can become conscious, and also that they are associated with somatotopic maps that are quite similar to the ones that support touch and thermal perception. In general, it is easy to adapt the positive supporting arguments that have been developed by advocates of somatic theories of emotion so as to obtain positive supporting arguments for somatic theories of emotional qualia.

It is also true that advocates of the latter theories can make use of some of the defensive moves that advocates of the former theories have devised. Earlier we took note of two standard objections to somatic theories of emotions – the "higher pleasure" objection that James considers, and the objection based on spinal patients. As the reader can easily appreciate, both of these objections have counterparts that are aimed at somatic theories of emotional qualia. For example, when spinal patients claim that they have continued to enjoy rich emotional lives after their injuries, part of what they are claiming is that they continue to experience many of the same emotional qualia. These counterpart objections are prima facie quite strong, but the replies that James and Damasio give to the original objections can easily be adapted so as to provide replies to the counterparts. The adapted replies take us at least part way towards adequate answers.

I would like now to expand on my claim that James's subtraction and induction arguments can be adapted so as to yield valuable support for somatic theories of qualia.

In presenting the subtraction argument, James invites us to "fancy" an emotion, which presumably means to imagine one, and to proceed to think away various components of the imagined state. I do not find the argument very convincing when it is based in this way on an imagined emotion. Whether they are produced by memory or the imagination, my images of emotions are too vague and insubstantial to permit delicate surgical excisions. What is worse, my images of emotions tend to be centered around representations of facial expressions and other overt behaviors. I can't easily synthesize internal weather in the imagination – in imagining how I might *feel* on a given occasion, I generally succeed only in imagining how I might *look* on that occasion. But the situation is quite different when I apply the subtraction technique to an *actual* emotion. I find, for example, that if I focus my attention on a passing surge of road rage, at the time when I am actually experiencing it, it is reasonably clear how to apply James's instruction to think away various somatic components. Thinking away presumably comes to the same thing as prescinding from, and I have no difficulty in prescinding from such features of my state as the increase in my pulse rate, the tightening of my grip on the wheel, and the facial expressions associated with glaring at the offending driver. The only difficulty in applying the procedure derives from the fact that it is easy to overlook somatic components of an emotion, or to misclassify them as mental. Thus, when I am in the grips of road rage, I often hurl mental curses and insults at the other driver. I may think, "Brilliant move, you execrable moron!" – or worse. Denunciations of this sort are internal, and it can seem that they proceed entirely at the level of pure thought. But in my case, at least, careful introspection reveals that there is a somatic involvement, amounting perhaps to a subvocalization that engages some of the same muscles as overt speech. Even in milder moods, my thoughts often have a somatic electricity of this sort. One must prescind from all such phenomena if one is to follow James's instructions to the letter.

Suppose one succeeds in following them. How much of the targeted emotion remains? James would say that virtually all of it disappears, but it is reasonably clear that this is wrong. Thus, for example, emotions influence a large range of mental processes, changing their speed, fluency, and cohesiveness, and also shaping content to a large degree. When one is excited one's thoughts come quickly and easily, and are likely to undergo spontaneous and even unpredictable changes in content. Further, if the excitement is positive, thought contents tend to lean in the direction of optimism. When one is sad about something, on the other hand, one's thinking is comparatively slow and sluggish, and contents are more likely to cleave to a restricted range of subject matters. There may also be a broadly systematic effect on contents. This is, anyway, what the depressing literature on "depressive realism" suggests. (There is some experimental support for the view that people suffering from mild depression are more accurate than others in evaluating such things as their reputation, abilities, and degree of control over external phenomena.[25] "Depressive

---

[25] See e.g., K. Dobson and R. L. Franche, "Conceptual and Empirical Review of the Depressive Realism Hypothesis," *Canadian Journal of Behavioral Science* 21 (1989), 419–433.

realism" is the name for this phenomenon.) These mental manifestations of emotions are left entirely intact by James's subtraction procedure.

Moreover, in addition to effects of these sorts, which are all accessible to introspection, it is now widely recognized that emotions have a number of unconscious manifestations. They shape memory, learning, and long-term motivation in ways that lie beyond our introspective ken.[26] Like the foregoing conscious manifestations, the subterranean dimensions of emotions are left intact by James's subtraction technique. Accordingly, insofar as it is meant to establish the correctness of somatic theories of emotion, the subtraction argument turns far short of the mark.

We arrive at a quite different evaluation, however, when we consider the argument in relation to somatic theories of emotional qualia. Or so it seems to me. When I am careful to prescind from *all* of the bodily sensations that accompany an emotion, I find that very little remains that could reasonably be described as both qualitative and proprietary to the emotion. Thus, as far as I can tell, the surviving conscious components or manifestations are limited to perceptual experiences of the eliciting stimulus, imagery of various kinds, conscious thoughts, including intentions and other occurrent propositional attitudes, and various adverbial determinations of mental processes. None of these surviving phenomena has a qualitative dimension that is somehow peculiarly emotional in character. To be sure, it seems that emotions influence one's perceptual take on the eliciting stimulus, and thereby have an effect on perceptual qualia. But these perceptual qualia have no proprietary relationship with the emotions. The emotions can cause them, by directing attention at one or another aspect of the eliciting stimulus; but their occurrence is not conditional on the occurrence of any specific emotions, and they play a role in cognition that is largely independent of emotional liaisons. The same is true of the imagery that accompanies emotions. The emotions play a role in determining what images we entertain, but the qualia associated with imagery have no proprietary connection with emotional experience. As for the other conscious phenomena that survive the "Jamesian reduction," thoughts and adverbial determinations of mental processes, I can see no grounds for thinking of them as qualitative. I will, however, say a bit more about this question in the next chapter.

---

[26] See, e.g., Jorge L. Armony and Joseph E. LeDoux, "How Danger is Encoded: Toward a Systems, Cellular, and Computational Understanding of Cognitive-Emotional Interactions in Fear," in Michael Gazzaniga (ed.), *The New Cognitive Neurosciences*, 2nd edition (Cambridge, MA: MIT Press, 2000), 1067–1080.

This brings us to James's induction argument, or rather, to the version of it that is designed to support somatic theories of emotional qualia. Unlike the corresponding version of the subtraction argument, this version of the induction argument makes no claim to *establish* somatic theories, but only to contribute to their plausibility. More particularly, it is designed to show that many of the most striking and characteristic emotional qualia are somatic in character. It does not argue directly for the more general claim that *all* emotional qualia are somatic. In practice, however, it has the effect of increasing our confidence in the more general claim. Once we appreciate the bodily nature of a broad array of emotional qualia, it becomes easier to appreciate the bodily nature of the others.

The argument consists of an invitation to adopt the facial expressions and other bodily manifestations of an emotion that are under voluntary control, and to note the extent to which the qualitative profile of the emotion is thereby induced. It does not claim that the entire profile will be brought into existence, for there is a background acknowledgment that many of the qualia that are associated with an emotion are associated with bodily states that are not under voluntary control. The claim is rather that, in many cases at least, the artificially induced qualia will be quite impressive in their number and variety, and will include many of the qualia that are most characteristic of the given emotion. The reader can easily confirm this claim by performing the following experiment. To set the stage, think of something sad and allow the natural emotional consequences of your thoughts to develop. Continue to think about the same topic until you feel genuinely sorrowful. Then, without changing the tenor of your thoughts, reconfigure your face into a broad grin, making sure both to smile and to "crinkle" the muscles around your eyes in the way that is characteristic of genuine amusement. At the same time, make the noises in your throat that normally accompany laughter, and allow your upper body to pulsate correspondingly. (The noises are produced by short bursts of air. One's throat, chest, and shoulders move when the air is expressed from the lungs.) As you do this, you will find, I predict, that your qualia are almost entirely transformed. Despite the fact that the bodily changes are produced artificially, the qualitative profile of sorrow will largely disappear, giving way to the qualitative profile of amusement. Of course, this is exactly what somatic theories of emotional qualia predict.

If you conduct some additional experiments of the same sort, you will find that it is possible to induce a large array of emotional qualia by miming the appropriate expressions, postures, and behaviors, including even a number of qualia that seem initially to have more to do with the mind than the body.

It may come as some surprise to realize how large a proportion of the qualitative profile of an emotion can be induced simply by forming the corresponding facial expression. To better appreciate the number and variety of such qualia, imitate the expressions in Figure 7.1 (on the next page) and pay close attention to the resulting qualitative changes.[27]

These new qualia form tapestries that are salient and intricate. Moreover, I find that the tapestries are sufficiently different from each other, and from other qualitative tapestries, that they uniquely determine a set of emotions – joy, anger, sadness, surprise, disgust, and fear. There are a number of other emotions that one can "read off" directly from tapestries of facial qualia.

In addition to being supported by armchair experiments of this sort, the claim that the qualitative profiles of emotions are largely determined by facial qualia has received a fair amount of support from scientific investigations. In one study, Strak, Martin, and Stepper found that the way one holds one's mouth when one is engaged in processing cartoons significantly influences one's degree of amusement. These investigators asked one group of subjects to hold a pen between their teeth while looking at a set of cartoons, and another group to hold a pen between their lips. The first condition produces an expression that is similar to a smile. The second produces something like a pout. The members of the first group found the cartoons more amusing than the members of the second group.[28] In another study, Zajonc, Murphy, and Inglehart asked subjects to read two stories containing a number of occurrences of the vowel "ü," whose pronunciation requires a configuration of lip and nostril muscles that is opposed to the configuration associated with smiling, and two other stories that contained no occurrences of "ü" or vowels with similar pronunciation patterns. The subjects liked the second pair of stories better than the first, and also described them as more pleasant.[29] In both of these experiments, facial expressions were found to contribute significantly to the emotional dimension and/or the hedonic dimension of experiences.

---

[27] I am indebted here to Paul Ekman and to Jesse Prinz, who use similar images. See P. Ekman and W. V. Friesen, "Constants across Cultures in the Face and Emotion," *Journal of Personality and Social Psychology* 17 (1971), 124–129, and Jesse J. Prinz, *Gut Reactions: A Perceptual Theory of Emotion* (Oxford: Oxford University Press, 2004), p. 107.

[28] See F. Strak, L. L. Martin, and S. Stepper, "Inhibiting and Facilitating Conditions of Facial Expressions: A Non-obtrusive Test of the Facial Feedback Hypothesis," *Journal of Personality and Social Psychology* 54 (1988), 768–777.

[29] R. B. Zajonc, S. T. Murphy, and M. Inglehart, "Feeling and Facial Efference: Implications of the Vascular Theory of Emotions," *Psychological Review* 96 (1989), 395–416.

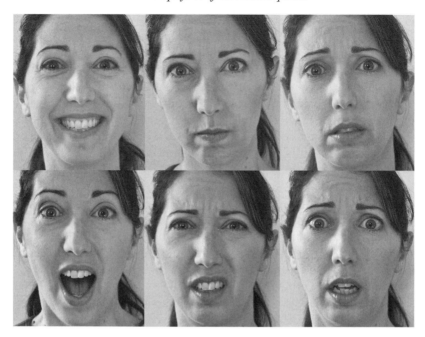

Figure 7.1 Facial expressions for joy, anger, sadness, surprise, disgust, and fear.

It is hard to see how this could be the case if they did not influence the qualitative nature of an experience to an equal degree.

It is time to take stock. We began by observing that if emotional qualia are bodily, and awareness of them is perceptual, then they can be explained in terms of the apparatus that is used to explain pain qualia in the previous chapter. Motivated by this observation, we decided to review two justly celebrated somatic theories of the emotions, due respectively to James and Damasio. It seemed that it might be possible to borrow useful ideas and arguments from these theories, and this has proved to be the case. In addition to the two Jamesian arguments for the somatic nature of emotional qualia that we have considered most recently, we are in possession of a powerful empirical argument, due to Damasio, for the perceptual character of awareness of emotional qualia, and also of plausible replies to two of the most challenging objections to somatic theories.

7.2 THE PERCEPTUAL/SOMATIC THESIS

I am now in a position to make a proposal about the nature of emotional qualia. Let us say that a category of qualia is *emotion-related* if it figures prominently in the etiology or development of one or more emotions. In terms of this notion, my proposal is that there are three categories, and only three categories, of emotional qualia: somatic qualia, perceptual qualia, and qualia associated with perceptual imagery.[30] We have already seen a case for including somatic qualia. Perceptual qualia must be included because perceptual states generally play a large and essential role in the etiology of emotions. Moreover, in many cases, perhaps most, it is a perceptual state that provides an emotion with its intentional object. Imagistic qualia must be included because imagery is often essential to the elaboration of emotions, and to their ability to determine actions. My claim, though, is that there are no other qualia that must be included.

Now as I see it, it is very plausible, both on introspective grounds and on grounds provided by contemporary scientific work on imagery, that the qualia associated with perceptual imagery are fundamentally akin to perceptual qualia.[31] Often they are neither as vivid nor as determinate as qualia that are actually associated with the standard perceptual modalities, but they are nonetheless sufficiently similar to the latter qualia to count as perceptual. Accordingly, it is not necessary to develop a separate metaphysical theory to account for them. Once we have explained perceptual qualia, we have in principle explained the qualia that are associated with perceptual imagery as well. Applying this view to our inventory of emotion-related qualia, we find that we can reduce the complexity of the inventory by a third. Thus, in its simplest and most basic form, the proposal I wish to make is that all emotion-related qualia are either somatic or perceptual in character. I will call this the *perceptual/somatic thesis*, and will say that any theory of emotional qualia that incorporates the thesis is a *perceptual/somatic theory*.

The previous section provides considerable motivation for this thesis, and it also provides some of the main fortifications that are required for its defense. But there are a couple of additional issues that warrant our attention. These issues will appear in the following sections in the form

---

[30] I should emphasize a feature of my use of the term "somatic qualia" that might otherwise escape notice. As I am using the term here, it stands not only for the qualia associated with such Jamesian phenomena as facial tension, strength of heartbeat, and rate of breathing, but also for the qualia associated with actions and the various forms of readiness to act. (Thus, for example, it applies both to the bodily qualia associated with shouting and to the bodily qualia associated with being on the verge of shouting.) Various psychological studies make it clear that action-related qualia generally accompany emotions (and perhaps partially constitute them). There are particularly illuminating discussions of this topic in John A. Lambie and Anthony J. Marcel, "Consciousness and the Varieties of Emotion Experience," *Psychological Review* 109 (2002), 219–259.

[31] See the appendix to Chapter 3.

of objections. In each case, I will try to show that the objection can be met. These replies will extend the theoretical machinery that is presented in Section 7.1, but they will not make any concessions. The perceptual/somatic thesis will emerge unscathed from our inquiries.

Before turning to consider the objections, however, it will be well to pause briefly to consider the perceptual qualia that are involved in emotions. What has been said so far is that awareness of the eliciting stimuli will generally be perceptual, that the intentional object is often furnished by perception, and that perceptual qualia are involved in the imagistic elaboration of an emotion. All of this is correct, but it seems that emotions often interact with perception in a further way. It is well known that interests and expectations can have a profound influence on perceptual processing, both by directing attention to various details of what is perceived, thereby allocating processing-energy to low level perceptual mechanisms, and by priming the higher level mechanisms that are involved in recognizing macrostructural properties of various kinds. Thus, for example, an expert on Velazquez will perceive details of brushwork that are invisible to the novice, and will also be more sensitive to the higher order features of attire and expression that signify the rank and personality of Velazquez's subjects. Again, a mother is more likely than the rest of us to recognize the higher order features of her child's expression that display its mood. It is easy to multiply examples of this sort. Now it is extremely plausible that emotions can shape perceptual processing in both of these ways – by enhancing the processing of details, and by facilitating the recognition of higher order patterns. This can be appreciated by observing that the emotions play a large role in determining our interests and expectations, for as we have just seen, interests and expectations do much to shape perceptual processing. An example: Suppose you become angry with a friend. You will then be more likely, won't you, to see opposition and perhaps even hostility in his countenance? In a case of this sort, your sense of his expression may be due entirely to expectation and therefore mildly hallucinatory, or it may be that your expectations have led you to do justice to real information about the actual state of his countenance that you would otherwise have neglected. But in either case, your anger brings with it a high level classification of your friend as negatively disposed to you, and this classification exerts a top-down influence on lower level perceptual processing, enhancing some aspects of it and inhibiting others.

Someday we will understand how an emotion like love endows us with the ability to see the faces of those we love as beautiful or noble, and how the aesthetic emotions enable us to see paintings and mathematical proofs as gorgeous or elegant. One conjecture is that the perception of beauty has to do with recognizing certain facial symmetries and giving them due weight. But we are at present a very long way from seeing into the heart of such matters. It is clear that the emotions play a significant role in shaping perceptual experience and therefore perceptual qualia, but we do not yet have a deep grasp of the details of the process.

7.3   THE HEDONIC DIMENSION OF EMOTION

An objection to perceptual/somatic theories, at least as they have been developed this far, is that they fail to do justice to the hedonic nature of emotional experience. Some emotions are pleasant or enjoyable while others are unpleasant or disagreeable. What is the difference? A theory of the emotions owes us a satisfactory answer to this question. Further, the objection continues, isn't it rather clear that the answer would have to appeal to qualia – that the difference between pleasant and unpleasant experiences is a qualitative one? Still further, isn't it rather clear that the qualia that make for pleasantness and unpleasantness are different in kind from all of the qualia we have considered this far? Consider the pleasantness of looking at a Vermeer. Is it at all plausible to say that the factors that make for the pleasantness of this experience are somatic qualia? Or that they are perceptual or imagistic qualia? It seems not. Thus, it seems quite wrong to say that this pleasantness derives from the bodily sensations that accompany one's perceptual experience. Moreover, if we think of perceptual and imagistic qualia as having to do with experiencing such perceptual qualities as colors and shapes, it seems quite wrong to say that the *pleasantness* of looking at a Vermeer is a matter of experiencing perceptual qualia. In general, it seems that the pleasantness or unpleasantness of an experience isn't a qualitative factor that is internal to perceptual awareness of one's body, or to perceptual awareness of the world, or to one's entertaining an image. It is something over and above the somatic qualia, perceptual qualia, and imagistic qualia of an experience. In view of this, isn't it rather clear that perceptual/somatic theories, as defined in the last section, lack the resources to explain pleasantness and unpleasantness? They have left important qualia out, and are incapable of correcting this error without making substantial revisions.

While this objection is initially plausible, I think it errs in taking the pleasantness and unpleasantness of experiences to be qualitative characteristics. Careful examination shows that there is no felt quality that is common to all experiences that are pleasant, or even to any large subset of those experiences. Nor is there a common qualitative component of the experiences that we find unpleasant. Consider the taste of a fine wine, the taste of chocolate, the smell of an orchid, the look of a Vermeer, the sound of a Bach cantata, the give and take of a conversation among people of like interests and supportive dispositions, and the touch of someone to whom one is romantically attached. All of these things are pleasant. Perhaps more fundamentally, one's experience of them is pleasant. But surely there is no qualitative characteristic uniting the experience of drinking wine, the experience of eating chocolate, and the experiences of all the other sorts. There is no quality that we can single out as a component of one or two of the experiences, attend to carefully, and then recognize as a component of all of the others.

As far as I can tell, the only thing that is common to all of the experiences I find pleasant is that I *like* or *enjoy* them. But what is it to like an experience? I see liking as a complex functional property that is more fundamental than desire but similar to it in certain ways. If one likes an experience, then, I suggest, one has a tendency to attend to the item that serves as its object, and a tendency to remember that item and how one came into contact with it, a tendency to engage in behaviors that are found to prolong the experience, a tendency to engage in behaviors that intensify it, and a tendency to engage in behaviors that promise to bring about similar experiences in the future. Further, liking an experience has a tendency to influence one's facial expression, by reducing severity and perhaps even promoting a smile, and it may have an effect on one's posture, causing one to adopt a more open stance. It also has a tendency to reduce such background somatic conditions as tension and agitation, while increasing one's sense of disposable energy. Finally, if one has the necessary conceptual resources, then liking an experience may cause one to have certain desires – specifically, a desire to prolong the experience, a desire to intensify it, and a desire to have similar experiences in the future. But it is possible to like an experience even if one's capacity to form desires is quite limited. Small children can like things, as can kittens and puppies.

Just as there is no qualitative element that is shared by all of the experiences one finds pleasant, so also there is no qualitative element that is shared by all the experiences one finds unpleasant. Any introspective search for such an element will end in frustration. What is common to unpleasant experiences is just that one *dislikes* them, where dislike is a complex functional state. As in the case of liking, disliking an experience includes a tendency to pay attention to the object of the experience, and a tendency to remember how one came into contact with that object. But all of the other tendencies that figure in dislike are the opposites of the tendencies that figure in liking. Thus, for example, instead of a tendency to pursue experiences that are similar to a given experience, dislike involves a tendency to avoid such experiences.

Although one might have reservations about the details of these proposals, I think we have no choice but to accept the view that pleasantness and unpleasantness are functional properties. They cannot be explained in terms of shared qualia or qualitative similarity. Explanations must therefore appeal to shared causal tendencies. It must be acknowledged, however, that the foregoing analyses have a couple of counterintuitive consequences. One of these consequences has to do with the causal powers that folk psychology attributes to pleasantness. According to folk psychology, we tend to pursue things *because* we find them pleasant. The foregoing analysis of pleasantness fails to sustain this view, for it implies that having a tendency to pursue something is *part of* what it is to find it pleasant. If this tendency is a component of pleasantness, then presumably it can't be caused by pleasantness. Thus, the analysis calls for a mild revision of folk psychology.[32] The other counterintuitive consequence has to do with masochism. The foregoing analysis of unpleasantness implies that finding an experience unpleasant involves a tendency to avoid similar experiences in the future. But it is natural to think of masochism as involving a tendency to pursue experiences that one finds unpleasant.

---

[32] My claim that this is a "mild" revision of folk psychology has been challenged both by Joseph Levine and an anonymous referee from Cambridge University Press.

   I acknowledge that we find it very natural to say things like the following: "I want this experience to continue *because* it is pleasant – I cherish it for its own sake." A theory would be abruptly at variance with our intuitions if it implied that such claims are always deeply inappropriate. But I think that my theory of pleasantness can accommodate a certain amount of this sort of talk.

   To be sure, the theory implies that it is inappropriate to attribute causal efficacy to pleasantness on occasions when a strict, Humean conception of causation is operative. A disposition to cause events of type E cannot be a Humean cause of a particular event of type E, for Humean causes are causes that are metaphysically independent of their effects. Since my theory of pleasantness implies that pleasantness consists, in part, in a disposition to try to prolong experiences, the theory implies that pleasantness cannot be a Humean cause of wanting a pleasant experience to continue. Reflection shows, however, that we sometimes have a more liberal conception of causation in mind, according to which a cause is anything that provides a certain amount of explanatory insight. And it also shows that when we are thinking of causation in this more inclusive way, we allow ourselves to say that dispositions are causes of particular events. Thus, for example, despite the fact that magnetism is a disposition to attract, we would allow ourselves to cite the magnetic nature of a certain object as causally relevant to the motions of certain particular iron filings. It is plausible, I think, that we generally have this inclusive conception of causation in mind when we attribute causal efficacy to pleasantness. If this is true, then my theory of pleasantness is broadly compatible with such attributions.

Clearly, if the foregoing analysis is to be accepted, this natural way of describing masochism must be set aside. To the layman, it is not apparent whether it should be replaced by the proposition that masochism involves a tendency to pursue experiences that are *normally regarded* as unpleasant, or by the proposition that masochism involves conflicting tendencies, tendencies of approach and also tendencies of avoidance, and that the tendencies of approach are dominant. All that can be said here is that one or the other of these two new descriptions, or some combination of them, *must* be accepted. We must learn to wear a shoe if it is the only one that fits, even if its style is not fully in harmony with the rest of our attire.

In summary, I wish to suggest that the hedonic features of experiences must be understood in functional terms. Hedonic features have to do with what we learn from experiences, with the action programs that they activate, with their effect on various background bodily conditions, and with their capacity to produce propositional attitudes. The view that they are qualitative fails to withstand close scrutiny.

7.4 MENTAL QUALIA

The foregoing objection begins by citing a specific dimension of emotional experience, and then goes on to challenge perceptual/somatic theories to account for it. The second objection I wish to consider is quite different. Instead of pointing to a particular dimension of emotional experience, it simply affirms the existence of emotional qualia that can't be explained in perceptual or somatic terms. In the versions I have encountered, the objection is expressed in something like the following way: "It is plausible that many if not most emotional qualia are somatic in nature, and it is of course true that emotions generally have perceptual and imagistic components. But introspection reveals that there are *mental* emotional qualia that are not reducible to perceptual and imagistic qualia. That is, there are emotional *feelings* that are purely psychological in character. It isn't possible to describe these feelings very precisely, or even to give precise instructions for locating them in one's experience. But isn't it just obvious that, for example, there are feelings of elevation, expansion, and energy that accompany joy, and that some of these feelings are purely psychological?"

I don't know whether this worry can ever be fully dispelled, but there are three responses that make it seem much less compelling and urgent. The first is just that it is often far from easy to appreciate the somatic nature of emotional qualia. This is particularly true, I feel, of the qualia that are associated with facial expressions, and of the qualia that are associated with such generalized bodily conditions as tension, agitation, relaxation, energy, harmony, and discord.[33] Thus, for example, as we noticed earlier, it is more than a little surprising to realize how large a proportion of the qualia that accompany joy can be attributed to facial expressions alone. What initially seems mental turns out to be bodily. The same is true of one's sense of being energized. I will acknowledge in a moment that when one is aware of being energized, some of the energy one experiences is mental in character. I believe, however, that the *qualia* that accompany being energized are entirely somatic. To appreciate the merits of this claim, perform a "Jamesian reduction" the next time you experience excitement. That is to say, blot out all of the bodily aspects of your excitement by focusing your attention narrowly on those aspects of it that are indisputably psychological. If you are like me, you will find that there is nothing left that has a strong claim on the adjective "qualitative."

The second response begins with what may initially appear to be a concession. I wish to acknowledge that it is genuinely appropriate to apply terms like "elevated," "expansive," and "energized" to the psychological component of joy, and to apply terms that have similarly "qualitative" connotations to the psychological dimensions of other emotions. I think, however, that the truth-makers for descriptions of mental states that involve these terms are not qualitative facts, but rather facts about the semantic contents of mental states and the adverbial determinations of mental processes. Thus, if one is in an "elevated" mental state when one is experiencing joy, this is because one's evaluations of the things one considers tend to be much higher than they would be in other contexts. When one is experiencing joy, one tends to look on the bright side of things. One focuses on the virtues of the things one is considering and applauds those things for being so wonderfully virtuous. Moreover, the structure of one's preferences undergoes a temporary change: one considers more things worth pursuing, and one is more ready to commit oneself fully to the pursuit of the things one prefers. The truth-makers for "expansive" are similar. When a person is experiencing joy, the sphere of his approval literally expands to include more people, more objects, more courses of action, more ideas, more theories, more sensations, and more ways of being. What about the truth-makers for "energized"? Here I think it is necessary to appeal to adverbial determinations of mental processes. When one is experiencing joy, or any other positive emotion for

[33] For discussions of these "background feelings," see Antonio Damasio, *Descartes' Error*, 2nd edition (London: Vintage Books, 2006), pp. 150–155, and Damasio, *Looking for Spinoza*, pp. 43–44.

that matter, one's thoughts flow more rapidly and fluently, and are also more robust, in the sense that one has more confidence in their correctness. Moreover, one is more inclined to undertake mental endeavors of various sorts, and to pursue those endeavors with purpose and efficiency. Thus, for example, when one is experiencing a positive emotion, one may be more willing to work on difficult chess problems, and one may approach the problems with more confidence and persistence. In combination, these facts can make it quite appropriate to apply "energized" and cognate expressions to one's state of mind.

Similar remarks apply to the other terms with vaguely qualitative connotations that we use to describe the psychological dimensions of emotions – terms like "constricted," "frozen," and "surging." These terms have qualitative connotations because they draw analogies between frames of mind and bodily conditions that have a proprietary phenomenology, or between frames of mind and external physical conditions that give rise to distinctive qualia when we encounter them perceptually. What I wish to claim, however, is that if we reflect on the facts that make the analogies or metaphors apt, we will find that they can be adequately characterized without invoking qualia. The metaphors can be replaced by descriptions that are concerned exclusively with facts involving contents and facts involving such properties of mental processes as speed, coherence, robustness, and autonomy (that is, independence of the agent's control).

My third response to the present objection is that it owes much of its plausibility to the vagueness and ambiguity of "qualia" and related expressions. In effect, the objection claims that when we perform the "Jamesian reduction" on an emotional state, we are left with a qualitative residue – a residue that is elusive and very hard to describe, but that can be partially captured, or at least gestured towards, by metaphors. The objection thus presupposes that the term "qualitative" has a fixed and determinate meaning. In fact, however, the use of this term becomes dangerously elastic in contexts in which it is not anchored by paradigms like pain and the way yellow things look. The present context belongs to this category. The context is defined by the question, "Are there emotional qualia that are neither bodily nor perceptual?" It is built into the content of this question that the usual paradigms will provide little useful guidance for attempts to answer it. Accordingly, it is impossible to *prove* that the answer to the question should be "no." But this is hardly a reason for thinking that the answer should be "yes." Rather, insofar as the intuitive, pre-theoretical notion of the qualitative is vague, we should not suppose that questions framed in terms of it admit of determinate answers. If we wish to have answers, we must rephrase the questions with others that make use of more determinate notions. I would urge that in framing such notions, we must be guided principally by the usual paradigms. If we are not to drift on the open seas, we must make full use of the anchors that are available to us.

For all of these reasons, it seems appropriate to set the present objection aside. Perhaps there is some way of reformulating it that will increase its effectiveness, but rather substantial improvements will have to be made in order for it to warrant further attention. I don't see what those improvements could be.

7.5   CONCLUSION

The realm of emotional qualia is vast and diverse. I have been mainly concerned in this chapter to chart its boundaries and subdivisions, and in particular, to examine the thesis that it is exhausted by the members of three categories – somatic qualia, perceptual qualia, and imagistic qualia. We have found several lines of thought that provide support for this thesis. We have also observed that several prima facie powerful objections to it can be answered. On the whole, it seems acceptable.[34] This is a welcome result, for it implies that the theoretical apparatus that has been developed

---

[34] Although I find the foregoing lines of thought fully persuasive, conversation has made me aware that there are others who feel differently. They remain convinced that there are solid introspective grounds for thinking that the phenomenological dimension of emotions includes a range of emotional qualia that are neither somatic nor associated with any of the standard perceptual modalities. Now I must allow that it is possible that they are right, for it is conceivable that my introspective powers are defective in one or more respects. I therefore add the following observation: If it is true that such residual emotional qualia exist, it may be possible to account for them by combining one of the guiding hypotheses of the present work with the theory of the representational content of emotional experience that has been developed by Jesse Prinz. The hypothesis in question is the claim that phenomenology can be fully explained by saying that qualia are properties that are objects of experiential awareness – that is, properties that are represented by perceptual or quasi-perceptual experiences. In order to apply this hypothesis to residual emotional qualia, it would be necessary to show that the limbic system produces representations that can be appropriately classified as perceptual or quasi-perceptual. But it might be possible to show this by invoking Prinz's theory of emotions, which maintains that emotions necessarily involve representations of properties that have biological and psychological significance. In effect, Prinz postulates a perceptual modality over and above vision, hearing, and the other standard forms of perception – a modality that might be called *emotional perception*. The chief difference between emotional perception and the standard forms is that it has the job of keeping the organism apprised of certain *normative* properties – more specifically, properties like *offensive, dangerous,* and *posing a threat to self-esteem.* It could perhaps be argued that residual emotional qualia are properties of this sort, and that they owe their status as qualia to the perceptual character of limbic representations. (Prinz's views are developed at length in his splendid book, *Gut Reactions: A Perceptual Theory of Emotions* (Cambridge, MA: MIT Press, 2004).)

in earlier chapters can be applied, without significant modifications, to emotional qualia. To be more specific, since imagistic qualia are reducible to perceptual qualia, it implies that all emotional qualia can be analyzed either in terms of the framework for explaining perceptual qualia that is presented in Chapter 5, or in terms of the framework for explaining somatic qualia that is presented in Chapter 6.

Accordingly, we have now obtained a more or less unified theory of all of the characteristics that are widely agreed to be qualitative – a theory that provides much encouragement to the hope that it will be possible to tell a comprehensive metaphysical story about reality that is unified and comparatively simple.

CHAPTER 8

Introspection and consciousness

8.1 INTRODUCTION

As we observed in Chapter 1, there is a sense of the word "conscious" according to which, roughly speaking, a mental state counts as conscious just in case the relevant agent is introspectively aware of it. The present chapter is concerned with the form of consciousness that is signified by this sense of the word.

This form of consciousness, *introspective consciousness*, is a relational property, like the property of being married and the property of being illuminated. It is widely distributed across the realm of mental phenomena. Thoughts, volitions, and other occurrent mental states can be introspectively conscious, but so can beliefs, long term plans, and other enduring phenomena that are stored in memory. Introspective consciousness can also be possessed by a range of mental processes, including planning, deciding, evaluating, and inferring.

Introspective consciousness has been recognized and discussed for centuries. For example, the contrast between introspectively conscious motivation and its opposite is very much in view, without being explicitly mentioned, in Austen's *Mansfield Park*. One of the characters in that book, Mrs. Norris, constantly rebukes, marginalizes, and assigns demeaning tasks to the young heroine, Fanny Pryce. Mrs. Norris consciously sees herself as helping Fanny, who has in effect been brought to Mansfield Park as an act of charity by her aunt and uncle. In Mrs. Norris's opinion, Fanny must be constantly reminded of the inferiority and fragility of her position in the household if she is to appreciate the nature of her situation and adapt to it. In fact, however, as is clear to the reader, and to some extent Fanny herself, Mrs. Norris's behavior is shaped by unconscious motivation that includes a certain amount of pure sadism and also a desire to make the comparative superiority of her own standing in the household more salient, both to herself and to Fanny. In a phrase,

Austen's descriptions of the interactions between Mrs. Norris and Fanny are a kind of constructive argument for the importance of motivation that is not introspectively conscious. Of course, Austen is presupposing that her readers are familiar with the contrast between mental states that are introspectively conscious and states that lack this feature. That the presupposition was fully warranted is shown by the esteem in which the novel has been held by generations of readers.

Although the notion of introspective consciousness is part of our folk psychological heritage, it was not until Freud developed a detailed theory of unconscious motivation that "conscious" came to be widely used as a term for mental states that are objects of introspective awareness. Freud was uncharacteristically taciturn about the nature of consciousness, perhaps because he regarded it as unanalyzable. (He wrote that consciousness "defies all explanation and description."[1]) Given the role that the notion of consciousness plays in his psychological theory, however, and in particular the role it plays in his description of the goals of therapy, it is reasonable to regard Freud as holding, or at least as committed to, the following views: (i) the conscious mind consists of mental phenomena that are objects of introspective awareness; (ii) the preconscious mind consists of mental phenomena that are not currently objects of introspective awareness but could easily acquire that status; and (iii) the unconscious mind consists of a variety of mental phenomena, including inappropriate sexual desires, shameful memories, and irrational wishes, that are actively repressed and therefore inaccessible to awareness. At all events, this is a familiar and widely shared interpretation of Freud's position. I cite it here to remind the reader of the centrality of the notion of introspective consciousness in contemporary discussions of consciousness.

I will be concerned in this chapter with three sets of questions. First, what is the internal nature of states of introspective awareness? Are they uniform or do they come in two or more varieties? To what extent are they conceptual and doxastic in character? To what extent are they sub-conceptual? More particularly, are they ever perceptual, and if so, to what extent? Second, what is the nature of the processes that produce states of introspective awareness? To what extent, if any, do they resemble the processes that are responsible for producing states of perceptual awareness? If perceptual models fail, what should we put in their place? Are the processes fundamentally similar to one another or are they diverse?

---

[1] Sigmund Freud, *An Outline of Psycho-Analysis* in James Strachey (ed.), *The Complete Psychological Works of Sigmund Freud* XXIII (London: Hogarth Press, 1966–74), p. 157.

Third, must a state of introspective awareness be conscious in order to be capable of bestowing introspective consciousness on its object? Of course, it could not be true that a state of consciousness must be *introspectively* conscious in order to bestow introspective consciousness, for on this principle, no state could be introspectively conscious unless it was embedded in an infinite series of introspectively conscious states, each of which was aware of the immediately succeeding member of the series. But it could be true that a state must possess *experiential* consciousness in order to be able to confer introspective consciousness on its object. *Is* this true? Does introspective consciousness presuppose consciousness of this other sort? (As the reader may recall from Chapter 1, a mental state counts as possessing experiential consciousness if it is available for use by a variety of high level cognitive agencies, including those that are responsible for fixing beliefs, establishing episodic memories, generating plans, guiding intentional actions, producing speech, and initiating inferences.)

In addition to discussing these three primary topics, I will devote some attention to epistemological issues. It has traditionally been held that introspective beliefs are different from beliefs of most other types in that they have a much higher degree of epistemic warrant. On the whole I am sympathetic with this view, because I think that the causal distance between introspective beliefs and the states of affairs that serve as their truth-makers tends to be much smaller than in other cases. Given that the causal distance is small, there is less room for error to occur. At the same time, however, it seems to me to be a mistake to hold that *all* introspective beliefs enjoy a highly privileged epistemic status, and also a mistake to hold that high privilege, where it exists, amounts to a kind of certainty. I will argue briefly for these reservations concerning the traditional picture at the end of Section 8.5, but I will not attempt to defend them systematically.

I conclude these introductory remarks with a few comments about the view, familiar from the contemporary literature, that introspective awareness of propositional attitudes involves *deliberation* about the world.[2] This view is much in evidence in discussions of introspective awareness of beliefs. For an agent to determine whether he believes that *p*, it is maintained, he must determine whether it is true that *p*, and the latter endeavor involves rational deliberation about the nature of extramental fact. To put the point somewhat paradoxically, it is claimed that introspection requires

[2] Richard Moran, *Authority and Estrangement: An Essay on Self-Knowledge* (Princeton: Princeton University Press, 2001).

extrospection, at least in a wide array of cases. I will not engage this view at any length in the present chapter, but will simply say now that it seems to me to rest on a confusion. I distinguish between explicit, actual beliefs and implicit, potential beliefs. In effect, an implicit belief is a belief that one is committed to holding on the basis of one's explicit beliefs. To illustrate: an agent's explicit beliefs will generally include the belief that his or her own name is such and such and the belief that Columbus arrived in the New World in 1492, but the agent can only be said to believe implicitly that his name has fewer than 267 letters or that Columbus never aspired to own a Corvette. Now as I see it, there is no need to engage in deliberation to become introspectively aware of one's explicit beliefs. To the extent that deliberation is connected with introspection at all, we deliberate because it is necessary to *fix* our beliefs about certain topics, to convert our implicit beliefs into explicit ones, before it can be appropriate to claim introspective awareness of them. But to say this is to say that there is no internal, necessary relation between deliberation and introspection. Deliberation is a precursor of introspection, an activity that often must occur before introspection is possible. One cannot become introspectively aware of a belief that one does not yet actually hold, just as one cannot perceive events that have not yet actually occurred.

This is not to deny that one often determines whether one has a belief by considering a question about the world. A friend recently asked me, "Do you believe that marijuana should be legalized?" In answering the question, I began by replacing it with a simpler question that was concerned with the world rather than the state of my opinion – viz., the question "Should marijuana be legalized?" At a certain much earlier point in my life it might have been necessary to engage in deliberation in order to answer this simpler question; but I have long held a settled opinion about the matter, so an answer ("Of course!") came immediately to mind. This answer led immediately to an answer to the first question. "Yes," I said, "I definitely do believe that marijuana should be legalized." What happened in this case is, I think, fairly typical. Often we arrive at second order judgments by asking first order questions. But this has no tendency to show that we arrive at second order judgments by engaging in first order deliberation. We know the answer to many questions about the world without deliberating.

8.2 DOXASTICISM AND PLURALISM

We know that introspective awareness takes the form of propositional knowledge in a large range of cases. Indeed, where M is any mental state that counts intuitively as accessible to introspection, it is plausible that the relevant agent can form an introspective judgment that provides him with propositional knowledge of *M*. Thus, we can easily acquire propositional knowledge of our beliefs, desires, intentions, occurrent thoughts, moods, emotions, perceptual experiences, images, and bodily sensations. Moreover, we can easily acquire propositional knowledge concerning a significant array of mental processes, including choosing, planning, calculating, deducing, explaining, and imagining.

In view of these facts, it is natural for inquiries into the nature of introspective awareness to take the form of attempts to determine the extent to which our introspective capacities are grounded in judgments. There are three possible positions here – *doxasticism*, *pluralism*, and *perceptualism.*

Doxasticism is the view that introspective awareness always takes the form of judgments or beliefs. (As I see it, a judgment is mental occurrence – a kind of occurrent belief. But beliefs also include semipermanent states that are located in various memory stores. Doxasticism claims that introspective awareness sometimes takes the form of a judgment and sometimes takes the form of an enduring belief. To simplify the exposition, however, I will henceforth only mention judgments in discussing doxasticism.)

In contrast to doxasticism, pluralism claims that introspective awareness can take the form of judgments and can also take the form of perceptual states. It claims, for example, that awareness of thoughts usually takes the form of judgments, and that awareness of qualitative states is often perceptual in character. Further, as I shall understand it here, it also maintains that there are certain types of mental state that can be known in more than one way. Where *M* is a mental state of one of these types, pluralism allows that it is possible to achieve awareness of *M* via an introspective judgment, but it maintains that it is also possible to achieve awareness of *M* via a subconceptual and subdoxastic state of some sort. Thus, for example, in the case of pain, pluralism allows that it is possible to be introspectively aware of a pain via a judgment to the effect that one is in pain, but it maintains that in a typical case the relevant agent will be perceptually aware of the pain, and also that any doxastic awareness of the pain will be epistemically and causally grounded in this perceptual awareness.

As its name indicates, perceptualism claims that *all* forms of introspection are fully perceptual in character. It seems to me that this view is quite implausible, so I will not discuss it here. After all, we *know* that introspective awareness takes the form of judgments in a broad array of cases.

Perceptualism is excluded by this fact. I will focus here on doxasticism and pluralism.

It can be shown, I think, that doxasticism is correct, but pluralism has a powerful initial appeal. Prima facie, at least, it *seems* that we are perceptually aware of many of our mental states. There are three main reasons why this is so. I will describe them briefly here, and will then evaluate them in Sections 8.3–8.4.

The first reason is that some of the forms of awareness that count intuitively as introspective have a proprietary phenomenology. This is true, for example, of awareness of pain. Although awareness of pain is complex and hard to characterize, it is clear that we are strongly inclined to think of it as introspective. Moreover, there is no gainsaying the fact that the states that count intuitively as states of awareness of pain have a vivid phenomenological dimension. Now if a state of awareness has a phenomenological dimension, it is more naturally construed as perceptual than as conceptual and doxastic. Hence, there is a strong prima facie case for saying both that awareness of pain is introspective and that it is perceptual (or quasi-perceptual). Further, the same is true of various other forms of awareness, including awareness of bodily sensations other than pain, and awareness of the qualitative characteristics of emotions. These forms of awareness count intuitively as introspective, and they also count as perceptual, due to their vivid phenomenological components. Of course, to the extent that they can be sustained, these views constitute a powerful case for pluralism.

The second reason for thinking that introspection is perceptual has to do with our access to imagery. For various reasons, it seems natural to say that we *see* visual images, that we *scan* them in the course of various cognitive tasks, and that we *zoom in* on them to acquire information about details. There must be something about our access to imagery that makes claims of these sorts appropriate. What could it be? The obvious answer is that we talk about perceiving images because we do in fact perceive them.

Third, we have some inclination to think that introspective awareness of occurrent propositional attitudes has a phenomenological dimension. This is true, for example, of introspective awareness of thoughts. Thus, we are strongly inclined to say that there is something that it is like to think that p, and it can be tempting to conclude from this that the experience of thinking that p has a phenomenal character of some kind. But if thinking that p has a phenomenal character, then awareness of thinking that p is arguably perceptual, for it is arguably perception, and only perception, that puts us in touch with qualitative properties.

Although they have a certain amount of prima facie appeal, it is possible to show that the three reasons for embracing pluralism should be rejected, and that doxasticism should be embraced as the correct view. The vehicles of introspective awareness are judgments and beliefs, not perceptual or quasi-perceptual representations. After arriving at this conclusion in Section 8.6, I will go on to consider an argument for the view that the *processes* leading to introspective judgments are perceptual in character. This view concedes the truth of doxasticism, but it maintains that the relationship between introspection and attention gives us a reason to think that we need a perceptual model of the mechanisms that are responsible for introspective judgments. I will argue in Section 8.7 that this view is misguided. Thus, by the end of Section 8.7, I will have presented a broad-based case for thinking that perceptual models of introspection are wrong.

8.3   AWARENESS OF BODILY SENSATIONS

It is acknowledged on all sides that that it feels a certain way to be aware of a pain, and that it feels a certain way to be aware of an itch. In general, where S is any bodily sensation, awareness of S has an associated phenomenology. In view of this fact, it is quite plausible that awareness of bodily sensations is perceptual. It is less clear, however, that awareness of a bodily sensation should be classified as a form of introspective awareness. According to the dictionary, to introspect is to examine one's own mind or its contents. Hence, if awareness of pain is a form of introspection, pain must be a mental state of some kind. But it is not at all clear that this is so. It is agreed on all sides that pain is internal to the subject who possesses the pain. But internal to what? The mind? Perhaps; but it can also be reasonably maintained that pain is a bodily state, and that a pain is internal to the subject only in the sense that it is internal to the subject's body.

In Chapter 6 we considered three theories concerning pain and awareness of pain. According to the first theory, to be in pain is to undergo a certain type of bodily disturbance, and to be aware of a pain is to be perceptually aware of a disturbance of that type. Assuming that "introspection" is used exclusively to stand for internal awareness of *mental* phenomena, as the dictionary maintains, this theory implies that awareness of pain is not a form of introspection. According to the second theory, to be in pain is to be in a certain sort of perceptual state – specifically, a perceptual state that is directed on a bodily disturbance of the given type. That is, according to this theory, a pain is identical with a state of perceptual awareness. The theory also claims that awareness of pain takes the form of a judgment – a judgment to the effect that one is in pain. The theory asserts that judgments of this sort can be seen on reflection to refer to the states of perceptual awareness that count as pains. It follows from the theory that awareness of pain is awareness of a mental state and is therefore introspective. Thus, the second theory sustains the intuition that awareness of pain is a form of introspective awareness. This brings me to the third theory. Unlike the first two theories, this one does not make a definite claim about the nature of pain. Rather, it asserts that there is no fact of the matter as to which of the first two theories is correct. It allows that each of these theories honors important strands in the account of pain that is embedded in folk psychology, but it denies that either of them honors all of these strands. Moreover, what is most important for our purposes, it claims that neither of these theories does a significantly better job than the other in capturing the folk psychological account. Neither counts as a uniquely best systematization of our thought and talk about pain. In effect, then, the third theory denies that there is such a thing as pain, and also that there is such a thing as awareness of pain.

After comparing the strengths and weaknesses of the first two theories, I argued in Chapter 6 that the third theory is correct. There is no fact of the matter as to what serves as the referent of the commonsense concept of pain. This claim carries an important implication concerning the concept of awareness of pain. If there is no fact of the matter as to what serves as the referent of the concept of pain, there can be no fact of the matter as to what serves as the referent of the concept of awareness of pain. It follows from this in turn that the concept of awareness of pain has no bearing on questions about the nature of introspection, including the question of whether there are subconceptual, subdoxastic forms of introspective awareness. Since it is itself indeterminate, the concept of awareness of pain cannot support determinate answers to questions about introspection.

In addition to arguing that the commonsense concept of pain is referentially indeterminate, I maintained in Chapter 6 that we should replace it with three new notions – one that stands only for bodily disturbances involving actual or potential damage (*D-states*), another that stands only for perceptual states that are directed on D-states (*D-perceptions*), and a third that stands only for pain-affect, the limbic activity that normally accompanies D-perceptions. Consider for a moment what will happen when conceptual utopia is at hand, and we are using three concepts that answer to these specifications. In those happy circumstances we will recognize four forms of awareness – perceptual awareness of D-states, judgments to the effect that one is in a D-state, judgments to the effect that one is enjoying a D-perception, and judgments to the effect that one is experiencing pain-affect. It will be true by definition that the first form of awareness is perceptual; but the first form will provide no support for the idea that introspection is perceptual, for it will also be true by definition that the first form is concerned with bodily states, and is therefore not introspective. On the other hand, we will have no reason to think that any of the other three forms of awareness is perceptual. They will all be conceptual rather than experiential, and will therefore lack the various features that we have found to be characteristic of perceptual states.

To summarize: There are two salient ways of conceptualizing pain and awareness of pain – our current way and a utopian alternative. Neither of these conceptualizations permits us to discern a form of awareness that is both perceptual and directed on a state that counts unequivocally as mental.

8.4 AWARENESS OF IMAGERY

As we observed in Section 8.2, from an everyday perspective it seems entirely natural and appropriate to say that one sees a visual image, that one scans its surface, and that one zooms in on one of its parts. Insofar as claims of this sort can be taken at face value, there is reason to think that introspective awareness of images is perceptual.

Let us agree to say that claims of the sort in question are *perceptualist interpretations* of certain facts about our possession and use of imagery. What I wish to propose is that there is an alternative interpretation of these facts that is more accurate. Thus, as I see it, instead of saying that one sees an image, one could with more justification say that one sees the imagined object, where "see" is used with an intensional sense (i.e., with a sense which permits speakers to make claims of the form "x sees an F" without committing themselves to existential claims of the form "An F exists"). Further, instead of saying that one is scanning an image, one could with more justification say that one is scanning the imagined object, where "scan" is used in an intensional sense. And instead of saying that one is zooming in on a part of an image, one could with more justification say that one is zooming in on part of the imagined object, where "zoom in on" is used in an intensional sense. In general, when one puts forward a perceptualist interpretation of a fact involving an image, one would do better to make an intensional claim about the imagined object.[3] There would be no loss of information, and one would avoid certain implications of the perceptualist interpretation that reflection shows to be unwelcome.

If it was genuinely appropriate to say that we see images, using "see" in an extensional, relational sense, then it would have to be true that we stand in a relation to images that shares a number of features with visual perception of the external world. Now everyday visual perception has the following characteristics: it involves experiences with proprietary phenomenologies; it makes use of a sense organ; it encodes information that is carried by light; it makes use of mechanisms that compute constancies; and it provides access to such intrinsic properties of objects as size, shape, and mereological structure. Our relationship to images is not characterized by any of these features. Thus, for example, "seeing" an image tells us nothing about the size, shape, or mereological structure *of the image*. If, for example, an agent is entertaining an image of a basketball, he will have an accurate grasp of the size and shape of the imagined ball, but he will have no sense of the size and shape of the image itself. I do not mean to claim here that our relationship to images would have to possess all of the defining features of ordinary vision in order to count as a form of seeing. After all, the visual systems of animals are often quite different from ours; and there is a form of human vision, known as blindsight, that differs from ordinary human vision in several key respects (e.g., it has no experiential dimension, and therefore does not involve phenomenology). But it seems fair to say that our relation to images should resemble

---

[3] It is independently plausible, I think, that "see" has an intensional sense. Thus, we find it is entirely natural to use this term in characterizing hallucinations, as when we say that Macbeth sees a dagger before him, and also in talking about afterimages, as when one says that one sees an afterimage on a nearby wall. Accordingly, it seems quite appropriate to propose, as I have done in the text, that when we speak of "seeing" visual images, our claims should be understood as statements to the effect that we are "seeing" (in the intensional sense) imagined physical objects. It is somewhat less clear, however, that expressions like "scan" and "zoom in on" have established intensional senses, for we do not normally use them in talking about hallucinations, dreams, afterimages, and the like. As I see it, the right way to respond to this observation is to say that when someone speaks, e.g., of "scanning" a visual image, he is presupposing that there is a way of defining a new sense of the term that will authorize his usage. And in fact, it is easy to provide definitions of expressions like "scan" that endow them with intensional senses. Thus, when someone says that he is scanning a visual image of an F, we can construe this as meaning that he is imagining that he is scanning an F, and when someone says that he is zooming in on a visual image of an F, we can take this to mean that he is imagining zooming in on an F. In general, where "V" is an extensional verb that denotes some form of visual awareness, we can understand statements of the form "X is V-ing an image of an F" as meaning that X is imagining that X is V-ing an F. (I have been helped considerably here by a conversation with Jaegwon Kim.)

ordinary vision in a number of important respects in order to count as a form of visual perception. And it also seems fair to say that we have no reason to think, and much reason to doubt, that our relation to images satisfies this basic requirement.

In view of these considerations, it seems best to view perceptualist interpretations of facts involving imagery as mere *façons de parler*. When we wish to be accurate, we should make use of the intensional senses of expressions like "see," "scan," "zoom in on," and "observe the rotation of." When used in their intensional senses, these expressions do not commit us to the existence of strong structural analogies between facts involving the possession and use of images and facts involving ordinary visual perception. Moreover, they are apt because they highlight the representational character of images. Images always have representational contents: my image of Bill Clinton is a quasi-perceptual representation *of Clinton*, and my image of a unicorn is a quasi-perceptual representation *of a unicorn*. But this means that it is always appropriate to use intensional language in characterizing images, for intensional language provides us with a way of attributing representational contents. In particular, if I wish to claim that I am currently entertaining an image of Clinton, it is appropriate to say that I *see* Clinton, using "see" in an intensional sense, for this is a way of attributing a certain representational content to the image. Equally, if I wish to claim that I am attending successively in imagination to different portions of the surface of a table, it is appropriate to say that I am *scanning* the table, using "scan" in an intensional sense, for this is a way of indicating that successive portions of the content of my image of the table are undergoing certain changes, such as increases in resolution.

In sum, while it is perfectly acceptable to use perceptualist interpretations of facts involving imagery in casual discourse, there is reason not to assign any metaphysical weight to such interpretations. There is an alternative way of describing the facts that is superior in two respects.

8.5 AWARENESS OF OCCURRENT PROPOSITIONAL ATTITUDES

I maintained in Chapter 1 that the qualitative dimension of occurrent attitudes is quite elusive, if it exists at all. I must now qualify this claim. There is a category of attitudes of which the claim is true, and we will be largely concerned with members of that category in this section. But it must be acknowledged that many attitudes are accompanied by *salient* qualia of various kinds. In some cases, they may even be partially constituted by such qualia. The qualia in question are sometimes visual, sometimes auditory, sometimes somatic, and sometimes multi-modal. To elaborate, with reference to the special case of thoughts: (1) Thoughts often combine with visual imagery to produce representations of complex scenes or series of events. In such cases the imagery may simply elaborate the contents of the thoughts, but there are occasions on which it contributes to thought-content, and therefore plays an individuative role. This happens, for example, when a demonstrative thought acquires some of its content from an image of an object. (Consider a case in which an agent thinks *He is still quite handsome* while entertaining an image of Bill Clinton.) (2) Further, many subjects find that their thoughts are often accompanied by auditory imagery: when they have these thoughts, they say, it is as if spoken sentences are running through their heads.[4] Apparently, it seems to them, or at least can seem to them, that their thoughts are constituted by this auditory imagery. (3) Still further, it often happens that thinking is accompanied by subvocalizations. For example, in thinking about what to say in the present chapter, I have on several occasions found my throat, tongue, and lips to be in motion. Some of these movements have closely resembled the ones that I would have made if I had actually been speaking, and others have been embryonic versions of such movements. From the point of view of the experiencing subject, it can seem that events of these sorts are constitutive of thoughts. Since subvocalizations entail somatic qualia, it follows from this that thoughts sometimes seem to have somatic qualia as constituents.

Insofar as the phenomenological dimension of occurrent attitudes consists of visual imagery, auditory imagery, and the somatic qualia associated with subvocalizations, it is naturally regarded as a *perceptual* phenomenology. But this has no bearing on the question of whether introspection can take the form of perceptual awareness, for the perceptual modalities that are associated with visual imagery and auditory imagery are concerned with extramental properties, and the perceptual modality that puts us in touch with somatic qualia is by definition a form

---

[4] Suppose it is true that thoughts are on occasion partially constituted by somatic qualia. Does it follow from this that introspection can take the form of bodily awareness? No; there is another, equally defensible interpretation. Instead of concluding that introspective awareness of some aspects of thoughts is perceptual, we could with as much right conclude that some aspects of thoughts are somatic, and awareness of them is therefore not introspective. It does not matter much what we say about this issue. The interesting question is whether there is a form of awareness of purely mental phenomena that is perceptual. That is, what is interesting is whether there is a form of awareness that is indisputably introspective and indisputably perceptual.

of bodily awareness.[5] The question before us at present is whether there is a distinctive perceptual modality that is in the service of introspection, a form that is trained exclusively on mental states. Clearly, if we are to find phenomenological grounds for supposing that a modality answering to this description exists, we must consider whether the phenomenological dimension of attitudes is exhausted by the comparatively *prosaic* qualia we have been considering. If attitudes are sometimes accompanied or constituted by non-prosaic qualia, then there will be a phenomenological argument for a perceptual faculty that is dedicated to the tracking of mental states. Prosaic qualia provide no reason to believe that such a faculty exists.

It will be useful, I think, to approach this issue by focusing on what might be called *pure* occurrent attitudes – that is, occurrent attitudes that are not accompanied by prosaic phenomenology. Introspection appears to attest to the existence of such attitudes. Certainly this is true in my own case, and also in the case of Charles Siewart, who invokes them in the following passage:

> [There are] instances in which a thought occurs to you, when not only do you not *image* what you think or are thinking of, but you also do not *verbalize* your thought, either silently or aloud... .[6]

They have also been reported by a number of subjects in Russell Hurlburt's controlled studies of introspection. Summarizing the data, Hurlburt says the following:

> I'm confident that people frequently think without any experience of words (spoken or heard), images, or other symbols; therefore experienced words can't be essential to thinking... .[7]

So it seems that pure attitudes exist. What exactly do we find when we consider them introspectively? By definition, they are not accompanied by visual qualia, auditory qualia, or somatic qualia, but are they entirely free from qualitative determinations? When we consider them, do we encounter qualia of a fourth sort? Perhaps qualia that are less vivid than prosaic ones?

It is sometimes maintained that *all* occurrent propositional attitudes, including pure ones, have distinctive qualitative profiles, and that we

[5] For discussion see Russell T. Hurlburt and Eric Schwitzgebel, *Describing Inner Experience? Proponent Meets Skeptic* (Cambridge, MA: MIT Press, 2007), pp. 60–66.
[6] Charles P. Siewart, *The Significance of Consciousness* (Princeton, NJ: Princeton University Press, 1998), p. 276.
[7] Hurlburt and Schwitzgebel, *Describing Inner Experience?*, p. 137.

arrive at introspective judgments about occurrent attitudes by inferences from such profiles. This view is not widely shared; but it has had some very able defenders, so it deserves to be taken seriously.[8]

To grasp the details of the view, we should recall the distinction between *attitude types* and *attitude contents*. Attitude types include judging, supposing, doubting, and wishing. Attitude contents include the proposition *the budget crisis will soon ease* and the proposition *I will be going to New York next weekend*. The *attitude qualia view* (the AQ view) asserts that each attitude type is associated with a distinctive qualitative character, and that the same is true of each attitude content. According to the AQ view, an agent forms an introspective judgment about the nature of an occurrent attitude by perceiving the type-qualia that are associated with it, perceiving the associated content-qualia, and then inferring a conceptual representation of it from these perceptions. In effect, then, the AQ view has two parts – a proposal concerning the process leading to conceptual classifications of types, and a proposal concerning the process leading to conceptual classifications of contents. I will discuss these two parts separately.

If it is true that we identify attitude types by perceiving associated qualia, then it should be within our power to answer questions about the nature, number, and relationships of qualia of the relevant sort. It seems, however, that we find it impossible to answer these questions. This casts doubt on the AQ view.

Consider, for example, the question of whether the qualitative profile of wishing consists of a single quale or a set of qualia that are related to one another in some way. In my own case, at any rate, there is no hope of answering this question. In particular, I cannot answer it by attending more closely to occurrent wishes. There is such a thing as attending to one's wishes; but in my case, anyway, attending to them provides no relevant information. Again, consider the question of whether judging with full conviction and judging with moderate confidence are two distinct qualia, similar qualia, or different intensities of a single quale. The AQ view implies that we should be able to answer this question, for it is clear that we can distinguish introspectively between judging with

---

[8] See, for example, Alvin I. Goldman, "The Psychology of Folk Psychology," *Behavioral and Brain Sciences* 16 (1993), 15–28. Goldman has abandoned this view in recent years. He continues to think that awareness of attitude types is perceptual, but he no longer holds that it has a qualitative dimension. Moreover, he denies that awareness of attitude contents is perceptual. See his *Simulating Minds: The Philosophy, Psychology, and Neuroscience of Mindreading* (Oxford: Oxford University Press, 2006), Chapter 9.

full conviction and judging with moderate confidence, and the AQ view implies that any introspective judgment about occurrent attitudes is based on perceptual awareness of a qualitative profile. But we are unable to answer the question. Or so I suppose, since I myself am unable to answer it, and the same is true of other people I have asked. Another such question is whether the space of attitude qualia is ordered by similarity relations, in the way that the space of color qualia is, so that it counts as a quality order, or it is instead a collection of incommensurable qualia, like, say, a set consisting of visual, auditory, olfactory, gustatory, and tactual qualia. Speaking for myself, there is no hope of answering this question. I do not even know where to look for an answer.

It appears, then, that the AQ view leads to unanswerable questions. This fact is not in itself problematic. There are many perfectly meaningful, perfectly appropriate questions about the remote past and distant galaxies that we are unable to answer. Rather, it poses a problem because the AQ view implies that we are on intimate terms with attitude qualia – that it is by possessing such qualia that we arrive at introspective judgments. If we are directly acquainted with attitude qualia, we should be able to tell whether they are simple or complex, similar or dissimilar, commensurable or incommensurable.

We encounter a similar problem when we turn to consider the implications of the AQ view concerning content-qualia. There is a potential infinity of attitude contents, so a theory of how we recognize contents should imply that the features that enable recognition have a compositional structure – or in other words, that they are generated by a recursive procedure of some sort. Accordingly, we should understand the AQ view to imply that qualitative profiles of attitude contents are generated from a finite set of base qualia by compositional rules. More specifically, we should expect it to imply that the profile of the proposition *the mother of Oedipus was a queen* is structurally simpler than, and is somehow embedded in, the profile of the proposition *the mother of Oedipus was a queen of Thebes*. We should also expect it to imply that while the profile of the proposition *the mother of Oedipus was a queen* has only one occurrence of the quale associated with the content *mother*, the profile associated with the proposition *the mother of the mother of Oedipus was the mother of a queen* has three occurrences of that quale. But if the AQ view has implications of this sort, then it must also imply that we are able to answer questions like the following: Are the base qualia associated with single contents like *mother* simple or complex? Are there inclusion relations among base qualia? Is it true, for example, that the qualitative profile associated with the content *grandmother* includes the profile associated with the content *mother* as a proper part? Are there similarity relations defined over base qualia, so that they occupy positions in a quality space? Do the compositional rules introduce new qualia (that is, qualia over and above base qualia), or do they simply arrange base qualia in arrays of various sorts? If the latter, what exactly is the nature of the arrays? How many dimensions do they have?

I find that I am unable to answer these questions. There are no pertinent introspective data.

In view of these difficulties, it is appropriate to conclude that the AQ view is false. Introspective awareness of occurrent attitudes is not grounded in perceptual awareness of qualia. But this is not necessarily the end of the road for the idea that attitudes have distinctive qualitative natures. It shows that we do not recognize individual attitudes by perceiving qualitative profiles, but it could still be true that attitudes *have* qualitative profiles, and that we can on occasion glimpse them. One might argue for this much weaker and less precise view in the following way: "Consider two thoughts – say, the thought that Christmas is just three months away and the thought that the stock market is in turmoil. Let both of these thoughts be pure. Now ask yourself: Isn't there a difference between what it is like to entertain the first thought and what it is like to entertain the second? Isn't there an *experiential* difference between entertaining the first thought and entertaining the second? The natural answer to these questions is 'yes.' But if there is a difference in what it is like to entertain the thoughts, then surely there is a phenomenological difference. After all, what it is like to be in a state is determined by the state's phenomenology."

As I understand him, Siewart is offering an argument of this sort in the following passage:

I think you will, if you try, be able to recognize examples from your own life ... of unverbalized noniconic thought. These are sometimes fairly primitive or simple, and sometimes remarkably complicated, so that to *say* what one was thinking would require a lengthy syntactically complex utterance – but in either event thought occurs, wordlessly, without imagery, condensed, and evanescent. If you agree that you have such unverbalized noniconic thoughts, and the way it seems to you to have them differs from the way it seems to have imagery and sensory experience, then you will agree that noniconic thinking has a phenomenal character distinct from that proper to iconic thinking and perception.[9]

According to Siewart, then, even when a thought is pure, there is a *way it seems* to the subject who is entertaining it. But what is it for a thought to

---

[9] Siewart, *The Significance of Consciousness*, pp. 277–8.

seem a certain way to a person? As far as I can tell, the idea that Siewart has in mind here is the same as the idea of *what it is like* for a person to have the thought.

I believe that many people are influenced by reflections of this sort, but I think that the appeal of such considerations dissipates when one observes, as we did in Chapter 1, that the notion of what it is like to be in a mental state comprehends a number of quite different phenomena. There is a qualitative component to what it is like to hear a piece of music, but there are also substantial components of other sorts. At any point in listening to a piece one has memories concerning preceding passages and expectations concerning future ones. These are not qualitative states. One also has desires of various sorts – desires concerning the future course of the piece, but also desires concerning one's relationship to it. For example, one may desire to attend more closely to the contribution of the violins. Further, one inevitably has thoughts of various kinds – about the composer, the quality of the performance, and many other things, including perhaps the party that one will be attending later that evening. When one notices the rich diversity of the items that combine to determine what it is like to have an experience, it becomes apparent that it can be true that there is something it is like to be in a state without its being true that the state has a qualitative dimension. In general, the notion of what it is like to be in a state is too broad to bear much weight in a discussion of phenomenology. Moreover, the vagueness of the notion poses another problem.

Still, it is true that the *experience* of thinking that Christmas is just three months away is different than the *experience* of thinking that the stock market is in turmoil. Does this fact show that the thoughts are different in point of phenomenal character? No. As we saw in Chapter 1, the notion of a conscious experience is plausibly understood as implicitly functional. Thoughts are experiences, and so are such paradigmatically qualitative states as perceptions, emotions, and feelings of pain. But it does not follow from this that thoughts are qualitative, for it is quite plausible that the ground for grouping these items together under the rubric "experience" is that they have a common causal role. Because this is plausible, it is impossible to establish phenomenological conclusions by appealing to the experiential nature of mental states.

8.6 THE TRIUMPH OF DOXASTICISM

In view of the lines of thought in Sections 8.3–8.5, it seems that there is no good reason to accept introspective awareness of mental phenomena sometimes takes the form of perceptual awareness. In other words, there is no obligation to accept the view I earlier called pluralism – the view that some of the vehicles of introspective awareness are perceptual or quasi-perceptual. But if there is no obligation to accept pluralism, we should accept doxasticism, which maintains that the vehicles of introspective awareness are always judgments or beliefs. Doxasticism is simpler than pluralism, since it recognizes only one form of introspective awareness. Accordingly, it enjoys a prima facie epistemic advantage. When arguments for pluralism are found to fail, doxasticism becomes more fully entrenched in its superior position.[10]

8.7   INTROSPECTION AND ATTENTION

William Lycan and Alvin Goldman are the two philosophers who have done the most in recent years to promote perceptual models of introspection. Both authors acknowledge that most forms of introspection differ from perception in that they have no phenomenological dimension. Moreover, as I understand them, they concede that introspective awareness generally takes the form of judgments or beliefs. It does not involve perceptual or quasi-perceptual representations. Even so, however, they maintain that introspection is fundamentally perceptual in character.

---

[10] It is claimed in the text that there are three main sources of the idea that introspection is perceptual – the perceptual character of awareness of bodily sensations, the fact that we are inclined to describe our cognitive access to imagery in visual terminology, and our sense that there is something it is like to have an occurrent propositional attitude, together with a confused impression that what it is likeness is essentially qualitative. I feel sure that these are indeed the main sources, but it should be acknowledged that there is also a fourth source. When we are introspectively aware of thoughts and other occurrent propositional attitudes, it seems to us that we are immediately aware of them as being in a certain *place* – more specifically, in a region of inner space that is roughly behind the eyes. Now in all other cases, immediate, non-inferential awareness of things as located is perceptual in character. This being so, it is natural for us to conclude that awareness of thoughts is perceptual.

What should we make of this conclusion? Or, more pertinently, what should we make of the impression that thoughts are located? Alas, I must confess to ignorance here. To complete my argument that introspection is non-perceptual, I need to explain the impression away. At present, however, I do not see how to do this. One possibility is that the impression is due to top-down influence of *beliefs* about the location of thoughts. Another possibility, which has been emphasized by my colleagues Justin Broackes and Bill Warren in conversation, is that it is due to a quasi-perceptual sense that the *self* is located in space. (We experience ourselves as located. Interestingly, the location seems to shift with the concerns of the moment. Thus, for example, when we are exploring an external object tactually, we experience the self as extending to our fingertips; and when we are exploring an object with a hand held instrument, say a blind person's cane, we experience the self as extending to the instrument's tip.) Unfortunately, I have no idea as to how to develop these hypotheses, and, a fortiori, no idea as to how to assess them.

For further discussion, see Hurlburt and Schwitzgebel, *Describing Inner Experience?*, p. 160.

Their reason for this view, I believe, is that, as they see it, the processes that produce introspective judgments are fundamentally akin to perceptual processes. I will examine the view, under the name *process perceptualism*, in the present section.

What is appealing about the view? Although there are various grounds for holding it, the principal one seems to be that introspection resembles perception in being governed in various ways by attention. Speaking of the higher-order representations that subserve introspection, Lycan says the following: "The relevant higher-order representations are characteristically produced by the exercise of attention. That makes them more like perceptions than like thoughts, since it is not characteristic of thoughts to be directly produced by the exercise of attention (though of course thoughts can happen to be produced by the exercise of attention, normally by way of a mediating perception)."[11] Goldman concurs. According to him, "[t]he 'organ' of introspection is attention, the orientation of which puts a subject in an appropriate relation to a targeted state."[12] He appears to hold that this fact is sufficient to establish that introspection is a form of perception. Attention-based considerations are the main common ground for these authors, and it is clear that they constitute the most substantial component of their case for process perceptualism. Accordingly, I will focus on these considerations here. More particularly, I will focus on whether there are persuasive attention-based arguments for the view that awareness of *occurrent thoughts* is essentially perceptual. Awareness of occurrent thoughts is an important test case, since it is widely held that perceptual models are most plausible when understood as theories of awareness of mental occurrences.

I will take it as given that there is a form of attention that plays a role in determining whether I am aware of my thoughts, and I will use the expression "introspective attention" as a name for it. We must consider two questions. First, is introspective attention identical with any of the things that scientists have in mind when they speak of perceptual attention? And second, is it importantly similar to any of those things?

It appears that there are three main forms of perceptual attention.

First, there is the form of attention that figures in Anne Treisman's feature integration theory of perceptual processing.[13] This form has the

[11]   William G. Lycan, "The Superiority of HOP to HOT," in Rocco J. Gennaro (ed.), *Higher-Order Theories of Consciousness: An Anthology* (Amsterdam: John Benjamins Publishing Company, 2004), p. 105.

[12]   Alvin I. Goldman, *Simulating Minds: The Philosophy, Psychology, and Neuroscience of Mindreading* (Oxford: Oxford University Press, 2006), p. 244.

[13]   See, e.g., Anne Treisman, "Features and Objects," *Quarterly Journal of Experimental Psychology* 40 (1988), 201–237.

job of binding together representations of various sensible characteristics to produce a unified representation of an object. In Treisman's familiar picture, visual processing begins with the activity of a large number of agencies that work in parallel. Each has the mission of producing a representation of a particular feature, and of assigning that feature to a location in the visual field. Attention has the job of selecting one of these locations. When it does so, all of the representations that assign features to that location are bound together to produce a unified representation of an object. The object is represented as having those features and as standing at the given location. Thus, this form of attention is in effect the agency that determines what objects the visual system will recognize. It is the great entifier.

I will use the expression "binding attention" as a name for this agency.

Second, there is a form of attention that has the job of increasing the accuracy and efficiency of perceptual processing, and also the job of heightening resolution and figure/ground contrast. In effect, it selects streams of information for preferential treatment, giving them access to processing resources that have limited capacity.

I will use the expression "processing attention" as a name for this second form of attention.

Third, there is a form of attention that determines which perceptual representations are accessible to the high level cognitive agencies that are responsible for such things as fixing perceptual beliefs, planning intentional actions, and laying down episodic memories.[14] The domain of accessibility needs a gate-keeper, and this form has that role.

I will use the expression "gate-keeper attention" to refer to this third agency.

Now insofar as these three forms of attention are associated with specific perceptual modalities, it would be unreasonable to suppose that they are identical with, or even strongly similar to, the form of attention that is associated with introspection. This is because it is the job of each of the three forms to influence the processing of purely perceptual information – that is, the processing of information about such properties as shape, color, sound volume, tone, and solidity. It is clear that introspective attention is concerned with the processing of information

---

[14] For a discussion of this form of attention, see, e.g., Nancy Kanwisher, "Neural Events and Perceptual Awareness," in Stanislas Dehaene (ed.), *The Cognitive Neuroscience of Consciousness* (Cambridge, MA: MIT Press, 2001). What I am calling the domain of accessibility is generally thought of as a form of memory – specifically, working memory. But I prefer to remain neutral on this question. For discussion, see the antepenultimate paragraph of Chapter 9.

that is altogether different in character. Mental states don't have shapes or colors or volumes or tones or degrees of solidity. Even though the three forms of perceptual attention are distinct from introspective attention, however, it could still be true that one or another of the former is *roughly* similar to the latter. Or, to put the point another way, it could still be true that it is possible to describe the three forms of perceptual attention in a sufficiently abstract way that one or another of the descriptions applies to introspective attention. And in fact, reflection shows that this *is* possible. Thus, reflection shows that processing attention admits of a characterization that makes no reference to perception. Instead of conceiving of it as an agency that enhances specifically perceptual processing, we can think of it as an agency, or a family of agencies, that is responsible for enhancing processing *of all kinds*. On this way of conceiving of it, in addition to accomplishing such goals as enhancing the accuracy and resolution of perceptual representations, it also facilitates and augments such activities as calculating, planning, evaluating, and inductive reasoning. Moreover, it is possible to give a similarly abstract characterization of gate-keeper attention, by saying that it makes representations *of all kinds* accessible to the high level cognitive agencies that are responsible for such things as fixing perceptual beliefs, planning intentional actions, and laying down episodic memories. But when they are described thus abstractly, it is easy to see that processing attention and gate-keeper attention play a role in introspection. In this respect, introspection resembles perception.[15]

These observations seem correct to me, but do they provide support for perceptualist models of introspection? I don't see that they do. When we conceive of processing attention and gate-keeper attention in the abstract way that is required for the parallels between perceptual attention and introspective attention to emerge, we are conceiving of them as cognitive agencies, or families of agencies, that can play roles in a range of quite different cognitive activities. Hence, it is no longer true that perception has a proprietary association with them. But this means that when they are conceived abstractly, processing attention and gate-keeper attention cannot play a role in arguments for perceptualist models of introspection.

---

[15] As far as I can tell, even when binding attention is described abstractly, there is no motivation for thinking that it plays a role in introspection. Certainly there is no motivation of the sort there is for Treisman's view that attention is responsible for visual binding. Treisman's view is supported by a wide array of studies, including Treisman's own investigations of pop out, conjunction search, and illusory binding. (See the reference in note 13.) There are no comparable results concerning introspective processing. That is to say, there are no results that provide reason to think that *attention* is responsible for the binding that is involved in introspective awareness.

To appreciate this point, recall that when processing attention is conceived in the present abstract way, it becomes natural to suppose that it is employed in calculating, planning, evaluating, and inductive reasoning. Reflection shows that the same is true of gate-keeper attention. Do these considerations make it reasonable to conclude that calculating, planning, evaluating, and inductive reasoning are forms of perception? Or that it might be fruitful to develop perceptual models of them? No. Each of these activities is as similar to the others as any of them are to perception, so it would be a mistake to think that their similarity to perception provides us with a special explanatory leverage in thinking about them. It would be no more reasonable to adopt a perceptual model of calculation than to adopt a calculational model of perception. To express the point in other terms, since processing attention and gate-keeper attention are no more closely associated with perception than with calculating, planning, evaluating, and inductive reasoning, there is no reason to prefer a perceptual model of introspection to a calculation-based model, a planning-based model, an evaluation-based model, or a reasoning-based model.

In sum, anyone who tries to justify perceptualist models of introspection by appeal to attention faces a dilemma. There are two ways of conceiving of the three forms of perceptual attention: we can conceive of them concretely, in terms of the roles they play in specifically perceptual processing, or we can conceive of them in abstract and generic terms. If we think of them as concrete, specifically perceptual agencies, we find that they are quite different in character than introspective attention. On the other hand, when we think of them in generic terms, as agencies, or families of agencies, that are broadly relevant to a diverse array of mental activities, we find that at least two of them are germane to introspective processing. But then we have no reason to say that perception is more relevant to introspection than are calculating, planning, and a number of other mental activities.

It appears, then, that it is inappropriate to argue from the fact that introspection is governed by attention to process perceptualism, the view that the processes that produce perceptual judgments are deeply similar to perceptual processes. Accordingly, it seems that we are entitled to reject process perceptualism. The attention-based arguments are not the only ones that count in favor of this theory, but they are the ones that advocates of the theory regard as the most robust. Moreover, process perceptualism commits us to the existence of strong structural analogies between the processes that subserve perception and the processes that are responsible for introspective judgments. There is good reason to doubt the existence of such analogies, for the task that perceptual systems face is quite different than the task that confronts the introspective system. Perceptual systems must infer experiential representations of extramental objects from traces of such objects in sense receptors. The introspective system must infer conceptual representations of mental states from the states themselves. It would be amazing if systems with such different responsibilities turned out to go about their tasks in the same way.

8.8 DIVERSITY

Doxasticism gives us a positive account of the internal nature of states of introspective awareness, implying both that the representations that figure in these states are built out of concepts, and that the states themselves have the form of judgments. We do not yet, however, have a positive account of the processes that are responsible for introspective awareness. Our only conclusion in this area is the negative thesis that the processes are not perceptual. I will make a few remarks about introspective processing in the present section. My goal is to sketch a case for a view that I call *diversity* – the view that the processes that are responsible for introspective judgments and beliefs are a highly heterogeneous lot, differing from one another significantly in internal organization. I will not be trying to achieve completeness or accuracy of detail, but only to indicate the general direction in which, as it seems to me, the truth about introspective processing is to be found.

Let us assume that doxasticism is correct, and accordingly, that it is judgments that provide us with introspective awareness of beliefs, and also that it is judgments that provide us with introspective awareness of perceptual experiences. What can we conclude about the processes that produce judgments of these two sorts? Let us say that the processes that produce introspective judgments about occurrent beliefs are *processes of type P1*, and that the processes that produce introspective judgments about perceptual experiences are *processes of type P2*. Clearly, since they both produce meta-representational judgments, processes of type *P1* resemble processes of type *P2* in point of outputs. But they are quite different in point of inputs. The inputs to processes of type *P1* are occurrent beliefs, and the inputs to processes of type *P2* are perceptual experiences. Beliefs are of course quite different than experiences. Among other things, they differ with respect to their constituent representations: the representations that figure in beliefs are built out of concepts and have logical structures, but the representations that figure in perceptual experiences are presumably analog, and, to some extent anyway, iconic. Processes that transform conceptually informed, logically structured representations into metarepresentational judgments will inevitably differ significantly from processes that transform analog representations into judgments. The internal organization of the former processes will inevitably be much simpler than the internal organization of the latter.

It is clear, then, that processes of type $P1$ are quite different than processes of type $P2$. But this is just the beginning of the story. The category of processes of type $P2$ divides into at least three different subcategories, for there are at least three quite different types of introspective judgment about perceptual experiences, and each of these types of judgment requires its own form of processing. Thus, introspective judgments about perception include judgments of the form *I am perceiving that p*, judgments of the form *x looks F to me* that deploy *looks* in its phenomenological sense, and judgments of the form *x looks F to me* that deploy *looks* in its epistemic sense. (Cf. the discussion in Section 5.3.) Judgments of these three different sorts differ from one another significantly in point of content. Hence, they could not be produced by the same processes, or even by similar processes. Diversity of content can only be explained by diversity of causal mechanisms.

Reflection shows that there must be a number of other large scale differences among the processes that are responsible for introspective judgments. I will just mention three of them. That will suffice to show that the processes underlying introspective judgments exhibit a significant degree of diversity.

First, the processes that produce judgments about enduring propositional attitudes must be much more complex than the processes that produce judgments about occurrent attitudes, for they must have access to long term memory stores, and what is more important, they must make use of procedures for searching those stores for particular propositions. These procedures must be quite complex. To see this, observe that the domains that fall within the purview of these search procedures are both vast and heterogeneous, and recall that it is quite difficult to design a computer search engine that will search comparable bodies of information. The processes that produce judgments about occurrent attitudes are inevitably much simpler, for they need only have the capacity to search one or another of the comparatively miniscule stores that constitute working memory. Their job is comparatively trivial.

Second, the processes that are responsible for introspective judgments about mental processes must be quite different than the processes that produce judgments about mental states. Consider the following processes: thinking about Vienna, fantasizing about heroic deeds, imagining a conversation with Leonardo da Vinci, trying to prove a lemma, figuring out how to get to New Haven, planning a trip to Russia, assessing the probability of p, trying to decide whether to mow the lawn today, and looking for an explanation of the fact that p. In addition to being able to engage in endeavors of these sorts, each of us has the ability to know that he or she is so engaged. Clearly, knowledge of this type requires more than knowledge of individual mental states. Knowledge of individual mental states is probably presupposed, but in addition, one must be able to appreciate the goals toward which sequences of mental states are progressing. Just as knowledge of such goals goes beyond knowledge of individual states, so also the processes that are responsible for knowledge of the former sort must be more inclusive than the processes that are responsible for knowledge of the latter sort. Among other things, the processes responsible for knowledge of goals must have access to the stores in which lists of goals are found, and to the agencies that regulate high level, goal directed activity.

Third, there must be a difference between the processes that are responsible for introspective awareness of simple, ungraded propositional attitudes and the processes that are responsible for awareness of the more complex attitudes that involve degrees. Indeed, we know this to be so, for these differences are largely manifest to introspection. Thus, to determine whether one believes a certain proposition – say, the proposition that New York has more than 8,000,000 inhabitants – one only has to ask oneself an appropriate probe question, such as *How many people live in New York?* The answer comes immediately, providing one with a ground for thinking that one does indeed believe the proposition. The task of determining whether one believes a proposition to a certain degree is generally much more complex. One cannot simply ask oneself whether one believes a proposition to a certain degree. No answer will be forthcoming. Instead one has to perform various thought experiments to determine the odds that one would accept in wagering on the proposition, or else try to determine whether one is more or less confident of the proposition than of a representative sample of other propositions, where the degrees that are respectively associated with these other propositions are known independently.

When, earlier, we considered the internal nature of states of introspective awareness, we arrived at the conclusion that such states have a similar character. They are all judgments. In contrast, our more recent reflections support a pluralistic view of introspective processing. The processes responsible for introspective awareness tend to be quite different from one another. We have concentrated thus far on differences in structure, but we should note that there are significant epistemological differences as well. Thus, for example, when we reflect on the differences between searching a long term memory store for a particular belief and searching the store with a view to locating the evidence on which the belief is based, we see that the additional complexity of the latter enterprise carries with it a greater risk of error. In general, introspective judgments about single beliefs are much more secure than judgments about the supporting rationale for such beliefs. Another example is afforded by the processes that provide us with judgments concerning degrees of belief. One does not have direct epistemic access to one's degrees, but must try to estimate them on the basis of thought experiments of various kinds – for example, thought experiments involving wagers. It is not easy to derive determinate judgments from such experiments, and anyway, any resulting judgments are intuitions rather than observations of fact. It would be absurd to claim anything like certainty for them. In general, it seems wise to be skeptical concerning generalizations about the epistemic credentials of introspective judgments. Many of the relevant processes are highly trustworthy, but others have only a modest degree of reliability.

I would like to make one further epistemological observation. According to a long tradition, our judgments about our thoughts and other occurrent propositional attitudes are essentially presupposition-less, and therefore enjoy an epistemic status that approaches certainty. This seems wrong to me. Note first that it is very difficult, and perhaps even impossible, to judge that one is thinking that p at the same time as one is simply thinking that p, or to judge that one is occurrently wishing that p at the same time as one is entertaining the wish. The general rule here seems to be that it is very difficult, if not impossible, to have a meta-cognitive propositional attitude in mind at the same time as one is entertaining an occurrent attitude to which the first attitude refers. It is as if the part of one's mind in which occurrent attitudes take place, the Humean stage on which they appear, has only enough room for a single attitude at any one time. Indeed, it seems that there is not enough room on the Humean stage for both an occurrent attitude and a question about it. If one asks oneself, *What am I thinking **right now**?* the question will inevitably have displaced the thought to which one means to refer. The only current thought will be the question itself.

Assuming that this is correct, introspective awareness of occurrent attitudes is generally, and perhaps even necessarily, retrospective. Even though it is not appropriate to ask, *What am I thinking **right now**?* (unless one means to refer to the question itself), it makes perfect sense to ask, *What was the nature of my **immediately preceding** thought?* Now in most cases, as soon as one has asked the question, the correct answer will appear before one's mind. But like the question itself, the answer will refer to a thought that exists in memory, not in one's present consciousness.

The moral of these reflections is that it is a mistake to hold, as the tradition encourages us to do, that introspection is presuppositionless. Far from being presuppositionless, introspection often presupposes the trust-worthiness of memory. Now as we all know, memory is fallible. No doubt its deliverances concerning the very recent past are highly reliable in most circumstances, but there may be occasional lapses, and there may also be circumstances (involving, say, priming, drugs, or divided attention) in which their reliability rating goes way down. Accordingly it would be a mistake to claim certainty for introspection, at least insofar as it is concerned with occurrent attitudes.

<h2 style="text-align:center">8.9   INTROSPECTIVE CONSCIOUSNESS AND
EXPERIENTIAL CONSCIOUSNESS</h2>

I turn now to a new question. Suppose that B is a belief that has another mental state M as its object; that is, suppose that B incorporates a representation of M and attributes one or more properties to it. Suppose further that B is obtained from M by an immediate inference. Now if B is itself conscious, then, I suggest, it will quite definitely confer introspective consciousness on M. But will B confer introspective consciousness on M if it lacks consciousness? I will urge in this section that the answer is "no." It would of course be absurd to say that a representing state must itself be *introspectively* conscious in order to confer introspective consciousness on the state it represents, for that claim in effect posits an infinite regress. But it is not absurd, and is in fact quite true, to say that a state must possess *experiential consciousness* to be capable of imparting introspective consciousness to a represented state. Or so I will maintain.

Our principal intuition about introspective awareness seems to be this: a mental state is introspectively conscious just in case the relevant agent has cognitive access to it – more precisely, just in case the agent has cognitive access to it that is direct. When we attempt to spell out the content of this intuition, we find, I think, that in order to count as having cognitive access to a mental state, an agent must be able to classify that state, to answer questions about it, where the questions may be posed in thought by the agent himself or posed in speech by an interlocutor, and to appreciate its relevance to a range of cognitive endeavors, such as planning, decision making, and predicting. Now in order to provide an agent with this sort of access to a state, a representational state must be available to a range of high level cognitive agencies. Thus, for example, if a representing state $R1$ is to support an ability to answer questions about a represented state $R2$, $R1$ must be available to agencies that can process various sorts of meta-cognitive information, including information about the representational content of $R2$, information about $R2$'s logical and probabilistic import, and to some extent, anyway, information about $R2$'s constituent structure. But a representation that is available to high level agencies of this sort will count as experientially conscious.[16]

It may be useful to illustrate this argument with a thought experiment. Suppose that a certain agent, Jones, believes that p, and that Jones also believes that he has this belief. Suppose further that neither of these beliefs enjoys experiential consciousness. To be more specific, suppose that the contents of both beliefs are in some sense shameful, and that they have therefore been repressed by a Freudian mechanism of some sort. They were conscious at one time, perhaps, but are no longer so. Moreover, they could not easily become conscious. To complete the picture, suppose that at the conscious level Jones now has rather strong evidence that he does *not* believe that p. He is moved by this evidence, and therefore actively doubts that he has the belief. Is it at all plausible, given these assumptions, that the belief that p is introspectively conscious? Surely not, for it would be most implausible to say that Jones is introspectively aware of the belief. He has no cognitive access to it. The relation he bears to it is like the relation a swimmer bears to a stone that lies far beneath the surface of a lake. It is nothing to him, and it could not easily become more than nothing. The moral here is clear: If a meta-cognitive belief is not experientially conscious, then it is powerless to bestow introspective consciousness on its object.

Incidentally, this result provides additional support for a conclusion we reached in Chapter 1. In that chapter we formed the opinion that experiential consciousness is a complex functional property – more specifically,

---

[16] In taking this position I diverge sharply from David Rosenthal, with whose views I am otherwise in broad agreement (though we use the term "introspection" in different ways). See Rosenthal, *Consciousness and Mind* (Oxford: Oxford University Press, 2005).

a property that mental states possess if they are available for use by a range of high level cognitive agencies. Before arriving at this view, however, we considered the idea that it might be possible to explain what it is for a state to have experiential consciousness by saying that a state is experientially conscious if it is actually or potentially an object of introspective awareness. This idea is initially plausible because the notion of experiential consciousness and the notion of being accessible to introspection seem roughly coextensive with respect to human beings. In the end, though, we found the idea unacceptable, due to our willingness to attribute experiential consciousness to mental states of animals. We are strongly inclined to think, for example, that the perceptual experiences of vervet monkeys are conscious, but we have no good reason to think that vervets are capable of forming introspective judgments about their experiences. We can now appreciate that there is another reason for doubting that experiential consciousness can be analyzed in terms of introspective awareness. We have just concluded that if a meta-cognitive belief is not experientially conscious, then it is powerless to bestow introspective consciousness on its object. Assuming that this is correct, if we were to attempt to explain experiential consciousness in terms of introspective awareness, we would wind up with an account that looked something like this: a mental state M is experientially conscious just in case M is the actual (or potential) object of a state of introspective awareness that is (or would be) experientially conscious. This account is not flatly circular, as it would be if it used the clause "M is experientially conscious" in explaining what it is for M to be experientially conscious. (It says that a certain *other* mental state must be experientially conscious if it is to be capable of conferring experiential consciousness on M.) It is clear, however, that it presupposes the very concept that it purports to explain, and that, because of this feature, it provides very little illumination concerning the nature of experiential consciousness.

8.10   CONCLUSION

In the early sections of this chapter we found reasons for departing from the tradition of trying to explain introspection in terms of perceptual models. These models fail, we found, to provide an adequate account of the internal nature of introspective awareness, and also to illuminate the cognitive processes that are responsible for such states. We have also taken note of several positive doctrines about introspection that seem collectively to provide an appealing alternative to traditional views. One of these doctrines is doxasticism, the view that introspective awareness always takes the form of judgments, and another is diversity, the claim that the processes that underlie introspective judgments are a highly heterogeneous assortment, differing from one another both in point of structure and in point of reliability. A third component of the alternative picture is the doctrine that a meta-representational belief must possess experiential consciousness in order to be capable of conferring introspective consciousness on its object. As we have seen, there are considerations that provide strong motivation for all three of these doctrines. Thus, while the picture of introspection that they offer is at best embryonic, and suffers from considerable vagueness, it seems reasonable to regard it as providing the skeleton of a correct theory of introspection, and correlatively, a correct theory of introspective consciousness.

CHAPTER 9

A summary, two supplements, and
a look beyond

This concluding chapter is concerned with phenomenal consciousness, perceptual consciousness *of*, and the future of philosophical and scientific work on consciousness. The story of phenomenal consciousness that I have told is spread over several chapters. I will begin by drawing the various components of that story together. Once they are assembled, I will go on, in Section 9.2, to discuss their implications for metaphysical questions about the simplicity and unity of the universe. I will then turn to consider perceptual consciousness. I argued at some length in Chapter 5 that experiential awareness of A-properties constitutes the ground floor of conscious perceptual awareness, and that this ground floor enables perceptual awareness of properties of other kinds. But nothing has been said thus far about perceptual consciousness *of objects*. Any work aiming at broad coverage of consciousness must address this topic, for consciousness *of* is one of the six fundamental forms of consciousness. I will say something about it in Section 9.3. Finally, I will call attention to some important questions about consciousness that the present work does not address. They are quite difficult. I wish I knew how to answer them, but I fear that it will be some time until they are resolved.

9.1 PHENOMENAL CONSCIOUSNESS

The foregoing theory of phenomenal consciousness has three main components.

First, there is a preliminary analysis of phenomenal consciousness in Chapter 1. It consists of two claims: one that represents phenomenal consciousness as conscious awareness of qualitative properties, where "conscious" is understood to stand for experiential consciousness, and another that explains experiential consciousness in terms of causal powers with respect to a range of high level cognitive agencies.

247

The second component is the critique of standard theories of qualia that occupies Chapters 2, 3, and 4. The theories that receive the most attention are central state physicalism (together with conceptual dualism) and property dualism. In Chapter 2 we found that the first of these views lacks an adequate account of awareness of qualia, and that it also lacks the resources to respond successfully to the arguments for property dualism. Further, since our conclusions about qualia in later chapters tend to associate them either with bodily disturbances or with external stimuli, we have in effect been accumulating evidence that it would be a mistake to identify qualitative states with neural phenomena in the brain. As for property dualism, we observed in Chapter 4 that despite initial appearances to the contrary, the motivation for embracing it is actually quite weak. This finding was sufficient to discredit the view, for in the absence of powerful supporting arguments, property dualism falls to considerations having to do with the desirability of simplicity and explanatory uniformity.

The third component is a positive theory of qualia and awareness of qualia that consists of the following ten doctrines:

(1) As is the case with all other forms of awareness, awareness of qualitative characteristics is representational.

(2) Awareness of qualitative characteristics is governed by an appearance/reality distinction. The realm of appearance consists of qualia-as-they-are-represented. The realm of reality consists of qualia-as-they-are-in-themselves.

(3) Accordingly, it isn't necessary to take our experience of qualia at face value. For example, a qualitative characteristic can be quite complex even though it seems to us to be simple.

(4) In general, it is possible to provide deflationary explanations of why qualia seem to us to have properties that would set them apart from the physical domain. It is possible to close the explanatory gap.

(5) Awareness of a qualitative characteristic is always either perceptual or quasi-perceptual in character. It is perceptual insofar as it either involves one of the standard perceptual modalities, such as hearing and sight, or involves a modality that is very similar to one or more of the standard modalities. It is quasi-perceptual if it resembles one or more of the standard modalities but also diverges from the standard modalities in significant respects. Relevant respects of comparison include the syntactic, functional, and semantic properties of the representations that are involved in a form of awareness.

(6) It is possible to bring the various forms of qualitative awareness under a single banner by appealing to the notion of experiential awareness that is introduced in Chapter 3. To be perceptually or quasi-perceptually aware of something is to be aware of it experientially.

(7) Accordingly, qualitative characteristics can be explained as characteristics that are objects of unqualifiedly direct (i.e., unqualifiedly non-inferential and unmediated) experiential awareness. Qualia are objects of experiential awareness whose conscious apprehension is cognitively and epistemically ground floor.

(8) Qualitative characteristics come in at least two different flavors. The qualia that are revealed by the standard perceptual forms of awareness are appearance properties – that is, viewpoint-dependent properties of external objects. On the other hand, the qualia that are revealed by bodily awareness, like pain, are independent of viewpoints or perspectives. They are forms of bodily activity.

(9) The qualia involved in emotional experience fall into three main categories: perceptual, imagistic, and somatic. Since imagistic qualia belong to the same general category as perceptual qualia, emotional qualia can all be accommodated within the binary classificatory framework described in (8).

(10) There is no essential connection between qualia and occurrent propositional attitudes, nor even a nomological connection. Thus, for example, thoughts can occur without any attendant qualia. Moreover, the qualia that sometimes accompany occcurrent attitudes do not constitute a separate domain. They are qualia that are familiar from various forms of perceptual experience – principally auditory qualia, visual qualia, and somatic qualia.

As we have seen, these doctrines are motivated by both philosophical and empirical considerations.

9.2 QUALIA AND PHYSICALISM

Qualia are either appearances of external objects or properties of bodily disturbances of various sorts. Accordingly, there is good reason to believe that they are reducible to physical properties. But what is the relevant form of reducibility? As we saw in Chapter 2, reducibility comes in three rather different flavors: a property P may be said to be reducible to a set of properties Σ if (i) P is identical with one of the members of Σ, or (ii) P is realized by the members of Σ, or (iii) P supervenes logically on the members of Σ. Assuming that qualia are reducible to physical properties, should we say that the reduction involves identity, realization, or supervenience?

The answer depends on what is meant by "physical property." According to the broadly inclusive conception of physical properties that we adopted in Chapter 2, physical properties include the properties recognized by the more basic special sciences, such as chemistry and biology, in addition to the properties recognized by physics itself. When physical properties are construed in this broadly inclusive way, it is plausible that qualia are identical with physical properties. Thus, for example, it is plausible that the types of bodily disturbance that we have equated with somatic qualia are biological properties. It follows, of course, that they are identical with physical properties, given the present broad understanding of physicality. This is not the whole story, however, for there is also a narrower construal of physical properties, according to which the only properties that count as genuinely physical are the ones that figure in the fundamental laws of physics. What follows from this second construal about the metaphysical status of qualia?

It is pretty clear that the construal excludes identity physicalism. Thus, we have reason to doubt that appearances can be identified with intrinsic physical properties of external objects. Rather, they are viewpoint-relative properties, depending on such contextual factors as the location and velocity of the observer, and the intensity and spectral distribution of the light source. Moreover, it seems likely that they can be defined only by applying rather baroque transformations to input data – transformations that are of importance only to organisms that have species-specific inferential mechanisms, and species-specific informational needs. Now on the narrow construal of physical properties, they are characteristics that come into view only when one is concerned to describe the interactions of broad categories of objects and events in terms of maximally simple and maximally general laws. It would be amazing if properties that are viewpoint-relative and that are recognized via species-specific transformations turned out to be *identical with* properties that figure in fundamental laws of nature. Much the same is true of sensational qualia. It would be amazing if properties that come into view when we study disturbances in the human body turned out to be *identical with* properties that have independently attracted the attention of physicists. This is not to deny that we could identify qualia with complex disjunctions of physical properties; but disjunctions of physical properties are not themselves physical, at least if we take involvement in the laws of physics as our criterion for whether a property is physical.

It is clear, then, that the narrow construal of physical properties precludes acceptance of identity physicalism. But it could still be true that qualia are *realized* by physical properties – or in other words, that instantiations of qualia are constituted by instantiations of physical properties. And in fact, reflection shows that realization physicalism is quite plausible. To appreciate the merits of this view, let us focus on the property that has been identified with pain in earlier discussions – the property of being a bodily disturbance that involves actual or potential damage. Prima facie, at least, this is an especially challenging case for realization physicalism, since the notion of damage has an obvious teleological content. But reflection suggests that a reduction is possible. Thus, damage is to be understood in terms of proper functioning: it is a physical condition that inhibits proper functioning in the area or areas where it occurs. Proper functioning, in turn, is presumably to be understood in terms of natural selection: a component of the organism is functioning properly when it is doing the job it was selected to do. And finally, it seems likely that whether a component of an organism is selected is, at the deepest level, a purely physical affair, having to do with changes in the physical constitution of genetic material over time. In view of these observations, it is natural to suppose that instantiations of the property of being a bodily disturbance that involves actual or potential damage are constituted by, or composed of, instantiations of physical properties. Certainly it seems that one could *fully explain* an instantiation of the former property by appealing to instantiations of physical properties – that is, explain it without logical residue, and without presupposing any contingent laws linking damage to physical conditions.

What about appearances? Is it plausible that they are realized by the properties that are involved in fundamental physical laws? In Chapter 5 I suggested that visual appearances can be seen as certain properties of external objects – specifically, properties that result from applying computable functions to such quantitative properties of external objects as visual angles and angular shapes. If we assume that this is correct, and assume also that quantitative properties of external objects are realized by physical properties, we can conclude that appearances are realized by physical properties.

Chapter 5 is concerned exclusively with visual appearances, but it seems likely that what it says about appearances of that sort applies to appearances of other sorts as well. That is, it seems likely that the appearances associated with other perceptual modalities are properties of external objects that the modalities keep track of by applying computable functions to quantitative properties of those objects. If this is right, then what has just been said about the constitution of visual appearances also holds for auditory appearances, tactual appearances, and the rest. Their instantiations are realized by physical properties.

In view of these considerations, I suggest, no matter how the expression "physical property" is construed, it is reasonable to embrace the view that qualia are reducible to physical properties. There are two standard construals of the expression. On the first, broadly inclusive construal, it is plausible that qualia are identical with physical properties; and on the second, narrow construal, it is plausible that they are realized by physical properties.[1]

9.3   PERCEPTUAL CONSCIOUSNESS *OF*

Chapter 5 makes two claims about the nature of perceptual consciousness. First, it asserts that when we are perceptually conscious of objects, we are thereby conscious of them as instantiating certain viewpoint-dependent properties that are naturally called *appearance properties* (*A-properties*). Second, it puts forward a tentative proposal about the nature of A-properties, urging that they can be identified with the results of applying computable functions to certain quantitative properties that are viewpoint dependent. These claims take us part way to a theory of perceptual consciousness, but they leave a number of important questions unanswered. Perceptual consciousness involves consciousness *of objects*. What does consciousness of objects consist in? What can be said about the representations that support this form of awareness? More specifically, what can be said about their contents? How is consciousness of objects related to consciousness of their A-properties? The present section is concerned with these questions.

My point of departure for seeking answers is the following doctrine, which derives from Roderick Chisholm's wonderful book, *Perceiving*:

(CT) Necessarily, a subject x perceives an object y just in case y appears some way to x.[2]

---

[1] For a discussion of many of the metaphysical questions involving realization, and a theory that proposes answers to a number of them, see Sydney Shoemaker, *Physical Realization* (Oxford: Oxford University Press, 2007). Admiring Shoemaker's theory as I do, I wish I could say that it provides an adequate account of the notion of realization I am presupposing in this work. Unfortunately, for various reasons, this is not the case.

[2] Roderick M. Chisholm, *Perceiving: A Philosophical Study* (Ithaca, NY: Cornell University Press, 1957), p. 149. Expressed in Chisholm's words, (CT) looks like this:
"'S *perceives x*' means: *x* appears in some way to S."

According to this proposal, a subject x sees an object y just in case y looks some way to x, and x hears a noise z just in case z sounds some way to x. In keeping with Chisholm's intent, "appears," "looks," and "sounds" are being used here with their phenomenological senses – that is, with the senses they have in statements like these:

> That truck up ahead appears small.
> When they are held right before my eyes, my fingers look quite big.
> Because it is occurring so far away, the throbbing of the plane's engines sounds quite faint.

Further, again in keeping with Chisholm's intent, (CT) is offered as a claim about perceptual *consciousness*. Someone with blindsight can be said to perceive objects even though objects do not present visual appearances to him. But blindsight poses no problem for Chisholm's thesis, for the thesis is concerned only with perception that has an experiential dimension.

(CT) implies that a subject can see an object even though the object is presenting only *one* appearance to him. This implication may be mistaken. Thus, we have some inclination to suppose, I think, that a subject should not be said to see an object unless the object appears to him in two or more ways, and the subject appreciates that the appearances have a common ground. To put the point in other terms, it may be that the perception of objects requires that the subject has bound together representations of several appearances. But I will not explore this possibility here. Whatever the outcome of the inquiry, the spirit of (CT) would remain substantially intact. What is essential to (CT) is the idea that perceiving necessarily involves phenomenological appearances. For our purposes it does not matter much whether perceiving requires only one mode of appearing-p or many.

At all events, I will proceed on the assumption that (CT) is substantially correct. Now it follows from this assumption that the way to arrive at a theory of perceptual consciousness *of* is to explain what it is for an object to appear-p to a subject. But we already have a key component of such an explanation in hand. For, assuming that the main lines of thought of Chapter 5 are sound, we know that the following principle is correct:

(L) If y looks-p a certain way W to x, then (i) x's experience represents an A-property, P, that corresponds to W, and (ii) y instantiates P.

I believe that other perceptual modalities are governed by similar principles, but I will not attempt to explain or justify this view here. In the interests of definiteness I will focus on visual consciousness and looking-p.

(L) cites two conditions as necessary for looking-p. Are the conditions also sufficient? Is it always true that when they are satisfied, an object looks-p a certain way to a subject? The answer is "no." To see this, observe that if A-properties are independent of the internal states of the visual system, as I maintained in Chapter 5, then an object can instantiate an A-property without standing in a causal relation of any sort to the visual experience of the subject. Since this is the case, it is possible for there to be *veridical hallucinations* – that is, situations with the following properties: (i) a subject represents several A-properties as co-instantiated by an object in front of him; (ii) there is in fact an object in front of the subject that instantiates those A-properties; (iii) the visual experience of the subject, and the tokens of visual representations that constitute his experience, are not due to the A-properties of the external object; (iv) rather, they are due to malfunctions in the subject's visual system. Now intuitively, in a situation of this sort, the object cannot be said to appear to the subject. Evidently, the reason is that the experience of the subject would have occurred, just as it did, even if the object had not been present, or it had been present but it had instantiated quite different A-properties. It follows that if we are to characterize looking-p in an adequate way, we must build in a condition calling for a causal relationship between the A-properties of the object and the experience of the subject.[3]

We now have three conditions that are individually necessary for looking-p: a condition that is concerned with representation of A-properties, a condition that is concerned with instantiation of A-properties, and a condition that is concerned with causation. (The second condition is redundant, given the third, but I will allow this harmless redundancy to stand. I value the emphasis that it provides.)

Are these three conditions the only ones that are necessary for looking-p? That is to say, are they jointly sufficient? I am inclined to think that the answer is "yes." Thus, (L*) looks right to me:

(L*) y looks-p a certain way W to x just in case (i) x's experience represents an A-property, P, that corresponds to W, (ii) y instantiates P, and (iii) x's experience is caused, in a normal way, by the fact that y instantiates P.

---

[3] H. P. Grice was the first philosopher to appeal to veridical hallucinations in arguing for the necessity of including causal components in explanations of perceptual access to the world. See Grice, "The Causal Theory of Perception," *Proceedings of the Aristotelian Society* 35 (1961), 121–168. Section V is the relevant part of this essay.

It is now widely recognized that analyses of consciousness of objects must include a causal condition, but some authors maintain, in addition, that causation is *sufficient* for consciousness of objects – that there is no need to include a condition that involves instantiation of represented properties. I discuss a view of this sort at http://ndpr.nd.edu/review.cfm?id=13585

Further, since we are assuming that (CT) is true, (L*) implies a parallel account of perceptual consciousness – namely, (PC):

(PC) x is perceptually conscious of y just in case (i) x's experience represents an A-property, P, (ii) y instantiates P, and (iii) x's experience is caused, in a normal way, by the fact that y instantiates P.

I am inclined to accept (L*) and (PC) because they seem to capture my intuitions about possible cases. Thus, when I reflect on possible situations in which (i)–(iii) are all fulfilled, I find that I am strongly inclined to describe them as situations in which y looks a certain way to x, and also as situations in which x is perceptually conscious of y. This is true even of situations that are fairly outré, and in which, therefore, one might expect accidental and merely nomological correlations to break down.

Still, there is an objection to (PC) (and by implication, to (L*)) that must be considered. This objection claims that (PC) fails to honor the principle that all awareness involves representation. (PC) purports to analyze perceptual consciousness of external objects, but it makes no reference to representation of such objects. Its only reference to representation is in the context of a requirement that is concerned with representation of properties. Hence, the objection concludes, it is inadequate.

It is of course true that (PC) has no separate clause to the effect that x's experience represents y, but as I see it, it does not follow from this that (PC) fails to do justice to the representational dimension of perceptual consciousness. On the contrary, (PC) *does* do justice to the representational dimension. This is because conditions (i)–(iii) *jointly imply* that x's experience represents y. Representation of y is not an extra component of perceptual consciousness – a component that is independent of representation of P, instantiation of P by y, and causation of x's experience by y. Rather, it *consists in* these three things. This can be seen as follows: "Since we know independently that all awareness involves representation, we know that perceptual consciousness of y constitutively involves a representation of y. Further, by the same token, we can be sure that any set of conditions that is sufficient for the truth of statements of the form 'x is perceptually conscious of y' is also sufficient for statements of the form 'x's perceptual experience represents y.' But there is reason to think that (i)–(iii) are sufficient for the truth of statements of the form 'x is perceptually conscious of y,' for the latter statements seem to be true in possible situations in which (i)–(iii) are true. Hence, it is very likely the case that (i)–(iii) provide a correct account of perceptual representation of objects."

Perhaps it will be useful to formulate this line of thought in a somewhat different way. The first objection attempts to pit the analysis of perceptual consciousness that is offered by (PC) against the thesis that all awareness is representational. In responding to the objection, I have maintained that just the opposite is the case – that the thesis can actually be used to show that (PC) implies that perceptual consciousness of y constitutively involves a representation of y. The central idea of the argument is this: since we know that perceptual consciousness of y involves a representation of y, any considerations which indicate that (PC) gives a correct account of perceptual consciousness provide us with a reason to think that (PC) succeeds in capturing what is involved in representing y. But intuitions about possible cases indicate that (PC) gives a correct account of perceptual consciousness. Accordingly, we have a reason to think that (i)–(iii) are sufficient for the truth of "x's experience represents y."[4]

9.4 CONCLUSION

Inevitably, since I am the author, I feel that this work makes substantial progress toward an explanation of consciousness. It discusses a broad range of questions, and in each case, it offers an answer that is

---

[4] Throughout this work I have presupposed the view that perceptual representation of properties is a *fundamental* form of representation. This view is not implausible, and anyway, there is a practical advantage to presupposing it, for it makes certain expository simplifications possible. There is, however, an alternative view, according to which perceptual representations of properties are an aspect or dimension of a more fundamental form of representation – representation of states of affairs. This is perhaps the right place to acknowledge that the presupposed view is not inevitable.

According to the alternative view, instead of supposing that perceptual representations have A-properties as their primary semantic values, we should suppose that they have semantic properties analogous to the linguistic meanings that David Kaplan calls *characters* – that is, functions from contexts to contents. (Kaplan maintains, for example, that the primary semantic value of the indexical "I" is a function which maps each context of utterance onto the person who is speaking in that context. See, e.g., Kaplan, "Dthat," in Peter Cole (ed.), *Syntax and Semantics*, Volume 9 (New York: Academic Press, 1978), pp. 221–253.) Let R be a perceptual representation that is partially constitutive of a certain type of visual experience. Then, according to the alternative view, there is an A-property P and a function f such that, for every context C that contains a token T of R, if there is an object y in C such that y has P and causes T in virtue of having P, then f maps C onto the state of affairs y *is* P; and if there is no such y, then $f(C)$ is undefined. Here f is the *character* of R. Let T be a concrete token of R, and let C be the context in which T occurs. T will have a character, which it will inherit from R. It will also have a *content* – provided that $f(C)$ is defined. The content of T will be a state of affairs of the form y *is* P. On this view, the notion of the property represented by R is derivative, being definable as the property that figures in the character of R. Moreover, the view denies that there is such a thing as the *object* that is represented by R. According to the view, representation of objects is a feature of *tokens* of R – different tokens represent different objects. The notion of the object represented by a token T of R is derivative, being definable as the object that figures in the content of T. Intensional predications of experiences, as when one says that a hallucination is an experience of a dagger, are explained by appeal to characters.

approximately correct. Or so I believe. Having said this, though, I must go on to acknowledge that the ambitions of the book are comparatively modest. The answers it proposes are often partial. Moreover, there are many issues that the book does not address, some of them quite important. I will conclude by noting several of these limitations.

Perhaps the most important limitation is that very little has been said in explanation of the doctrine that awareness necessarily involves representation. To be sure, we have found a number of reasons for thinking that the doctrine is *true*. One is that it is intuitively plausible. Another is that it is presupposed by cognitive science. A third reason is that it enjoys significant explanatory advantages over its main rival, the view that awareness is acquaintance. Fourth, the doctrine enables us to explain what is common to veridical perceptual experiences and the corresponding hallucinations, and to explain the truth conditions of statements describing hallucinations in terms of what they are *of*. Fifth, it enables us to end the standoff between physicalists and dualists. And sixth, it proves useful in developing positive accounts of such otherwise opaque forms of awareness as awareness of perceptual qualia and awareness of pain. In view of these considerations, we can, I think, claim to *know* that all awareness is representational. But it is not clear what this knowledge amounts to, for I have not offered a general theory of the nature of representation, nor even an account of experiential representation, the form of representation that figures most prominently in the foregoing pages. Moreover, while there are a number of highly engaging ideas about representation in the literature, there is no developed theory that commands wide assent.[5] Accordingly, I cannot close this gap in the present work by referring the reader to other sources.

Further, while there has been much discussion of visual qualia in the foregoing pages, I have actually done little more than scratch the surface of this large and complex topic. There is a significant incompleteness even in the account of shape qualia, which, together with size qualia, are the only visual qualia that have received much attention. Thus, as is pointed out in notes 22 and 31 to Chapter 5, the only shape qualia that can be explicated as Thouless properties are the ones that are associated with the silhouettes of objects – the boundaries of facing surfaces. Nothing is said

---

[5] See, e.g., Ruth Millikan, "Biosemantics," *The Journal of Philosophy* 86 (1989), 281–297, Fred Dretske, *Naturalizing the Mind* (Cambridge, MA: MIT Press, 1995), Michael Tye, *Ten Problems of Consciousness* (Cambridge, MA: MIT Press, 1995), and Karen Neander, "Naturalistic Theories of Reference," in Michael Devitt and Richard Hanley (eds.), *Philosophy of Language* (Oxford: Blackwell, 2006), pp. 374–391.

about the three-dimensional shape qualia associated with concavities and convexities on the surfaces of objects. Also, what is more important, there is very little discussion of the category of visual qualia that many believe to pose the most serious challenges to philosophy – the category of color qualia. Indeed, my discussion of this topic is confined to a single note (note 31 to Chapter 5). Anyone who wishes to investigate this important realm must take the work of others as his point of departure.[6]

Visual qualia are the perceptual qualia that have received the most attention from philosophers, but the qualia associated with the other perceptual modalities pose challenging problems of their own. Aside from a few promissory notes, nothing has been said about these other qualia. There has been important work on them by other philosophers, but we are still a long way from understanding them.[7]

The discussion of introspection is also incomplete. To mention only the largest lacuna, I have said very little in a positive vein about the meta-cognitive mechanisms that are responsible for introspective judgments. Chapter 8 provides arguments for the view that these mechanisms are not perceptual, and also for the view that they are quite diverse. But these views are largely negative. What, we want to know, is the nature of the mechanism that provides awareness of occurrent propositional attitudes? What exactly is its structure, and how does it work? Further, how exactly does it differ from the mechanism that is responsible for awareness of enduring propositional attitudes? Still further, how exactly do these mechanisms differ from the one that advises us as to the direction and efficiency of mental processes? Any account of introspective consciousness that aims to be comprehensive must answer these questions and a number of others of the same sort.

I turn now to experiential consciousness, the form of consciousness that is shared by occurrent propositional attitudes and events with a proprietary phenomenology. This form of consciousness been largely neglected since Chapter 1. According to the account that is given there, a mental event *x* is experientially conscious just in case *x* is, potentially, at least, a maximally proximal causal trigger for several of the high level cognitive agencies that are recognized by folk psychology. Having said

---

[6] See, e.g., Clyde L. Hardin, *Color for Philosophers: Unweaving the Rainbow* (Indianapolis: Hackett, 1993), Alex Byrne and David Hilbert (eds.), *Readings on Color*, Volume I: *The Philosophy of Color* (Cambridge, MA: MIT Press, 1997), and Mohan Matthen, *Seeing, Doing, and Knowing: A Philosophical Theory of Sense Perception* (Oxford: Oxford University Press, 2005).

[7] For a discussion of the qualia associated with thermal perception, see Kathleen Akins, "Of Sensory Systems and the 'Aboutness' of Mental States," *The Journal of Philosophy* 93 (1996), 337–372; for a discussion of auditory qualia, see Casey O'Callaghan, *Sounds* (Oxford: Oxford University Press, 2007); and for a discussion of olfactory qualia, see Clare Batty, "Lessons in Smelling: Essays in Olfactory Perception," MIT Ph.D. Dissertation, 2007.

this, the account goes on to list the relevant agencies, citing the ones that are responsible for producing speech, forming beliefs and other propositional attitudes, making choices, elaborating plans, exercising on-line control of intentional actions, creating memories, monitoring mental states, and producing introspective judgments. Regrettably, the account says no more than this. Hence, while it captures some of the main features of experiential consciousness, it is clear that it raises more questions than it answers.

Some of these questions are concerned with the relationship between experiential consciousness and memory. It takes time to express a thought in speech; it takes time to make a choice; and it takes time for an episodic memory to be established. In general, it takes time for the cognitive agencies specified in the definition of experiential consciousness to become active and undertake a given task. Accordingly, a mental event must persist for a certain length of time, or leave a trace that persists for a certain length of time, in order to have the power to trigger specific processes involving the agencies that figure in the definition of experiential consciousness. It follows that memory is required to support the causal powers that figure in that definition, and it follows from this in turn that a theory of experiential consciousness must specify the memory store or stores that support the relevant powers. Can the store be identified with working memory?[8] Or is it perhaps a store whose contents are more ephemeral than those of working memory? We have reason to believe that the mind has at least two very short term stores – iconic memory[9] and the faculty that Mary Potter calls *conceptual short term memory*.[10] Could it be that these two stores work in tandem to endow mental events with experiential consciousness, with iconic memory lending consciousness to qualitative events, and conceptual short term memory lending it to occurrent propositional attitudes? It is clear that these are empirical questions. Moreover, they are entirely open. Science must advance on several fronts before they can be answered.

Another set of questions is concerned with the causal conditions that enable representations to achieve experiential consciousness. A great deal

---

[8] For a summary of the literature on working memory, see Daniel Reisberg, *Cognition: Exploring the Science of the Mind*, 3rd edition (New York, NY: Norton, 2005).

[9] The notion of iconic memory was introduced by George Sperling in 1960. See his "The Information Available in Brief Visual Presentations," *Psychological Monographs* 10. For a relatively up to date discussion of the topic, see Stephen Palmer, *Vision Science* (Cambridge, MA: MIT Press, 1999), pp. 575–580.

[10] See Mary C. Potter, "Understanding Sentences and Scenes: The Role of Conceptual Short Term Memory," in Veronika Coltheart (ed.), *Fleeting Memories: Cognition of Brief Visual Stimuli* (Cambridge, MA: MIT Press, 1999), pp. 13–46.

of recent clinical and experimental work suggests that *attention* is required for experiential consciousness in many cases, at least for perceptual states. This is true, for example, of clinical work on Balint's syndrome and hemineglect, and of experimental work on change blindness and inattentional blindness.[11] These results have led some researchers to claim that attention is required for *any* perceptual state to be conscious, but everyday experience suggests that this is an overstatement. I am not now attending to the keyboard of the computer in front of me. Rather, I am focusing on the screen. But I seem to have *some* awareness of the keyboard. So we must ask: To what extent is attention necessary for perceptual states to achieve experiential consciousness? What distinguishes the cases in which attention is required from the cases in which it is not? And what exactly is the form of attention that plays the relevant causal role? Further, most of the contemporary research linking attention and experiential consciousness is concerned with perceptual states. What exactly is the role of attention in endowing states of other kinds with experiential consciousness, and what exactly are the forms of attention that play this role?

As these reflections remind us, consciousness is a vast topic. If you want to understand it, not just in part but comprehensively, you will be busy as long as you live.[12]

---

[11] For richly informative discussions of these topics, see Stephen Palmer, *Vision Science* (Cambridge, MA: MIT Press, 1999).

[12] I am here echoing a remark that Warren McCulloch attributed to Rufus Jones, a Quaker philosopher who was one of his early teachers:

In the fall of 1917, I entered Haverford College ... That winter Rufus Jones called me in. "Warren," said he, "what is thee going to be?" And I said, "I don't know." "And what is thee going to do?" And again I said, "I have no idea; but there is one question I would like to answer: What is a number, that a man may know it, and a man, that he may know a number?" He smiled and said, "Friend, thee will be busy as long as thee lives."

This passage appears on p. 2 of Warren S. McCulloch, *Embodiments of Mind* (Cambridge, MA: MIT Press, 1965).

Index